The Occult A

ALSO BY DAVID HUCKVALE
AND FROM MCFARLAND

*Hammer Films' Psychological Thrillers, 1950–1972* (2013)

*James Bernard, Composer to Count Dracula:*
*A Critical Biography* (2006; paperback 2012)

*Ancient Egypt in the Popular Imagination:*
*Building a Fantasy in Film, Literature, Music and Art* (2012)

*Visconti and the German Dream: Romanticism,*
*Wagner and the Nazi Catastrophe in Film* (2012)

*Touchstones of Gothic Horror: A Film Genealogy*
*of Eleven Motifs and Images* (2010)

*Hammer Film Scores and the Musical Avant-Garde* (2008)

# The Occult Arts of Music

*An Esoteric Survey
from Pythagoras to Pop Culture*

DAVID HUCKVALE

McFarland & Company, Inc., Publishers
*Jefferson, North Carolina, and London*

LIBRARY OF CONGRESS CATALOGUING-IN-PUBLICATION DATA

Huckvale, David, author.
    The occult arts of music : an esoteric survey from Pythagoras
to pop culture / David Huckvale.
        p.      cm.
    Includes bibliographical references and index.

    ISBN 978-0-7864-7324-3
    softcover : acid free paper ∞

    1. Music and occultism.    2. Mysticism in music.
    3. Music—Philosophy and aesthetics.    I. Title.
    ML3800.H77 2013
    781.1—dc23                              2013030588

BRITISH LIBRARY CATALOGUING DATA ARE AVAILABLE

© 2013 David Huckvale. All rights reserved

*No part of this book may be reproduced or transmitted in any form
or by any means, electronic or mechanical, including photocopying
or recording, or by any information storage and retrieval system,
without permission in writing from the publisher.*

On the cover: Barbara Parkins from the 1971 film *The Mephisto Waltz*
(Twentieth Century Fox/Photofest)

Manufactured in the United States of America

*McFarland & Company, Inc., Publishers
    Box 611, Jefferson, North Carolina 28640
    www.mcfarlandpub.com*

# Table of Contents

| | |
|---|---|
| *Preface* | 1 |
| One — The Music of the Spheres | 5 |
| Two — Masonic Music | 27 |
| Three — The Birth of the Demonic | 44 |
| Four — Wagner's Racial Mysticism and Schoenberg's Numerical Superstition | 71 |
| Five — Synesthesia | 98 |
| Six — Theosophy | 108 |
| Seven — Phantoms at the Opera | 131 |
| Eight — Dancing with Death | 150 |
| Nine — Fairy Music | 161 |
| Ten — Satan Rocks: Popular Music and the Occult | 176 |
| *Epilogue* | 190 |
| *Chapter Notes* | 193 |
| *Bibliography* | 201 |
| *Index* | 207 |

"Music is the only embodied entrance into a higher sphere of knowledge, which possesses mankind, but he will never be able to possess it."—Ludwig van Beethoven, quoted by Bettina von Arnim, letter to Goethe, May 28, 1810, in Bettina von Arnim/Johann Wolfgang von Goethe, *Goethe's Correspondence with a Child*, p. 286.

"[Music] is only connected with men, in so much as it bears witness to the divine mediation in him."—Beethoven, quoted by von Arnim, letter to Goethe, May 28, 1810, in *Goethe's Correspondence with a Child*, p. 287.

"*Musica est exercitium metaphysices occultum nescientis se philosophari animi*" ("Music is an unconscious exercise in metaphysics in which the mind does not know it is philosophizing").—Arthur Schopenhauer (trans. E. F. J. Payne), *The World as Will and Representation*, Vol. 1, p. 264.

"In Magic there is neither good nor evil; it is merely a science, the science of causing change to occur by means of one's will."—Mr. Mocata (Charles Gray) in *The Devil Rides Out* (dir. Terence Fisher, 1968).

# *Preface*

The very word "occult" has had very bad press over the years. Derived from the Latin *occultus* (the past participle of *occulere*), it entered the English language in the early sixteenth century and originally meant, simply, "hidden from sight," but its connotation is now, like that similarly once-benign mystical symbol, the swastika, charged with connotations of evil — usually involving sexually charged, scantily clad, morally depraved devil worship, Dennis Wheatley–style. Consequently, there is still a reluctance among resolute champions of reason to admit that such an irrational, backward-looking mind-set can have anything serious to say about art and the human spirit. Scientists blush to admit that Sir Isaac Newton was primarily an alchemist. Champions of modernism are embarrassed by Mondrian's interest in theosophy and have been known to sideline his early esoteric paintings; certain musicologists like to emphasize that it is Scriabin's *music* that matters, rather than the ideas which he attempted to express by means of it. Occult fiction is still very popular, but, like the word itself, is still not really respectable in the Jane Austen sense of the term. Occult movies have never aimed to be respectable, and while they often perpetuate the Dennis Wheatley syndrome, it is ironic that their accompanying musical scores either look back to a perfectly respectable "demonic" tradition formulated by Berlioz, Liszt and Weber in the nineteenth century or look forward to the even more intellectually fashionable avant-garde inventions of Ligeti and Penderecki, thus applying "occult" connotations to music that originally had nothing to do with such things. Sometimes, as in the case of Jerry Goldsmith's score for *The Mephisto Waltz* (dir. Paul Wendkos, 1971), they combine both approaches, which makes the situation even more delightfully complex.

Even qualified uses of the word "occultism" can still cause a social *frisson*, much as a dinner-party guest's confession of "atheism" can cause an awkward hiatus. One is no longer expelled from British universities for professing atheism, as was famously the case with Percy Bysshe Shelley at Oxford University

1

in 1811, but having said that, I have been asked to avoid the word "occult" when preparing the publicity for an adult education course about the musical aspects of the subject run by another university of similar standing.

Shelley turned to occultism before his conversion to atheism, but even after his rejection of established religion, he maintained his interest in metaphysical speculation. So too did his anarchistic mentor, William Godwin (the father of Mary Shelley), who published *Lives of the Necromancers* in 1834, toward the end of a life otherwise devoted to the championing of reason and rational education. This is not as surprising as it might seem; not only is atheism a form of belief, but atheists also often take religion and belief in the supernatural rather more seriously than many a casual believer.

Shelley's interest in the supernatural can be traced to his earliest works, and in his "Hymn to Intellectual Beauty" of 1816 he himself reminisced

> While yet a boy I sought for ghosts, and sped
> Through many a listening chamber, cave, and ruin,
> And starlight wood, with fearful steps pursuing
> Hopes of high talk with the departed dead.[1]

While at Eton he read Pliny, Lucretius, Albertus Magnus and Paracelsus, whose occult philosophies perhaps first inspired his skepticism with regard to the orthodox Christian deity. These writers, after all, suggest that men, by controlling the forces of the natural world, are potential gods themselves. Shelley came to regard the Christian God as a tyrant, and the mythological beings who defied God, such as Prometheus and Satan, as prototypical freedom fighters. Indeed, Shelley was the first major writer to suggest that "Milton's Devil as a moral being is as far superior to his God, as one who perseveres in some purpose which he has conceived to be excellent in spite of adversity and torture, is to one who in the cold security of undoubted triumph inflicts the most horrible revenge upon his enemy, not from any mistaken notion of inducing him to repent of a perseverance in enmity, but with the alleged design of exasperating him to deserve new torments."[2]

It was, perhaps, with her husband's intellectual history in mind that Mary Shelley had Baron Victor Frankenstein, a character closely modeled on the poet in many ways, also read Paracelcus and Albertus Magnus, along with the works of Cornelius Agrippa. Frankenstein confesses:

> I read and studied the wild fancies of these writers with delight; they appeared to me treasures known to few beside myself. I have described myself as always having been embued with a fervent longing to penetrate the secrets of nature.[3]

Frankenstein, originally inspired by the occult, later turns to the science of electricity to create his god-like pyrrhic victory over life and death; it is

# Preface

this blend of the occult, Gothic romance and science, not to mention its subtextual criticism of Romantic idealism, as personified by the irresponsible behavior of Shelley himself, that makes *Frankenstein* such a compelling and perennial tale. Occultism has always regarded itself as a science as much as an art, and the trappings of science, the emotional impact of art and the excitement of the supernatural also collided less than a century later with the rise of theosophy, anthroposophy, Rosicrucianism, and even the spurious racial theories of Nazism.

The role of music in the history of occultism is perhaps less often discussed, but it is one of the most significant manifestations of occultism, particularly in the case of occult and science fiction cinema, where music plays a vital role in the creation of the respective ambiences of those two sometimes-overlapping genres. However, film music has developed out of an art music tradition that has its own complex relationship to occult philosophy, and that tradition needs to be understood before attempting to explore how music is used in such films.

I am neither an occultist nor an atheist. I have no metaphysical beliefs of my own but neither I do reject the possibility of so-called occult phenomena, even though I have never experienced any personally. I have approached this particular subject accordingly and aim merely to demonstrate, in the name of the history of ideas, some of the major parallels between music and the occult, encompassing both the art-music tradition and music in popular culture. I do, however, think that occultism as an idea has certain things in its favor, not only because it has inspired musical ingenuity and sometimes musical masterpieces, but also because it presents many agreeable fictions, which express genuine emotional needs and psychological realities.

And so I invite you to throw open this book on the occult philosophy of music and in the end perhaps agree with Doctor Faust, who, on opening a book of magical law by Nostradamus in Goethe's famous play, exclaims:

> Ha! as I look, what sudden ecstasy
> Floods all my senses, how I feel it flowing
> Through every vein, through every nerve in me,
> Life's sacred joy and youth's renewal glowing!
> [...]
> That sage's words at last I understand:
> "The spirit-world is open wide,
> Only your heart has closed and died."[4]

# Chapter One
## *The Music of the Spheres*

Aliens have made contact with the earth. The mothership descends, and humanity attempts to communicate with the visitors by means of music. In this celebrated scene from *Close Encounters of the Third Kind* (dir. Steven Spielberg, 1977), John Williams' decision to use the basic building blocks of the harmonic series (thirds, fifths and octaves) as the basis of a musical conversation is reminiscent of the well-known story of Pythagoras entering a forge in which he observed four smiths hammering on anvils. The philosopher was said to have been intrigued by the different pitches given off by the hammers, and on weighing them he discovered proportions that resulted in the corresponding musical intervals of a fourth, fifth and octave. The story was recorded by the Syrian philosopher Iamblichus (245–325 A.D.) in his *Life of Pythagoras*:

> When, therefore, he had accurately examined the weights and the equal counterpoise of the hammers, he returned home, and fixed one stake diagonally to the walls, lest if there were many, a certain difference should arise from this circumstance, or in short, lest the peculiar nature of each of the stakes should cause a suspicion of mutation. Afterwards, from this stake he suspended four chords consisting of the same materials, and of the same magnitude and thickness, and likewise equally twisted. To the extremity of each chord also he tied a weight. And when he had so contrived, that the chords were perfectly equal to each other in length, he afterwards alternately struck two chords at once, and found the before mentioned symphonies, viz. a different symphony in a different combination. For he discovered that the chord which was stretched by the greatest weight, produced, when compared with that which was stretched by the smallest, the symphony diapason; which the weights themselves rendered apparent.[1]

The aliens in *Close Encounters* are quick to respond to the musical relationships offered to them, and they triumphantly answer musical questions (i.e., D, E, C from the humans is followed by the aliens with the lower octave C rising a fifth to G). This leads to a complex piece of counterpoint between the two, all scored by Williams for a conventional orchestra rather than the electronic instruments implied by the film itself, with its array of keyboards, synthesizers and loudspeakers. What exactly is being said, though? Recognition of the overtone series and its resulting musical conventions? Certainly, and that is, after all, quite sufficient. As Eduard Hanslick (1825–1904), the Viennese music critic (and later enemy of Richard Wagner [1813–1883]), insisted, "In the pure act of listening, we enjoy the music alone, and do not think of importing into it any extraneous matter."[2] Hanslick violently disagreed with Wagner's approach to music drama, arguing that "an Opera [...] in which the music is really and truly employed *solely as a medium* for dramatic expression is a musical monstrosity."[3] Hanslick would no doubt have agreed with Mendelssohn's words—that music is "a more precise language than words or letters."[4] Such a view argues that music is autonomous and is not necessarily (or even desirably) a symbol of something extra-musical. This is no doubt why the scientists who make contact with the aliens in *Close Encounters* choose musical relationships as the means of their conversation rather than any kind of conceptual language. Music may not be a universally understood "language," as some Romantic theorists would have us believe, but basic relationships like fifths and octaves are certainly naturally occurring phenomena that are more likely to be recognized by alien life forms than purely human concepts. We (and presumably they) respond to such musical relationships just as we respond to other natural patterns and proportions.

The *Close Encounters* scientists might alternatively have considered showing the aliens examples of the Golden Section or the Fibonacci sequence, both of which are indeed related to the proportions required to create fifths and octaves. These ideas, incidentally, are explored in Walt Disney's inspirational film *Donald Duck in Mathmagic Land* (dir. Hamilton Luske, 1959), in which Donald Duck explores the outlines of Pythagorean theories of proportion and their connection to music, architecture and naturally occurring forms and structures. The Golden Section is dependent upon the ratio of *phi*, which is approximately 1.618, and is most easily expressed when a rope is divided in such a way that the ratio of the longer part of the rope to the entire length is exactly the same ratio as the shorter part of the rope to the longer part. From this proportion we can construct Golden Rectangles, which, as Donald learns, form the basis of the Parthenon's proportions, to name just the most famous architectural example. Golden Spirals can also be constructed from Golden Rectangles, which have a great deal in common with the Fibonacci sequence of 1, 1, 2, 3, 5, 8, 13, 21, 34, 55, 89, 144, and so forth. Donald also learns that the pentangle, the secret symbol of the Pythagoreans, is related to the proportions of the Golden Section, and the pentangle, of course, has become one of the most potent of all occult symbols, representing either Humanity, with head and arms outstretched above two legs, or, reversed, the Devil, with his two horns and goat's beard.

We respond emotionally to the proportions of the Golden Section because they form our own physical proportions. They are, indeed, part of us. The natural harmonics that form the basis of musical harmony could therefore also be said to be part of our genetic heritage. Having said that, no one has ever arrived at a successful definition of music, let alone an explanation of its immense emotional effect. Aristotle realized that "it is not easy to say precisely what potency it possesses, nor yet for the sake of what object one should participate in it — whether for amusement and relaxation, as one indulges in sleep and deep drinking (for these in themselves are not serious pursuits but merely pleasant, and 'relax our cares,' as Euripides says; owing to which people actually class music with them and employ all of these things, sleep, deep drinking, and music, in the same way, and they also place dancing in the same class); or whether we ought rather to think that music tends in some degree to virtue ... or that it contributes something to intellectual entertainment and culture."[5] There have been cynics, of course. Alexandre Dumas (1802–1870) is attributed with having said that music is the only noise for which one is obliged to pay, whereas the Polish-American musician, Josef Hofmann (1870–1956), put it more bluntly as "the most expensive noise." But the more serious inquirers into the nature of music usually connect it with some aspect of proportion or mathematics. Debussy (1862–1918), for example, suggested that "music is the 'arithmetic of sound' just as optics is the 'geometry of light'"[6]— a metaphor that also raises the interesting subject of synesthesia, which we will be considering in due course. Similarly, Arthur Honegger (1892–1955) defined it as "geometry in time,"[7] while Heinrich Heine (1792–1856) and Thomas Mann (1875–1955) injected an element of the noumenal into their definitions. Heine regarded music as standing "half way between thought and phenomena, between spirit and matter, a sort of nebulous mediator, like and unlike each of the things it mediates— spirit that requires manifestation in time, and matter that can do without space. We do not know what music is."[8] For the fictional composer Adrian Leverkühn in Mann's novel, *Doctor Faustus* (1947), music is "a magic marriage between theology and the so diverting mathematic. Item, she has much of the laboratory and the insistent activity of the alchemists and nigromancers [*sic*] of yore."[9] Francis Barrett, in his largely plagiarized occult compendium, *The Magus, or Celestial Intelligencer* (1801), was of the same opinion:

> The doctrines of mathematics are so necessary to and have such an affinity with magic, that they who profess it without them are quite out of the way, and labour in vain, and shall in no wise obtain their desired effect. For whatsoever things are, and are done in these inferior natural virtues, are all done and gov-

erned by *number, weight, measure, harmony, motion,* and *light:* and all things which we see in these inferiors have root and foundation in them.... Hence a magician (expert in natural philosophy and mathematics, and knowing the middle sciences, consisting of both these, viz. arithmetic, music, geometry, optics, astronomy, and such sciences that are of weights measures, proportions articles, and joints; knowing, also, mechanical arts resulting from these), may, without any wonder, if he excel other men in the art and wit, do many wonderful things, which men may much admire.[10]

It is no doubt the central importance of mathematical proportion in magical theory that lies at the heart of one of the most influential explanations about the power of music upon human emotions, which ultimately derives from the ideas of Pythagoras. Pythagoras left no writings but his ideas were recorded by his disciples, and his concept of a music of the spheres was immortalized by Plato in *The Republic*. While telling of the journey to heaven by the soul of the Pamphylian solider, Er, after having been slain in battle, the narrator, Socrates, discusses the structure of the universe:

> They came to a place where they could see from above a line of light, straight as a column, extending right through the whole heaven and through the earth, in colour resembling a rainbow, only brighter and purer; another day's journey brought them to the place, and there, in the midst of the light, they saw the ends of the chains of heaven let down from above: for this light is the belt of heaven, and holds together the circle of the universe, like the under-girders of a trireme. From these ends is extended the spindle of Necessity, on which all the revolutions turn.[11]

This, in effect, is a kind of ancient Greek science fiction movie, and Socrates wastes no time in adding a soundtrack, for spinning around the spindle are eight whorls, which represent the eight planets known at the time:

> On the upper surface of each circle is a siren, who goes round with them, hymning a single tone or note. The eight together form one harmony; and round about, at equal intervals, there is another band, three in number, each sitting upon her throne: these are the fates, daughters of Necessity, who are clothed in white robes and have chaplets upon their heads, who accompany with their voices the harmony of the sirens.[12]

Composers of science fiction movie scores usually take their cue from Plato's Socrates here, though there are, of course, exceptions to the rule. John Williams wrote something much more earth-bound and militaristic for *Star Wars* (dir. George Lucas, 1977), a film that treated deep space as a human battlefield, but Alexander Courage's famous theme for the *Star Trek* TV series and spin-off movies begins in a highly Platonic way. *Star Trek* certainly had its militaristic and "Wild West" elements ("Space: the final frontier," as the

## One. The Music of the Spheres

famous opening words of the title sequence put it), but it also stressed the element of "strange new worlds" along with the awe and majesty of the universe, and this more mystical element was emphasized by Courage's music. High, "celestial" A-naturals, an octave apart, open the piece, and continue as a sustained drone. A-natural is also the first note of a group of four that is next presented as an evocation of the vastness of the universe. So, we move from A-natural down to E-natural, up to G-natural and then down a minor sixth to B-natural. As the original A-natural continues throughout this sequence, we could think of it as an approximation of the "hum" of the universe, and the next three notes as representing Plato's three fates. These three notes appear again in the following introduction to the main theme. This introduction is based on fourths (which, like the fifths and octaves of the *Close Encounters* theme, are one of the three fundamental intervals discovered by Pythagoras in the forge), and Courage's introductory phrase consists of eight notes, which nicely correspond to the eight sirens. Though they share the same notes, Courage's fates and the sirens do not technically form a chord or sustained harmony, as Plato would have wanted them to. This "eternal harmony" is merely suggested by the sustained opening A-natural octaves, but the general effect is, I think, analogous to what Plato has Socrates describe in *The Republic*. I am not, of course, suggesting that Courage had Plato in mind when he wrote this theme (though it is possible, of course), but the *Star Trek* music does provide us with a powerful manifestation of the idea of a music of the spheres in the context of popular culture, which demonstrates how pervasive these ideas have been and still are in relation to our emotional response to the universe.

However, according to Plato, the celestial harmony of the sirens is eternal and inaudible to humanity. Our earthly music is but a diluted reflection of it. In Plato's *Phaedo* the analogy is explained:

> Might not a person say that harmony is a thing invisible, incorporeal, fair, divine, abiding in the lyre which is harmonized, but that the lyre and the strings are matter and material, composite, earthy, and akin to mortality? And when someone breaks the lyre, or cuts and rends the strings, then he who takes this view would argue as you do, and on the same analogy, that the harmony survives and has not perished; for you cannot imagine, as we would say, that the lyre without the strings, and the broken strings themselves, remain, and yet that the harmony, which is of heavenly and immortal nature and kindred, has perished — and perished too before the mortal. The harmony, he would say, certainly exists somewhere, and the wood and strings will decay before that decays.[13]

Later, the fifth-century philosopher Boethius (480–524) elaborated upon these ancient Greek principles in his influential treatise, *De institutione musica* (*Principles of Music*, first printed in 1491–1492), by introducing the tripartite categorization of *musica mundana, musica humana* and *musica instrumentalis* (the music of the universe, human music and instrumental music). Boethius accepted Pythagoras' idea that the universe made a harmonious sound:

> How indeed could the swift mechanism of the sky move silently in its course? And although this sound does not reach our ears (as for many reasons be the case), the extremely rapid motion of such great bodies could not be altogether without sound, especially since the courses of the stars are joined together by such mutual adaptation that nothing more equally compacted or united could be imagined.[14]

Of *musica humana*, Boethius writes, "What human music is, anyone may understand by examining his own nature. For what is that which unites the incorporeal activity of the reason with the body, unless it be a certain mutual adaptation and as it were a tempering of low and high sounds into a single consonance?"[15] Just as the universe is perfect, so we too can be perfect in our bodies and souls, for we are a microcosm of the macrocosm. Of primary importance, however, is the music of the universe, of which mere instrumental music is but a poor imitation, with *musica humana* being somewhere in between. Thus musical theorists were originally held in higher esteem than practitioners—yet another example of humanity's over-valuation of the intellect. This idea was still in circulation in the nineteenth century, when it informed a telling passage in Jens Peter Jacobsen's 1880 novel *Niels Lynne*. Another of Jacobsen's works went on to form the basis of Schoenberg's *Gurreleider* (indeed, the legend of Gurre is also briefly mentioned in *Niels Lynne*), so it is appropriate that this musical reference to Boethius can be found in Jacobsen's work. In *Niels Lynne*, a rather pompous theology graduate, Herr Bigum, is an instinctive follower of Boethius' tripartite categorization of music and a passionate violinist:

> In the long run, all audible notes were false anyway, but whoever had the gift of perfect pitch had an invisible instrument within (compared with which the loveliest Cremona was like the calabash violin of the savage), and on that instrument played the soul, from its strings rang the ideal tones, and on that instrument the great composers had created their immortal works. The external music, that which quavered through the air of reality and which the ear heard, was merely a poor imitation, a stammering attempt to say the unsayable.[16]

Even in the 1960s, popular culture continued to echo this theme. A particularly effective cinematic manifestation of the musical nature of the human soul and its microcosmic reflection of divine harmony can be found in James Bernard's music for Hammer Films' *Frankenstein Created Woman* (dir. Terence Fisher, 1967). In it, Peter Cushing's Baron Frankenstein isolates the soul of an executed man in a spiritual forcefield before transplanting it into a

## One. The Music of the Spheres 11

female body. Martin Scorsese famously cited this movie as one of his personal favorites, because "the implied metaphysics are close to something sublime."[17] When Fisher shows us the soul (a glowing sphere of light), Bernard's accompanying musical effect helps make such a metaphysical phenomenon convincing. A soul without music would have been quite out of the question, and the combination of oscillating vibraphones with string harmonics, which forms the effect of a note cluster in the style of Penderecki, indeed suggests Plato's eight planetary sirens humming "one harmony."

Even the greatest earthly music is thus but an echo of the divine harmony, and this idea eventually found its way into Milos Forman's 1984 film adaptation of Peter Schaffer's play *Amadeus,* when F. Murray Abraham's Salieri examines the manuscripts of Mozart and exclaims:

> It was beyond belief. These were first and only drafts of music, but they showed no corrections of any kind — not one. He had simply written down music already finished in his head — page after page of it — as if he was just taking dictation — and music finished as no music is ever finished. Displace one note and there would be diminishment. Displace one phrase and the structure would fall. It was clear to me that the sound I heard in the Archbishop's palace had been no accident. Here again was the very voice of God. I was staring through the cage of those meticulous ink strokes at an absolute beauty.

It is important to bear in mind, however, that *Amadeus* is a highly romanticized account of Mozart's life and death, and, in fact, there are many examples of preparatory sketches for his work, which suggests that the composition process wasn't quite the divine dictation the film and play would have us believe. It was a much more human phenomenon. But it is the perfection of Mozart's classical structures as much as the lack of corrections on his manuscripts that suggests to Schaffer's Salieri that this music is somehow supra-human, that it not only expresses the human condition but also echoes the divine harmonies that Plato supposed were generated as a consequence of divine proportions. We might regard such a correlation as a mere metaphor, as a way of attempting to express our wonder at human creativity, but philosophers like Pythagoras, Plato, Boethius and, later, Heinrich Cornelius Agrippa (1486–1535) were convinced that the universe does indeed make a musical sound as it moves through its various cycles. Agrippa states, "Moreover we shall not dent, that there is in Sounds a vertue to receive the heavenly gift; if with *Pythagoras* and *Plato* we thought the heavens to consist by an Harmonial composition, and to rule and cause all things by Harmonial tones and motions."[18]

Indeed, long before Pythagoras, many world-creation myths suggested that the universe was summoned into being by means of sound. Pythagoras inherited his idea from the ancient Babylonians, who believed the following:

# 12                    The Occult Arts of Music

When on high the heaven had not been named
Firm ground below had not been called by name,
Naught but primeval Apsu, their begetter....
No reed huts had been matted, no marsh land brought into being,
Uncalled by name, their destinies undetermined.[19]

The ancient Egyptians also believed that the universe began when the great Creative Principle opened its mouth and proclaimed itself:

I, am he who came into being as Khepri (i.e., the Becoming One). When I came into being, the beings came into being, all the beings came into being after I became. Numerous are those who became, who came out of my mouth, before heaven ever existed, nor earth came into being, nor the worms, nor snakes were created in this place. I, being in weariness, was bound to them in the Watery Abyss. I found no place to stand. I thought in my heart, I planned in myself, I made all forms being alone, before I ejected Shu, before I spat out Tefnut, before any other who was in me had become. Then I planned in my own heart, and many forms of beings came into being as forms of children, as forms of their children. I conceived by my hand, I united myself with my hand, I poured out of my mouth.[20]

Judaism shared the idea of sound as a generator of existence, as we learn in the book of Genesis: "And God said, 'Let there be Light' and there was light." All these creation myths influenced C. S. Lewis in his account of the creation of Narnia in *The Magician's Nephew* (1955), where Aslan, the Christ-like lion, *sings* Narnia into being. The power of Aslan's music generates everything, and makes everything so fecund that when the wicked witch, Queen Jadis, throws the iron rod of a gas lamp into the ground of Narnia, it grows into the full-size lamp-post that illuminates the Lantern Waste, which the children encountered in *The Lion, the Witch and the Wardrobe* (1950).

Chanting is directly related to this. The singer, vina player, and founder of the Sufi movement, Hazrat Inyat Khan (1882–1927), believed that

every syllable has a certain effect. As the form of every sound is different, so every syllable has a special effect; and therefore every sound made or word spoken before an object has charged that object with a certain magnetism.... Besides that, many masters of occult sciences, who have communicated with the unseen beings by the power of sound, have done still greater things. By the power of sound they have created beings; in other words by the power of sound they gave a body to a soul, to a spirit, making it into a kind of being which is not yet a physical being but a being of a higher kind.[21]

Jill Purce, a twenty-first-century follower of Khan, explains, "I found myself looking for the kind of sound that really did create form. If, as we're

## One. The Music of the Spheres 13

told, 'In the beginning was the word, in the beginning was the Logos, in the beginning was sound,' what sound is it that creates form?" For Purce, the most magical sound is based on a chant from the remote regions of Tibet and Mongolia, centered on a single note:

> But the miraculous thing about the singing of this one note is through the modulation of the vocal cavities, through the modulation of the resonant cavities, it's possible to split this note open and to reveal the harmonies of the universe; to reveal the very structure of the universe; to reveal what are called the overtones or the harmonics. So what you hear, then, is a fundamental note, a base note, and then over it you hear these high, flute-like sounds, which have a very pure, bell-like quality and which, when people hear them, remind them in some way of what they think of as the music of the spheres. Plato tells us that the Pamphylian soldier saw the system of the seven planets and the fixed stars with the sirens standing on each sphere, and he says "uttering one tone varied by diverse modulations, and the whole eight of them together composed a single harmony." I think this to me suggests overtone chanting.[22]

The magical power of sound found one of its most impressive manifestations in film in Jerzy Skolimowski's *The Shout* (1978), starring Alan Bates as a man who has learned how to kill by means of a "terror Shout" that has apparently been taught to him by an aboriginal magician during his eighteen years in the Australian outback. Based on a short story by Robert Graves, the film is really a disquisition about the spiritual basis of sound, as well as its physical effects. Bates' character, Charles Crossley, believes his soul has been shattered into four pieces, and the film in general is also concerned with the idea of the soul being out of joint, of society being dislocated, of relationships breaking down, and ultimately of the madness that results from this disharmonious state of affairs. This is why the film begins and ends in a lunatic asylum.

Throughout the film there are some specific references to the soul, which Skolimowski symbolizes by means of insects and insect sounds in the manner of the Greek idea of equating the soul with a butterfly. This insect symbolism is introduced in the scene in which Crossley invites himself to lunch in the Devon home of a musician called Anthony (John Hurt) and his wife (Susannah York). Anthony is an avant-garde composer specializing in *musique concrète* techniques. His taped compositions are constructed by means of amplified acoustic sounds, rather than electronically generated material. We later see him experimenting with close-miking: rolling marbles in water, drawing a violin bow over an empty sardine can and inhaling cigarette smoke — all clichés of musical modernism at the time. Another sound is that of a bee buzzing in a jam jar, but the first insect/soul reference occurs when Crossley crushes a wasp against Anthony's kitchen window. They have been

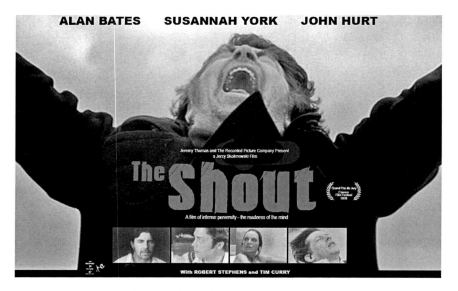

Poster for *The Shout* (dir. Jerzy Skolimowski, 1976).

discussing a sermon delivered in the church that morning, where Anthony also plays the organ. Just before the insect is crushed, Crossley says, "All religions have to answer the same question: has the human a soul and, if he has, where does he keep it?" The priest who gave the sermon clearly doesn't believe what he preaches. He speaks of society being a rudderless ship in a period of moral starvation: "Our faith in Jesus Christ is the only thing we have to hold on to. We must believe again." The trouble is that no one does. The soul is no longer in harmony with the universe. It would appear that the universal music of the spheres is not being channelled by the soul, and Anthony's avant-garde experiments are symptomatic of this dislocation. Later in the film, Crossley points this out, when he says to Anthony, "I heard your music. It's nothing. It's empty." A bee mobile hangs in Anthony's kitchen as a reminder that his soul, like those of other superficially fashionable (and, indeed, unbelieving) people, is suspended in a sterile world of meaningless sounds. Composers like Anthony, lost in their own private worlds, have abandoned their audience. This is made more explicit when we are shown the congregation at the church where Anthony plays the organ. Anthony has been so wrapped up in his tape recorders and introverted sound effects that he is late for the morning service. The congregation have started singing the hymns without him, and when Anthony eventually arrives and begins to accompany them with the organ, we discover they are all out of pitch — out of tune not just with the organ but perhaps with the universe itself.

## One. The Music of the Spheres          15

By contrast, Crossley's "terror Shout" is fully in tune with the universe. Indeed, he is able to command the universe with it. Not only can he cause thunderstorms, but he can also summon dreams, seduce those whom he desires, and kill those who get in his way. Another element of the film concerns his seduction of Anthony's wife — an occurrence that Anthony should have been prepared for, as his studio also contains reproductions of Munch's painting "The Vampire" and one of Francis Bacon's "Screaming Popes." Crossley is indeed a combination of both these images — a vampire and a screamer with an interest in religion. He argues that "in periods of spiritual starvation, the soul might take refuge in a tree or a stone," and this seems to have been the case with his own soul because Anthony eventually destroys Crossley by finding a stone on the beach. This he subsequently shatters, thus apparently shattering Crossley's soul into four pieces. Before that, however, Crossley does his best to destroy Anthony's marriage. He announces this intention by running his finger over the rim of a glass tumbler in the bathroom and causing it to ring. He later repeats the process with a wine glass over lunch, to such an extent that it too shatters. The implication here seems to be that he who commands sound commands the universe. The shattering of the wine glass accompanies Crossley's confession that he killed his children while married to an Australian aboriginal woman, who was bound to him by magical means, much as he is now binding Anthony's wife to him by means of stealing the buckle from her sandal (a well-established technique of sympathetic magic often used in witchcraft). The story is particularly upsetting to Anthony's wife, as she is unable to have children herself, but Crossley has more to impart: he has watched aboriginal magicians kill people by pointing a bone at them.

Crossley also explains that he has the power to kill by means of his Shout, and he eventually agrees to demonstrate this power to Anthony. They go out onto the sand dunes together and Anthony stuffs his ears with wax. This is a wise precaution, as the terrible sound kills a shepherd and his sheep outright, but before he releases it, Crossley inhales in a manner that suggests he is inhaling the daemonic spirit of the universe itself. Skolimowski films him from below and against the sky to monumentalize his god-like pose, as he gathers forces for the sonic eruption. Crossley's magical nature has already been suggested by a master-stroke of Skolimowski, who has Crossley's reflection appear in the dark surface of an oval mirror above the double bed in which Anthony and his wife are sleeping, prior to taking Anthony out on the dunes. The shot is reminiscent of Klingsor staring into his scrying glass in Act II of Wagner's *Parsifal,* summoning Kundry's alter-ego from its schizophrenic sleep.

As a consequence of Anthony's brush with death after experiencing

Crossley's Shout, all he can hear for a while is the muffled sound of pealing church bells—an echo, perhaps, of the faith he has lost. To reinforce this interpretation, Skolimowski makes sure that on the sand dunes and in the grounds of the lunatic asylum where the film's framing scenes of a cricket match take place, we see the tower of the local church. It dominates the horizon, but is ignored by all the characters. The church bells are either distant or, in Anthony's post–Shout condition, muffled. Crossley's Shout, however, is terrifyingly loud. Another character, later in the film, refers to it as "like a terrible music," and though it is not music of a conventional kind, its effect is far more powerful. Though Skolimowski commissioned two members of the progressive rock band Genesis to compose the film's main theme (Michael Rutherford and Tony Banks), he tends to favor heightened sound effects rather than music itself to emphasize this point. Sound is revealed here to be both Siva and Brahma — both destroyer and creator — and Crossley's Shout is an extreme kind of chant, which channels these elemental forces of the universe.

The word "enchant" means to make magical by chanting, so music is the most obvious medium with which to suggest the beginning of things. Wagner began his *Ring* cycle with the same basic building blocks of musical harmony (the octave, fifth and third) that we have already encountered for slightly different reasons in Williams' music for *Close Encounters*. This "acoustic idea," as Thomas Mann put it,[23] creates a powerful sense of the first cause — the creation of the world itself—and it was probably inspired by the opening of Beethoven's Ninth Symphony, the initial bars of which, with their open fifths, always suggested something mystical and magical to Wagner. He himself wrote that they played "a spectral role in my earliest impressions of music."[24] Even at the rather less exalted level of Hammer's prehistoric epic, *One Million Years B.C.* (dir. Don Chaffey, 1966), the composer Mario Nascimbene again resorts to a common chord (tonic rising to fifth, then dropping a third) to accompany the film's main title sequence, with its shots of volcanoes, fire and general "world creation."

We now know that sound cannot exist in a vacuum ("In space no one can hear you scream," as the publicists of *Alien* [dir. Ridley Scott, 1979] put it), but the universe and sound have always been united in mythological terms. In Plato's *Republic*, Socrates suggests that music and astronomy are fundamentally expressions of the same thing: cosmic harmony and proportion. He therefore argues that they should be studied together: "I conceive that as the eyes are designed to look up at the stars, so are the ears to hear harmonious motions; and these are sister sciences—as the Pythagoreans say."[25] The legacy of Pythagoras and Plato later influenced music during the Renaissance. The fifteenth-century philosopher Marsilio Ficino (1433–1499) extended Plato's analogy in his *De vita coelitus comparanda (On Obtaining*

# One. The Music of the Spheres

*Life from the Heavens)*, in which he explained:

> We attribute to Saturn voices that are slow, deep, harsh, and plaintive; to Mars voices that are the opposite — quick, sharp, fierce, and menacing; the Moon has the voices in between. The music, however, of Jupiter is deep, earnest, sweet, and joyful with stability. To Venus, on the contrary, we ascribe songs voluptuous with wantonness and softness. The songs between these two extremes we ascribe to the Sun and Mercury; if with their grace and smoothness they are reverential, simple, and earnest, the songs are judged to be Apollo's; if they are somewhat more relaxed, along with their gaiety, but vigorous and complex, they are Mercury's.[26]

Ficino's approach was shared by Agrippa, whose *Occult Philosophy* attributed "hoarse, heavy, and slow words and sounds" to Saturn and "rough, sharp, threatening, great and wrathful words" to Mars, with the Moon as mediator between the two. Jupiter "hath grave, constant, fixed, sweet, merry and pleasant" harmonies, while Venus has "lascivious, luxuries, delicate, voluptuous, dissolute and fluent" sounds.[27] These ideas of association were, of course, later musically elaborated by Gustav Holst (1874–1934) in his *Planets* suite, which we will be exploring later.

A famous realization of the concept of a music of the spheres was organized by the musician-soldier-poet-critic, Giovanni de' Bardi (1534–1612), who hosted meetings of the Florentine Camerata (which included Vincenzo Galileo, the father of the astronomer, and Giulio Caccini [1551–1618], one of the first opera composers). To celebrate the marriage in 1589 of Ferdinand de' Medici, Grand Duke of Tuscany, to Christine of Lorraine, a comedy (*La Pellegrina*, by Girolamo Bargagli) was performed. Between the scenes of the play, six unconnected *intermedi* were inserted, the sixth of which was called "L'armonia della sfere." Bardi was commissioned to organize the proceedings, which took place in what is now the Uffizi Gallery in Florence and were decidedly lavish in terms of special effects, stagecraft, and, of course, music. This sixth *intermedi* was, as its title suggests, a dramatization of Plato's Myth of Er from *The Republic*. Jamie James quotes from the account of one of the participants in this performance, Bastiano de' Rossi:

> A woman was descending on the cloud very slowly. She was playing the lute and singing the following madrigal:
>
> > *From the highest sphere,*
> > *friendly escort of the celestial Sirens*
> > *come I, Harmony, to you, O mortals:*
> > *for the winged messenger has brought to Heaven*
> > *a report of the greatest important,*

# The Occult Arts of Music

*that the Sun never saw a couple noble as you,*
*O new Minerva and strong Hercules.*[28]

The Sirens were next revealed on their clouds, singing and playing a variety of instruments, before the three Fates appeared along with Necessity, who held between her knees the spindle mentioned by Plato. It was altogether one of the most elaborate responses to the Platonic/Pythagorean idea of Universal Harmony, which, as we shall see, would be repeated centuries later in 1957 by Paul Hindemith in his opera, *Die Harmonie der Welt* (*The Harmony of the World*).

William Shakespeare (1564–1616) was equally fond of cosmic musical metaphors. A particularly notable one occurs in *Troilus and Cressida*, when Ulysses, advocating discipline in the war against the Trojans, begins his speech with an astronomical metaphor and ends it with a musical one:

> Degree being vizarded,
> The unworthiest shows as fairly in the mask.
> The heavens themselves, the planets, and this centre
> Observe degree, priority, and place,
> Insisture, course, proportion, season, form,
> Office, and custom, in all line of order.
> And therefore is the glorious planet Sol
> In noble essence enthroned and sphered
> Amidst the other; whose medicinable eye
> Corrects the influence of evil planets,
> And posts, like the commandment of a king
> Sans check, to good or bad. But when the planets
> In evil mixture to disorder wander,
> What plagues, and what portents, what mutiny,
> What raging of the sea, shaking of earth,
> Commotion of winds, frights, changes, horrors,
> Divert and wrack, rend and deracinate
> The unity and married calm of states
> Quite from their fixtures? O, when degree is shak'd,
> Which is the ladder to all high designs,
> The enterprise is sick. How could communities,
> Degrees in school, and brotherhoods in cities,
> Peaceful commerce from dividable shores,
> The primogenitive and due of birth,
> Prerogative of age, crowns, sceptres, laurels,
> But by degree, stand in authentic place?
> Take but degree away, untune that string,
> And hark what discord follows.[29]

# One. The Music of the Spheres

Indeed, so significant is music as a reflection of cosmic harmony that Shakespeare, in *The Merchant of Venice,* goes so far as to distrust men who do not respond to it. Such people are out of tune with humanity and, therefore, out of tune with the universe as a whole:

> The man that hath no music in himself,
> Nor is not mov'd with concord of sweet sounds,
> Is fit for treason, stratagems, and spoils;
> The motions of his spirit are dull as night,
> And his affections dark as Erebus:
> Let no such man be trusted.[30]

The result is truly disastrous in the original meaning of that word: *dis-astro* (ill-starred). The harmonies of music reflect the harmonies of the universe, of which man's society is but a microcosmic reflection.

The discord of an untuned universe, and the importance of restoring divine harmony here on earth, found expression in the twentieth century in both H. P. Lovecraft's 1922 short story, "The Music of Erich Zann" (which was filmed by John Strysik in 1980), and Jamil Dehlavi's 1986 film, *Born of Fire.* Both Lovecraft's story and Dehlavi's film have in common the concept of a musical duel in which supernatural forces of evil and disintegration, along with their concomitant disharmonious music, are kept at bay by the right kind of music. This benevolent music, in Shakespeare's terms, re-tunes the string of the universe, restores degree, and resolves, if only temporarily, a dangerous discord. Lovecraft's Erich Zann lives in the top floor of a boarding house, presumably in Paris, and plays the viol (though Strysik's film shows him playing an ordinary violin). A fellow boarder, who lives below Zann's attic room, is disturbed by Zann's weird improvisations, which sound unlike any music he has ever heard before. He visits the old man and asks to sit with him as he practices. When he requests a repetition of the weird music he has heard drifting from Zann's attic on so many occasions, Zann is terrified. He prevents the narrator of the tale from humming the tune and looks nervously at the curtained window at the back of the room. The dénouement reveals what is behind the curtain: Zann, who is a mute, has begun to write down the nature of his terrible secret, and implores the narrator to remain with him as he writes, but suddenly Zann starts with terror in response to "an exquisitely low and infinitely distant musical note."[31] At once, Zann picks up his instrument and begins to play his weird music. The narrator then plucks up the courage to peer behind the mysterious curtain, which reveals not the gigantic panorama of the city below but rather "the blackness of space illimitable; unimagined space alive with motion and music, and having no semblance to anything on earth." Zann's strange music therefore has a purpose:

"to ward something off or drown something out — what, I could not imagine, awesome though I felt it must be."[32] The strength of the tale's atmosphere lies in its non-specificity, which is almost impossible to translate into cinematic terms. Strysik makes a laudable attempt, but, of course, is faced with the problem of making utter blackness visually thrilling. He therefore changes it to brilliant light from behind the curtains, the silhouette of a dancing female figure, spinning circles of light and, finally, a light show reminiscent of the opening credits of the Jon Pertwee–era *Dr. Who*. Also, there was another problem for the composer, André Caporaso, who had to create music the like of which no human has ever heard before. Ostinati seem to do the job reasonably well and do indeed suggest the unstoppable power of whatever cosmic horror Zann is trying to keep at bay with his hard-pressed violin.

Jamil Dehlavi's *Born of Fire* has less narrative coherence than Lovecraft's tale, but the imagery is rather more compelling than the low budget of Strysik's nonetheless admirable homage to Lovecraft allowed. Basically, *Born of Fire* concerns the attempt of a flautist, Paul Bergson (played by Peter Firth), to defeat the power of a mythical creature known as "The Master Musician" (who is played by the oddly named Oh-Tee). The idea of a Magic Flute had, of course, been explored by Mozart at the end of the eighteenth century (and I will be exploring the occult aspects of that opera in the next chapter), but in *Born of Fire* the flute is a channel of both good and evil music. In the Islamic context of this film, the Master Musician is an Iblis, or evil spirit, intent on destroying the earth with fire. An unnamed female astronomer (played by Suzan Crowley, a distant relative of Aleister) attends one of Bergson's concerts at the Wigmore Hall in London, where he has been performing Poulenc's Flute Sonata, but the astronomer's presence makes him hear a much stranger kind of Oriental music, accompanying a vision of mosaics. The astronomer is convinced that the eruption of a volcano in Turkey, previously thought to have been extinct, is related to the recent sudden surges of solar activity. Obviously something is out of joint with the universe, so Bergson travels to the surreally beautiful region of Cappadocia in Turkey to search for the Master Musician, with whom his father had also had mystical dealings.

One imagines these to have been somewhat like those between Faust and Mephistopheles, for Bergson's father died in Turkey, having been taught mystical breathing techniques by the demonic flautist. Bergson's vision of mosaics is now explained, for they belong to the ancient church in Turkey where his father took refuge from the Iblis so many years ago. A Muslim holy man (Stefan Kalipha) is also involved, and he summons the Iblis with sacred chanting in preparation for the final showdown. He explains that Bergson must learn to control the hidden forces of the earth and that the will of the earth must burn within him. Only by finding the never-ending note

## One. The Music of the Spheres 21

will the Iblis bow down before the will of Allah and cosmic order be restored.

The narrative of the film is largely sacrificed in the name of its strikingly surreal imagery and Dehlavi's high-flown theological agenda, but the film's similarities to "The Music of Erich Zann" are nonetheless apparent. The suggestion is that there is a disruptive aspect in music that reflects chaos. A balance must therefore be maintained: the world can only be saved by the right kind of music. It is hard to say what this is, for Bergson plays conventional musical Orientalisms just as well as the Iblis in the crucial final duel. Earlier, he (or rather James Galway, who provided the soundtrack) intones Debussy's *Syrinx*, a piece devoted to Pan and *fin de siècle* neo-paganism. However, the idea that music is both a reflection of the universe and a powerful corrective of any imbalance within it goes right to the heart of the Pythagorean and Platonic concept of a music of the spheres, which originally resurfaced in Europe during the Renaissance and influenced so many musical theorists.

Among the most musical of Elizabethan thinkers was the Hermetic philosopher, Robert Fludd (1574–1637). In his *Tractatus on the Arts and Sciences,* published in 1618, he included a beautifully elaborate design for a Temple of Music in which the entire theory of this art as it was then understood is schematically displayed by means of architectural metaphor. It didn't add anything new to what was already known (or at least assumed), however, and, as Jamie James put it, in an age that was by then enjoying the sophistications of Monteverdi, "'The Temple of Music' must have seemed as quaint as Grandma's bloomers."[33] Significantly, however, in the lower portion of this temple, Fludd depicted Pythagoras entering the forge, relating the art of music to the divine proportions of the universe. The Jesuit philosopher, Athanasius Kircher (1601/2–1680), also included this famous Pythagorean scene in the frontispiece of the first volume of his *Musurgia Universalis* of 1650.

Other works by Fludd illustrate the divine order of the cosmos by means of a monochord. This instrument consists of a single string, stretched over a wooden sound box. It has a moveable bridge and was often used in the Middle Ages as a means of instructing students on the relationship between musical intervals and differing divisions of the string. Pythagoras realized that if you divide the string of a monochord in two, you have an octave, but an octave is not enough with which to make music. If you divide the string into three, however, you have a perfect fifth, and if you divide that again in three, you have another perfect fifth, and so on, every time you divide or multiply the string by three. This is why the number three was so important to Pythagoras, for it is the generative number of music.

Fludd provides us with what he called a Great Monochord, in which a complex table of cosmic relationships is structured around an engraving of this instrument. Next to the tuning peg, he includes a triangle in which resides the symbol, Alpha. At the opposite end there is another triangle containing Omega, thus visualizing the idea that the proportions of the universe are ordained and contained by God. Over the entire design, Fludd inscribed three resonant lines of explanation:

> The One is all things and all things are One.
> God is all that there is; from him all things
> proceed and to him all things must return.

Fludd was so fond of the metaphor of the monochord that we find a "Divine Monochord" in his *Tractatus on Metaphysics and Cosmic Origins* of 1617, in which the hand of God Himself, emerging from a symbolic cloud, turns the tuning peg of the instrument. For Fludd, different pitches are symbolic of the hierarchy of the universe. The lowest note on the monochord is C and represents the earth. Water is represented by A, air by B, fire by C, and then we move through the planets: D for the moon, E for Mercury, and F for Venus. The octave G (the midpoint between earth and heaven, as it were) is the place for the sun. Mars follows as we continue with the octave A, then Jupiter on B and Saturn on C. The remainder of the octave takes us out into the ether and up toward the hand of God.

Fludd's famous contemporary, Johannes Kepler (1571–1630), went so far as to suggest what the music of the spheres actually sounded like. Kepler's theory of the solar system was that the closer a planet is to the sun, the faster it moves. Conversely, the further away it is, the slower it moves. He attempted to express this in musical terms. Planets that moved in circular orbits, like Venus, kept one tone. Planets that moved in eccentric orbits, like the moon and Mars, created arpeggios. Rapid planets, like the moon, moved in semiquavers. Slow movers, like Saturn, moved in breves. Kepler believed that the planets also had specific intervals based on the difference between the maximum and minimum angular speeds of the various planets when measured from the sun. In other words, the closer to a circle around the sun the orbit is, the closer it is to a unison at each end of the orbit. Earth's interval, whose orbit is very nearly a circle but not quite, is a semitone: mi to fa. (He also glossed the names of these pitches theologically by suggesting that they also stood for the words "misery" and "famine"—our lot on earth.) Venus is almost a perfect circle and therefore the interval for Venus is a quarter tone. Thus do the orbits of the planets eventually build up a cosmic chord.

Sir Thomas Browne dwelt at some length on the concept of a music of the spheres in his 1642 *Religio Medici*: "There is music wherever there is harmony, order, or proportion: and thus far we may maintain the music of the spheres; for those well-ordained motions and regular paces, though they give

# One. The Music of the Spheres

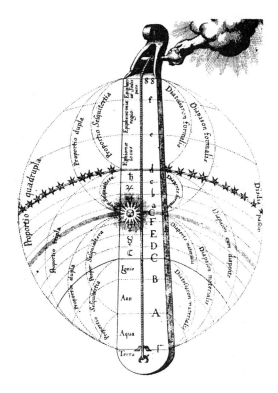

Robert Fludd, "The Divine Monochord," from *Utriusque Cosmi Maioris scilicet et Minoris Metaphysica, Physica Atque Technica Historia In duo Volumina secundum Cosmii differentian divisa* (Oppenheim: Johann Theodore de Bry, 1617), p. 90.

no sound to the ear, yet to the understanding they strike a note most full of harmony."[34]

Milton also followed the Pythagorean tradition in *Paradise Lost*:

> That day, as other solemn days, they spent
> In song and dance about the sacred hill,
> Mystical dance, which yonder starry sphere
> Of planets and of fixed in all her wheels
> Resembles nearest mazes intricate,
> Eccentric, intervolved, yet regular
> Then most, when most irregular they seem;
> And in their motions harmony divine
> So smoothes her charming tones, that God's own ear
> Listens delighted.[35]

# The Occult Arts of Music

For obvious reasons, the idea of an ordered, clockwork universe became very popular in the Age of Reason. John Dryden (1631–1700) anticipated this approach in his *Ode for St. Cecilia's Day*, with its lines "From harmony, from heavenly harmony/This universal frame began." Despite that, very little of the music composed by eighteenth-century composers was concerned with the classical idea of a music of the spheres. It is true that one of Haydn's most adventurous pieces of orchestral writing occurs at the opening of his most celestial piece, *The Creation* (1798) (in which he depicts Chaos by means of musical discords, which were considered to be very advanced in their day), but Haydn makes no attempt specifically to reflect the music of the spheres, and this lack of interest in what had once been so central an idea of musical theory continued throughout the nineteenth century. In the wake of the Romantic movement and impact of scientific inquiry, the concept of a music of the spheres came to look increasingly quaint and irrelevant. Composers did continue to respond to the grandeur of the universe but in less classically Pythagorean ways. It was left to late twentieth-century composers and film makers to revive the great theme.

Kepler had hoped to reconcile science and religion and demonstrate that everything in the world is but a part of a greater cosmic order, and Hindemith's *Die Harmonie der Welt* is largely an attempt to express Kepler's elaboration of the idea of a music of the spheres on stage. The various characters represent the seven planets: Kepler, for example, is the earth, while the Emperor is the sun, and Kepler's wife is Venus. Hindemith identified himself with Kepler, an identification that, as Hindemith scholar James D'Angelo explains, had many ramifications:

> He began to feel that music had a moral and ethical dimension, and he then began to look into the ancients and the medieval musical philosophers, and most especially Boethius and the idea that there were three levels of music.... Then he met a man named Hans Kayser. He was a philosopher who had a theory of world harmonics, which was the idea that the whole of the universe — everything — could be seen in number ratios and in a large Pythagorian Lambdoma table; so this got Hindemith thinking about a musical theory that was basically planetary in nature, that you could start from a single tone and in that tone there is an overtone series in which you have in a sense planetary relationships: near-ness and far-ness from a kind of sun. Now all of that was a background, and once he had discovered Kepler, well then, that was a great moment in his life, but it took him a very long time to realize this Kepler opera. I don't think he was creating any sort of literal music of the spheres at the end of that opera. It's a wonderful, wonderful piece of sound gathering and collecting, with that Passacaglia actually acting as a constant, as though that is the universal that always remains the same and everything else is changing. So it is metaphysical — metaphorical — but what can possibly be the literal music of the spheres?[36]

## One. The Music of the Spheres

Hindemith also composed a companion symphony dating from 1951, which bore the same name as the opera. Its three movements are named after Boethius' tripartite categorization of *musica instrumentalis, musica humana* and *musica mundana*. The final movement of the symphony forms the basis for the opera's Passacaglia finale, which sets the following imposing text:

Our gaze into the infinite cosmos encircling us with rich and gentle harmonies, inclines us through vision, ardor and faithful prayer, to uplift our imperfect selves higher than through logic and erudition, until the spirit of ultimate majesty grants to our soul the grace to be merged into the exalted harmony of the world.

As Ian Kemp suggests, in these works "Hindemith can be seen struggling with the idea that his theoretical concepts might give rise to music of such purity that it could provide a gateway into the secrets of the universe."[37]

The later twentieth-century British composer David Bedford (1937–2011) was also inspired by Kepler in his choral work, *From the City to the Stars* (2000), based on words by Arthur C. Clarke, telling the story of man's conquest of space billions of years in the future. Bedford even went so far as to ask the Royal Observatory at Greenwich to work out the orbits for Neptune and Pluto (unknown to Kepler in his lifetime) in order to create an even more complete universal harmony for the truly cosmic chord in his composition.

Arthur C. Clarke was also responsible for the scenario of Stanley Kubrick's *2001: A Space Odyssey* (1968), in which the idea of a music of the spheres is suggested by Kubrick's use of Johann Strauss' *Blue Danube* waltz during shots of humanity's space stations gracefully moving through the vacuum of the universe. Like the planets, they too move in a kind of dance, which the waltz rhythm emphasizes. Here, humanity and the cosmos move in harmony with each other, just as the medieval and Renaissance philosophers would have us believe. Significantly, the opening phrase of *The Blue Danube* is also based on a common chord, which brings with it the cosmic connotations of divine proportion with which we started.

An ongoing footnote to all this concerns the late twentieth-century phenomenon of crop circles, which, of course, continue to appear in the new century. Many people regard these as elaborate hoaxes, but some observers still interpret them along more esoteric lines. The Cymatics theory of Swiss scientist Hans Jenny (1904–1972), for example, which was elaborated in his 1967 book, *Kymatik,* has been applied to crop-circle analysis, and suggests a correlation between cosmic sound vibration and the crop circles' complex geometric patterns. Some crop circles have even been interpreted as expressions of the Pythagorean Lambdoma table (the table of ratios based on the overtone series that has been credited with being a numerical representation of the World Soul) to which James D'Angelo referred with regard to Hindemith and Hans Kayser. In the introduction to his magnum opus, *Textbook of Harmonics* (1944), Kayser advocated a distinctly regressive approach to the problems of modern life, creating an almost medieval ideal of contemplative retreat, complete with a medieval monochord and a distinctly Boethian kind of "music without notes" (a *musica mundana),* which he himself admits is "anachronistic," and all the better for that:

> We stand facing the inevitable destiny of ever more overpowering collectivism. The demands made on the individual by a profession, his duties to society, the ever growing difficulty of quiet self-reflection amidst the din of modern times, will require strong counterweights lest unfettered depersonalization drive humanity into a universal ant-like existence. One of these counterweights can be the harmonist's silent work for himself, without any aspiration to the outside. Just a small room, a table, a chair, and a monochord within reach: here, immersing oneself in harmonic problems, meditating upon the diagrams and tables one has drawn, upon each fine and subtle tone of the scales, chords, melodies, and rhythms—those who are called to this will become creators of a music without notes, which is sheer anachronism in contrast to the greater part of our so-called modern music! All this imparts, to those who know how to "hear," a harmonic state of soul and spirit that will automatically affect the conduct of the entire person in his professional and exterior life.[38]

Significantly, Kayser dated his introduction, "Near Bern at the sixth wartime Christmas 1944," and it is hard not to contextualize his vision as a response to the chaotic and threatening times in which he was writing. Similarly, the application of the Lambdoma table to mystical interpretations of crop circles should not be divorced from the millennial anxiety, and now post–9/11 context, that in part generated them. Neither should the suggestion that crop circles are a visual representation of a music of the spheres, created not by humans with planks but rather by some kind of cosmic musical vibration. Whatever the reality or absurdity of these claims, the popular interest in such an interpretation of the crop-circle phenomenon is certainly evidence of the continuation of Pythagoras' idea in the twenty-first century.

# Chapter Two
## *Masonic Music*

The original Brotherhood of Masonry first emerged at the end of the sixteenth century under the auspices of William Schaw, the "Maister o' Wark" under King James VI. In the eighteenth century, Guiseppe (or Joseph) Balsamo (a.k.a. Count Alesandro Cagliostro) (1743–1795), built on these traditions with his Egyptian Rite, which, indebted as it was to the Hermetic tradition, was not, in fact, anything particularly new, as he himself pointed out. He felt that he was merely restoring the ancient teachings to their original importance. In their engaging study of Cagliostro's Egyptian Rite, Philippa Faulks and Robert L.D. Cooper point out that Cagliostro went so far as to call himself "Grand Copht," a designation for the high priests of ancient Egypt. This is significant, according to their theory that ancient Egyptian stonemasons were an organized society, and that aspects of later Masonic symbolism are directly related to the way in which Egyptian temples were constructed.[1] The pyramid, for example, is a profoundly significant Masonic symbol. The four corners of its base represent the four elements, while the fifth point — the tip of the pyramid — represents the spirit, which rules the elements. The trials of fire, air and water, which form part of the initiation rituals of Freemasonry, were to play an important role in Jean Terrasson's Masonic novel *The Life of Sethos*. This, in turn, was to be a considerable influence on Mozart's Masonic opera, *Die Zauberflöte* (*The Magic Flute*, 1791).

Terrasson (1670–1750) was an obscure French abbé who published his novel in 1731. Despite its apparently biographical title, *The Life of Sethos* is, in fact, a hoax, wholly written by Terrasson himself, concerning the initiation of Sethos, an imaginary Egyptian prince, into the mystery religion of Isis and Osiris. Even so, *The Life of Sethos* was originally regarded by many as an authentic document from ancient times. Terrasson claimed that the book was a translation of a text by a Greek author living in Alexandria under the reign of Marcus Aurelius. While simultaneously describing that supposedly original text as a work of fiction, Terrasson claimed that he had also drawn upon sacred Egyptian wisdom, and to increase the sense of occult revelation, he added that the library in which the original text was located is in a foreign country that is "extremely jealous of this sort of treasure."[2] Disguised under such complex veils of dissimulation, it was not until well into the nineteenth century that *Sethos* was unmasked as a fake. It was also believed to be the foundation on which much Masonic ritual was later based, but in fact most of the rituals in the book were themselves taken from existing Masonic lore. (Terrasson was a Mason himself.) The book nonetheless made a considerable impact on the development of Freemasonry (and according to Faulks and Cooper, Cagliostro may well have been familiar with the novel, basing parts of his Egyptian Masonic Rite upon it[3]). It not only provided much of the Masonic ritual we see in *The Magic Flute* but also informed the play *Thämos, König in Aegypten (Thämos, King of Egypt),* by Tobias von Gebler, for which Mozart wrote incidental music in 1780.

Mozart was himself a member of the Viennese Masonic Lodge "zur Gekrönten Hoffnung," as a painting from 1789 by Ignaz Unterberger in the Vienna Historical Museum suggests. It shows the interior of the lodge and probably depicts Mozart sitting on the far right of the picture, next to Emmanuel Schikaneder (1751–1812), the librettist of *The Magic Flute.* The Master of Ceremonies is often assumed to be Prince Nicolaus Esterházy, Haydn's famous patron, and at the back of the chamber, a painting of a setting sun and a rainbow symbolizes the fact that Masons traditionally meet together after sunset and, like that symbol of purity, the rainbow, are themselves pure in heart and spirit. The two columns that flank the painting are symbolic of Jachin and Boaz, the two columns of Solomon's Temple, and the snakes coiling around them represent the enlightening influence of Mercury and consciousness.

Sarastro, the high priest of *The Magic Flute,* is often said to have been based variously on the Persian philosopher Zoroaster, Cagliostro himself and also the Freemason and mineralogist Ignaz Edler von Born (1742–1791). Eric Hornung suggests that Mozart and Schikaneder may have been familiar with Born's article "Über die Mysterien der Aegyptier," which was published in Born's Masonic journal, *Journal für Freimaurer.*[4] Mozart and Schikaneder were also keen players of the card game Tarock, and M. F. M. van den Berk has suggested that the Overture and 21 sections of *The Magic Flute* correspond to the 22 major arcana cards of the tarot deck, following the mystical plan of a fellow Freemason, Antoine Court de Gébelin (1719–1784), whose *Le Monde primitif, analysé et comparé avec le monde moderne (The Primitive World, Analyzed and Compared to the Modern World,* 1781) suggests that the tarot cards are in fact a symbolic representation of the Lost Book of Thoth, its 21 cards representing the 21 steps to higher states of consciousness (with its zero card representing the Fool).[5] This, however, is a contentious theory. As Colin Wilson points out, "Subsequent investigation has unearthed no sign of the Tarot pack in ancient Egypt. The Egyptian notion may have arisen from the known fact that the Tarot was used by gypsy fortune-tellers in the fifteenth century. But the notion that it was invented by the gypsies is contradicted by evidence that it was known in Spain, Germany and France at least a century earlier."[6]

Supposition or not, there is no doubt that the opera itself is far more than a pantomime. Technically it is not an opera, but rather a *Singspiel*, or singing play, as it contains lengthy sections of purely spoken dialogue. Singspiel was a popular form of entertainment in its day in Germany, and it is significant that the premiere of *The Magic Flute* took place in a popular theater on the outskirts of Vienna that was frequented by ordinary people rather than aristocrats and courtiers. Its audience was, indeed, more like that of a modern cinema, and with its spectacular stage effects, exotic scenery and varied action, *The Magic Flute* has all the ingredients of a popular movie—a kind of eighteenth-century

Ignaz Alberti, frontispiece for the first edition of *Die Zauberflöte*, Vienna, 1791.

*Indiana Jones* film in many ways. What's more, it was all performed in German rather than the courtly norm of Italian, and this made it much more appealing to Mozart's original German-speaking audience of ordinary people. Mozart, who longed to escape from the courtly confines of *opera seria*, with its Italian libretti and worthy classical subject matter, was at heart a populist.

*The Magic Flute* tells how the hero, Tamino, attains spiritual enlightenment under the guidance of the high priest, Sarastro. The Queen of the Night, whom we are at first led to believe is a force for good, tells Tamino that her daughter, Pamina, has been abducted by Sarastro. She charges Tamino with the task of rescuing Pamina, and presents him with the eponymous magic flute to help him. To his companion, Papageno, she presents a set of magic bells, and Tamino and Papageno set off together to find Sarastro's temple. We later learn that the Queen of the Night is quite the opposite of a good character and that Sarastro is equally the opposite of evil. Tamino and Pamina then undergo the trials of fire and water that will initiate them into Sarastro's magical Masonic circle of enlightenment. Papageno also finds his own true love in Papagena, who has been disguised until then as an old woman. The Queen of the Night is vanquished by the rays of light and wisdom that emanate from Sarastro, and everything ends in happiness, love and understanding.

The libretto's frequent references to Isis and Osiris, and the various temples we are shown, derive from passages in *Sethos* such as this one:

> In the middle of the sanctuary, upon a very high pedestal, and all on one single piece of cast metal, were plac'd these three deities, in such sort, that Osiris, whose image was the highest, held Isis standing before him, and she Horus in the same manner: For what Strabo says of the temples of Egypt being without statues, or at most having only the figure of some animal in the middle of them, is not to be understood of the times antecedent to the invasion of Cambyses. The head of Osiris was incircled with a radiant sun. Isis was crown'd with a bushel, and had her face cover'd with a veil. Under her left arm she held an urn bow'd downwards, and at her feet lay the bird Ibis. And Horus was describ'd holding his finger upon his lips.[7]

It is also revealing to compare what Sarastro has to say in his hymn "O Isis und Osiris," performed in Act II, with a similar prayer in Terrasson's *Life of Sethos*. Sarastro asks the gods to protect Tamino and Pamina as they undergo their initiation trials. He sings (in my translation of the original German text):

> O Isis and Osiris, hear us;
> Give wisdom to this pair.
> Lead their path away from temptations,

# Two. Masonic Music 31

> Give them patience in times of danger.
> Let them be victorious in their trial,
> But if they fail and Death should claim them
> Take them to your abode.

Here is Lepsius' translation of a similar invocation to Isis in *The Life of Sethos:*

> Isis, great goddess of the Egyptians, pour down thy spirit upon thy new votary, who has gone thro' so many perils and laborious trials to come before thee: Make him victorious also over his passions, by rendring him tractable to thy laws, that he may be worthy to be admitted to thy mysteries.[8]

The initiation trials endured by Sethos in the novel and by Tamino in *The Magic Flute* also have much in common. Once inside the temple, Sethos reads an inscription engraved in black letters on white marble:

> *Whoever goes thro' this passage alone, and without looking behind him, shall be purify'd by fire, by water, and by air; and if he can vanquish the fears of death, he shall return from the bowels of the earth, he shall see light again, and he shall be intitled to the privilege of preparing his mind for the revelation of the mysteries of the great goddess Isis.[9]*

In *The Magic Flute,* Tamino encounters three men in armor who say much the same thing:

> He who walks this path full of troubles will be purified through fire, water, air and earth; if he can overcome the terror of death he will soar heavenwards from the earth. He will then be enlightened and dedicate himself to the mysteries of Isis.[10]

Perhaps the three armed men of *The Magic Flute* were Schikaneder's version of the Anubis-headed priests encountered by Sethos in this passage from the novel:

> One of these three men said to the candidate; We are not posted here to stop your passage: Go on, if the gods have given you the courage: but if you be so unfortunate as to return, we shall then stop your passage: As yet you may go back, but from this moment you'll never get out of this place, unless you go on, without turning or looking back.[11]

The trials of earth, fire and water endured by Tamino also have their origin in *Sethos.* Early in the novel, Sethos enters a subterranean chamber beneath a pyramid, and has to pass over a grate of red-hot iron. He then crosses a canal of Nile water that is fed by a waterfall, and finally has to work out how to cross a chasm by means of two gigantic wheels that operate a drawbridge (this latter challenge is a particular test of courage, even though no actual harm can come to him). Schikaneder's stage directions for

# The Occult Arts of Music

scene 28 in Act II of *The Magic Flute* are surely indebted to the imagery in *Sethos*:

> Two high mountains. From one mountain, the rushing and roaring of a waterfall may be heard; the other spits out fire. Through a grill in each mountain, the fire and water can be seen — where the fire burns the horizon should be red as hell, while a thick mist lies on the water. There are rocks all over the stage, which is divided into two separate parts, each enclosed within an iron grate. Tamino is lightly clothed, without sandals. Two men in black armor accompany Tamino; on their helmets, flames burn. They read him the inscription, illuminated from within, on a pyramid high up in the centre, above the grills.[12]

The number 3 is of great importance to the story. It is reflected in the three-fold chord Mozart employs throughout, along with the key signature of E-flat (comprising three flats) in which the overture is composed. There is more to the three-fold chord of the overture, however. As Jacques Chailley explains, it is actually a five-fold chord (the second and third chords are each repeated). The significance of 5 is that it represents Woman. As Chailley points out, "The number 5 has a very precise meaning. In the symbolism adopted by Masonry, it is opposed to the number 3 of the male principle, and thus represents its opposite, the female principle."[13] The opening five chords therefore establish the feminine principle of the introductory adagio that opens the overture. The adagio also represents "the Kingdom of Darkness and Chaos (the 'Kingdom of the Night'),"[14] which is ruled over by the Queen of the Night. The fugue that follows the adagio represents the domain of the male, with its sun-illuminated logic and order. And in this section we indeed hear a three-fold chord, which certainly does represent the male principle. The entire thrust of the opera, therefore, is concerned with the mystical union of male and female. Without the male to provide guidance and control, according to Chailley's interpretation, women have a tendency to become proud and destructive. Chailley sums up Mozart's essentially misogynistic Masonic worldview by describing the Queen of the Night as being in opposition to the solar masculine kingdom. Wisdom is equated with the sun; the Queen of the Night can therefore only ever rule over a realm of folly. At first, she resists Sarastro's "manly" nature but must learn that the duty of women is to submit themselves to the rule of wise men. Her mistake lies in her pride — her belief that she can exist independently of men.[15] Thus, the mystical atmosphere of the work can essentially be reduced to a disquisition on sexual politics.

This theme subsequently found a rather more sensationalist expression in the Sherlock Holmes adventure *Murder by Decree* (dir. Bob Clark, 1979) and the film adaptation of Alan Moore's graphic novel, *From Hell* (dir. Albert and Allen Hughes, 2001). Both films cover much the same ground, and follow the now disproved theory that the Jack the Ripper murders were carried out by Queen Victoria's personal physician, Sir William Gull (1816–1890). The Masonic element is, however, consistent with Mozart's misogynistic agenda, as both films suggest that Sir William was driven by the desire to revenge himself on a group of prostitutes who witnessed the secret Roman Catholic wedding of the queen's grandson, Prince Edward, to one of their number. Not only did the girl in question give birth to a legitimate heir to the throne, but she also infected the prince with syphilis. Commissioned by the queen herself to murder all the women involved, Gull's unhinged mind becomes obsessed with the idea of ensuring the continuance of male dominance in society. The murders, therefore, become symbolic, and symbolic in a specifically Masonic manner. Gull is a Mason, and the Masons, it is suggested, were fully aware of the conspiracy — indeed, actively in support of it. Rather than allow Gull's dreadful secret to possibly come to light, the Masonic brotherhood to which Gull belongs ultimately orders that he be lobotomized.

Cagliostro has also appeared on screen, principally in *The Affair of the Necklace* (dir. Charles Shyer, 2001), in which he was played by Christopher Walken. Before that, a French TV series based on Alexandre Dumas' novel *Joseph Balsamo* (dir. André Hunebelle, 1973) had Jean Marais in the title role. Even earlier, the character had formed the basis of Johann Strauss' operetta, *Cagliostro in Wien* (1875), but these are all incidental to his possible influence on *The Magic Flute*. A rather more specific reference to that opera was imaginatively woven into one of the *Inspector Morse* TV episodes, "Masonic Murders," directed by Danny Boyle and starring John Thaw in the title role, which was first screened on British television in 1990. Julian Mitchell's script based a murder mystery around the rehearsal of an amateur production of *The Magic Flute*. The production of the opera itself is distinctly Masonic in its regalia — the choir wears vaguely Egyptian robes with Masonic medallions, and we even see an Anubis *couchant*. (Later, the opera is specifically referred to by one of the characters as a "Masonic opera.") A telephone call summons a female member of the cast away from the stage, and as the Queen of the Night reaches her top F, we hear, instead, the screams of the murder victim. Morse rushes to her aid, but when he is discovered holding the body in one hand and a kitchen knife in the other, the knife having been left on the floor beside her, he is suspended by his commanding officer. His replacement is a member of the local Masonic lodge, and Morse eventually suspects he is being victimized by a Masonic conspiracy against him, especially when he is later stopped in his car by another Masonic police officer and, in a separate incident, his car is scratched with Masonic symbols. In fact, the Masonic element is a red herring, but the opera is not. The episode's main title sequence is accompanied by Mozart's overture, and the plot of the opera runs throughout the story. Comparisons are made between characters in the opera and those in the series: Morse seeks help from his former superior, one Desmond McNutt (played by Iain Cuthbertson), whom he calls "Sarastro," explaining to the confused Sergeant Lewis (Kevin Whatley) that Sarastro—"the fount of all wisdom"—is based on Zoroaster. Morse later refers to Lewis as Papageno and to Lewis' wife as Papagena, and ultimately the real mastermind behind the murderous mysteries, the criminal confidence trickster Hugo De Vries (Ian McDiarmid), reveals that Morse himself is Monostatos, the foolish villain. "You made an elementary mistake, you see," he explains. "You thought you were the hero—you were meant to think that. You were meant to think your frustrations were ordeals, but the villain undergoes frustrations too, until he and his mistress are overwhelmed by the truth. I am the high priest, Morse. You are the evil spirit. I am Sarastro, you are Monostatos and now the earth is about to swallow you up." During this speech, we hear a recording of the magic bells that make Monostatos dance toward the end of the first act: De Vries is obviously making Morse dance to his tune.

But De Vries is only Sarastro in his own perverted imagination. He is much more suited to the role of Queen of the Night. He has set the whole thing up. It was he who scratched the Masonic symbols on Morse's car, and it was he who thought up the two "ordeals" by fire and water, echoing those in the opera. (McNutt is found dead in Morse's airing cupboard, drenched by a burst water main. Later, Morse's house is set on fire, ruining his beloved collection of opera recordings. The fire is started by an incendiary device that first sets fire to a recording of Toscanini's version of *The Magic Flute*—"the worst recording in history," according to Morse.) De Vries does all this to exact revenge on Morse for having put him in prison for an earlier crime. He wants Morse to suffer, to know what it's like to be put in prison himself. (In fact, the closest Morse gets to prison is a few nights in a police cell, when the circumstantial evidence against him, arranged by De Vries, proves almost conclusive.) The murder that started the whole process was carried out by De Vries' accomplice. Together, she and De Vries were engaged in a massive fraud of charity funds, and the murder victim was about to find out what was going on. These are the explanations, but the real interest of the episode lies in its manipulation of Mozart's Masonic imagery. It also echoes the long-established conspiracy theory that Mozart himself was murdered by his fellow Masons in revenge for his having exposed Masonic rituals to the public gaze in a popular work for the stage—not that Sergeant Lewis and his wife think much of it when they attend the belated performance. "What does he see in it?" Lewis complains, leaving halfway through. "I still couldn't understand a bloody word."

The same might be said of the Aleister Crowley romp, *Chemical Wedding*

## Two. Masonic Music 35

(dir. Julian Doyle, 2008), which has nothing to do with Mozart, but does rather effectively convey the sinister atmosphere of a Masonic meeting, thus perpetuating the public's general belief that the Brotherhood is the most likely suspect when it comes to conspiracy theories. *From Hell,* however, does the job rather more lavishly.

Movie versions of Mozart's opera tend to play down the Masonic elements. Ingmar Bergman's 1975 film emphasizes the theatrical nature of the drama, with pantomime dragons, backstage scenes, and a general sense of "Verfremdungseffekt," while Kenneth Branagh's 2006 version is set in a stylized World War I setting (blue uniforms rather than khaki) and concentrates upon more general ideas of good and evil as typified by war in the trenches rather than the more mystical variety. The misogynistic subtext is also carefully avoided.

For all Mozart's Masonic concerns in *The Magic Flute,* his general approach to composition was not so esoteric. For Mozart, a concerto was a concerto, a symphony a symphony. With the exception of sacred choral works and occasional pieces for specific functions, such as the Masonic Funeral Music of 1785, only in opera did conceptual meaning enter into the process, and only in *The Magic Flute* and *Don Giovanni* did he incorporate elements of what we now call "the occult." Beethoven's interweaving of music, mysticism and Freemasonry was somewhat more esoteric, however. In the finale of the Ninth Symphony, he set these lines by Schiller:

> Ahnest du den Schöpfer, Welt?
> Sach' ihn über'm Sternenzelt!
> Über Sternen muss er wohnen.
>
> (World, do you feel the Creator present?
> Seek Him beyond the firmament of stars
> Above the stars He surely dwells.)

Beethoven's setting of the third line, in particular, set the precedent for many a science fiction film composer in its evocation of the starry vastness of the heavens. To create the required sense of eternity, all harmonic movement is suspended and a single chord (in fact, no more than a straightforward diminished seventh) is repeated, with the singers and instrumentalists playing in very high registers (top G-sharp for the sopranos). The marking is *fortissimo* to suggest immensity and grandeur, but when the line "über'm Sternenzelt muss ein lieber Vater wohnen" is sung, Beethoven instructs everyone to play (and sing) *pianissimo* while retaining similarly high pitches. A feeling of movement is created by the tremolo strings and rapidly repeated triplets in the wind, with the phrase ending on a *fermata* as the last note is held, to suggest a mystical sense of timelessness.

High pitches are invariably employed in science fiction film scores to evoke the immensity above us, along with similarly sustained harmonies or note clusters. The opening bars of Jerry Goldsmith's score for *Alien,* for example, are a suitably modernized version of this Beethovenian moment. The *Dr. Who* composer Tristram Cary also matched shots of the starry skies in Hammer's *Blood from the Mummy's Tomb* (dir. Seth Holt, 1971) with high-pitched strings working to similar effect. Thus we see another active connection between high art and popular culture through the medium of music.

Beethoven's first teacher was the Bonn court organist, Christian Gottlob Neefe (1748–1798). Neefe was also a prominent Freemason and the leader of the Bonn Illuminati lodge, Stagira. Many of Beethoven's supporters and patrons were also Masons. Haydn, who became his teacher in Vienna, was one. So was Karl Lichnowsky (1756–1814), who was a lodge brother of Mozart and a member of the Illuminati. The poets Johann Gottfried von Herder (1744–1803) and Gottfried August Bürger (1747–1794) and Johann Wolfgang von Goethe (1749–1832), whose poetry Beethoven set to music, were also Masons or Illuminists. So was Gottlieb Friedrich Klopstock (1724–1803), whose poetry Beethoven much admired and whose complete works were part of his private library. ("I carried him about with me for years while walking," Beethoven wrote, "and also at other times. Well, I did not always understand him, of course. He leaps about so much and he begins at too lofty an elevation. Always *Maestoso,* D-flat major! Isn't it just so? But he is great and uplifts the soul nevertheless."[16])

There are rumors, so far uncorroborated, that Beethoven was a Mason himself. Whether he was or not, he was certainly often in the company of Masons and genuinely interested in esoteric ideas. On the last page of the sketch for the Adagio of the Razumovsky Quartet op. 59, no. 1, for example, Beethoven wrote, "A weeping willow or acacia tree on my brother's grave."[17] ("Einen Trauenweiden oder Akazien-Baum aufs Grab meines Bruders.") This could, of course, refer to one of his own brothers, but it is often considered that he was using the term "brother" in its Masonic sense. The acacia is certainly a Masonic symbol of initiation and the immortality of the soul. Beethoven also copied out passages from Schiller's essay, *Die Sendung Moses.*[18]

Ich bin, was da ist.
Ich bin alles, was ist, was war, und was sein wird, kein sterblicher Mensch had meiner Schleier aufgehoben.
Er ist enzig und von ihm selbst, und diesem Einzigen sind alle Dinge ihr Dasein schuldig.
(I am that which is.
I am everything that is, that was, and that shall be. No mortal man has lifted my veil.

He is unique unto himself, and it is to this singularity that all things owe their existence.)

Beethoven kept these sentences under a glass on his desk, and they served as daily inspirations for him. The first one allegedly originates from a statue of Isis, the second from a pyramid at Sais, while the third is an Orphic hymn used for rites of the Eleusinian Mysteries, and these ideas, largely due to their apparent Egyptian origin, also have Masonic connotations.

As Beethoven's biographer, Anton Schindler, pointed out, Beethoven's religious views were hardly orthodox. They "rested less upon the creed of the church, than that they had their origin in deism. Without having a manufactured theory before him he plainly recognized the existence of God in the world as well as the world in God. This theory he found in the whole of Nature, and his guides seem to have been the oft-mentioned book, Christian Sturm's *Betrachtungen der Werke Gottes in der Natur*, and the philosophical systems of the Greek wise men."[19] And Beethoven was also interested in Persian and Indian philosophy and mythology. He read Herder's translation of Persian poetry and owned a copy of the *Bhagavad Gita*. Indeed, Indian thought was fashionable at the time, later influencing Schopenhauer and Wagner. Beethoven was part of this general trend, and the following mystical opinions, derived from his studies of Hindu literature, were found among his personal effects, written out in his own hand:

God is immaterial; since he is invisible he can have no form, but from what we observe in his works we may conclude that he is eternal, omnipotent, omniscient and omnipresent — The mighty one is he who is free from all desire; he alone; there is no greater than he.

Brahma; his spirit is enwrapped in himself. He, the mighty one, is present in every part of space — his omniscience is in spirit by himself and the conception of his comprehends every other one; of all comprehensive attributes that of omniscience is the greatest. For there is no threefold existence. It is independent of everything. O God, thou are the true, eternal, blessed, immutable light of all times and all spaces.[20]

Beethoven may even have considered setting an Indian shepherd play called *Dewajani* by the Austrian orientalist Joseph von Hammer-Purgstall (1774–1856) in 1819, for in an undated and unaddressed note, evidently written to Hammer-Purgstall, Beethoven wrote:

I am almost put to shame by your courtesy and kindness showing me your still unknown literary treasures in manuscript. I thank you, Sir, most sincerely as I return both opera texts— Since I am overwhelmed by work in my own art, it is impossible for me just now to go into details about the Indian opera particularly.[21]

In addition, Beethoven's Conversation Books contain references to Egyptian mystery religion. In March 1826, for example, the violinist Karl Holz wrote, "Dear fellow! If you leave behind nothing but your sketchbooks, they won't lead to any such quarrel because they are hieroglyphics, from which no man will derive wisdom!—These are the Mysteries of Isis and Osiris."[22]

Beethoven also set songs with overtly Masonic meanings. These include G. C. Pfeffel's, "Der Freie Mann" (WoO 117):

> Wer, wer ist ein freier Mann?
> Dem nicht Geburt noch Titel,
> Nicht Sammtrock oder Kittel
> Den Bruder bergen kann;
> Der ist ein freier Mann!
> Ein freier, freier Mann!

(Who, who is a free man? He from whom neither birth nor title, peasant smock nor uniform, hides his brother man.)

Another important text was the "Opferlied" of Friedrich von Matthisson (1761–1831), in which a young man offers a sacrifice to Zeus in the hope that the god will be the protector of liberty. The final line—"Das Schöne zu dem Guten!" ("The beautiful to the good")—was particularly important to Beethoven, and he often wrote these words on the pages of his manuscripts toward the end of his life. Goethe's "Bundeslied" also has particularly Masonic ideals in its emphasis on brotherly comradeship:

> Wer lebt in unserm Kreise,
> Und lebt nicht selig drin?
> Genießt die freie Weise
> Und treuen Brudersinn!
> So bleibt durch alle Zeiten
> Herz Herzen zugekehrt;
> Von keinen Kleinigkeiten
> Wird unser Bund gestört.

(Who lives in our circle but is not happy? Relish the free ways and faithful brotherly love! So we remain through all time, heart turned toward heart; and through no trifle will our bond ever be broken.)

Not only do these words share the same sentiment as Schiller's *Ode to Joy*, which Beethoven set to music in the finale of his Ninth Symphony, but they also reflect the words sung by Don Fernando in Beethoven's only opera, *Fidelio* ("The brother seeks his brethren and if he can help them he gladly does so"), and it is perfectly reasonable to interpret them along Masonic lines. Beethoven's *Funeral Cantata for Joseph II* also has Masonic connotations with its text by Severin Anton Averdonk, which at one point expresses a very Masonic plea for political and religious tolerance:

> Ein Ungeheuer, sein Name Fanatismus,
> stieg aus den Tiefen der Hölle,
> dehnte sich zwischen Erd' und Sonne,
> und es ward Nacht!

> (A monstrous creature, its name Fanaticism,
> Arose from the depths of Hell,
> Stretched itself between earth and sun
> And it was Night.)

Averdonk was a government employee and inevitably, given the social conventions of the time, in contact with Freemasonry. The dancer and choreographer Salvatore Vigano came from a rather different background, born as he was in Naples, but it was his idea, perhaps inspired by the success of Haydn's *The Creation,* to commission music from Beethoven for a ballet about Prometheus. It was a subject well suited to Beethoven's idealistic concerns, and the resulting work, *The Creatures of Prometheus* (1801), reflected Beethoven's mission to encourage the elevation and perfection of mankind — a very Masonic theme, which also runs through his "Eroica" symphony. This is one of the reasons why the German symbolist artist Max Klinger (1857–1920) chose to represent Beethoven as a modern Prometheus in his famous polychrome monument to the composer in 1902.

Brian S. Gaona's thesis, "Through the Lens of Freemasonry: The Influence of Ancient Esoteric Thought in Beethoven's Late Works,"[23] suggests that Beethoven's music is sometimes a symbolic expression of esoteric thought. He cites the Op. 119 Bagatelles, the seventh of which shares its Masonic "magic" number significance with the theme of submission and self-sacrifice, which we read about in the *Bhagavad Gita.* In this mystical text, Krishna's student, Arjuna, must transform himself into a higher consciousness by means of yoga, thus breaking free from the illusion of Maya and ultimately finding unity in Nirvana. Gaona equates the trill in the last Bagatelle to this process. The theme of the Bagatelle gradually evolves until it becomes so rapid and brilliant that it resembles the trill that originally only accompanied it. The theme has thus been transformed into the trill itself. Gaona also equates the "Arietta" of the 32nd Piano Sonata (Op. 111) with Nirvana in its attempt to create a sense of timelessness. As Beethoven wrote in his Tagebuch, "For God, time absolutely does not exist."[24] In his novel, *Doctor Faustus,* Thomas Mann similarly describes the effect of the "Arietta" as being "of awe-inspiring unearthliness."[25]

40 The Occult Arts of Music

According to William Kinderman, Plato's *Republic* might well have influenced the choral finale of the Ninth Symphony. There is evidence in the Conversation Books that Beethoven may have read the text, as there is an entry by one of Beethoven's friends, Friedrich Wähner, full of enthusiasm for Plato's work: "Philosophie und Musik sollen leben! Den Plato müssen Sie in der Deutsche Übersetzung von Schliermachen lesen. Sie müssen. Ich bringe ihn ihnen." ("Long live philosophy and music! You must read Plato in the German translation by Schliermachen. You must. I'll bring it to you.") As Kinderman points out, "One of Plato's fundamental points in *The Republic* concerns the need for common human experience as the basis for common action, based on agreement about ends and means. In Book 5 Socrates asks 'Is there any worse ill for a state than to be divided or a greater good than being united?'"[26] These ideas sit very comfortably with Masonic ideals and complement the utopian sentiments of Schiller's "An die Freude," which provided the text for Beethoven's famous finale, with its highly Masonic lines:

> Alle Menschen werden Brüder
> wo dein sanfter Flügel weilt....
> Brüder! übern Sternenzelt
> muss ein lieber Vater wohnen.
>
> (All mankind become brothers
> Where thy gentle wings tarry....
> Brothers! above the vault of the stars
> There surely dwells a loving Father.)

Schiller was not himself a Mason, but this particular poem was much used by the Masons[27] and Schiller had personal links with Masonry through his Masonic and Illuminatist friend, the lawyer Christian Gottfried Körner (1756–1831).

Gaona regards the culmination of Beethoven's musical evocations of Masonic thought to be achieved in the Op. 131 string quartet in C-sharp minor, a work that has long been regarded as transcendental in its effect and intention. As Marion M. Scott put it as long ago as 1934, this is "serene, otherworld music."[28] The spiritual content of the three late quartets, of which the Op. 131 is the third, equates to the three Masses Beethoven planned but never wrote: "The C sharp minor Mass—projected and apparently abandoned—became the C sharp minor Quartet."[29] Scott adds, "I know of few things in music which seem so to transcend temporal existence as the passage beginning at bar 56 and its counterpoint later on."[30]

There is also evidence that Plato's concept of a music of the spheres may have influenced the Op. 131 quartet. It has seven movements, which are intended to be played without a break. The first is a fugue in C-sharp. The

## Two. Masonic Music 41

second is in suite form in D. The third is a recitative in B, followed by an andante in A, a scherzo in E, and aria form in G-sharp and finally a sonata movement in the opening key of C-sharp. Put them all together in the right order and you very nearly have a descending scale of C-sharp natural minor (though, technically, the D should be a D-sharp). The only missing note is the F-sharp, which could be interpreted symbolically: Although there are seven (planetary) movements, there are only six pitches. The relationship between 6 + 1 is also mystical in its own way, reminding us of the six days of creation followed by the Sabbath. (Unity was central to Beethoven's ideas at this time, reflecting his reading of Indian philosophy, which stresses the unity of all things. According to this idea, all things are in reality Vishnu: "All this visible universe comes from my invisible Being. All beings have their rest in me, but I have not my rest in them."[31]) Marion Scott concludes:

> So here we have *seven* (the perfect number in the lore of numbers), forming a circle (which is a symbol of eternity), and the motto fugue theme (probably symbolizing Life) all combined by Beethoven. Still further, the motto theme with its characteristic interval of the sixth is now below the threshold of consciousness, merged as it were in the new order, but in its reversed form — with the *third* as its characteristic, it dominates the thematic matter of the Quartet. Thus the third (which might symbolize God since it is the number of the Trinity) and its inversion the sixth — Man — are seen like reality and its reflection.[32]

Gaona also suggests that the motto theme that unites all three quartets is vaguely Indian/Oriental in its mixture of augmented and diminished intervals (C-sharp, D, B, A). He relates the motto theme to a similar theme in Bach's *Musical Offering*, which was written by the Masonic/Rosicrucian King Friedrich the Great for Bach to work his magic on. Gaona argues that Beethoven may well have been making a reference to this connection in his own motto theme.

The strange, diffused passage toward the end of the coda suggests that all the energy that precedes it must be relinquished along with our earthly striving if we are to enter the eighth sphere and become united with God or enter Nirvana. No earthly illusions must remain. The oddness of the passage suggests that the time for mere *musica instrumentalis* is over and we are ready to experience the true music of the spheres.

Various films have appeared over the years with Beethoven's life and legend as their subject, but few have grappled with the esoteric element. From Abel Gance's 1936 *Un Grand Amour de Beethoven* to Agnieszka Holland's *Copying Beethoven* in 2006, most of these films present merely a romanticized account of the well-worn biography of this musical Titan. *Immortal Beloved* (dir. Bernard Rose, 1994) went further, mixing fact with supposition. Perhaps, therefore, the most interesting film from an esoteric point of view is Stanley Kubrick's 1971 adaptation of Anthony Burgess' *A Clockwork Orange,* because the whole premise of the story concerns free-will, good and evil. Burgess even included some esoteric numerical symbolism in the structure of the book, as he explained in his autobiography: "I had structured the work with some care. It was divided into three sections of seven chapters each, the total figure being, in traditional arithmology, the symbol of human maturity."[33] Unfortunately, the American publisher insisted that the final chapter be removed, so when it came to Kubrick's film, "A vindication of free will had become an exultation of the urge to sin. I was worried," Burgess confessed. "The British version of the book shows Alex growing up and putting violence by as a childish toy; Kubrick confessed that he did not know this version: an American, though settled in England, he had followed the only version that Americans were permitted to know."[34]

Even so, Burgess' novel was understood more by American reviewers than their English counterparts. As one of the original American reviews of the novel put it, "Goodness is nothing if evil is not accepted as a possibility."[35] Burgess himself explained, "Brought up as a Catholic (and the book is more Catholic or Judaic than Protestant), I naturally considered that humanity is defined by its capacity for St. Augustine's *liberum arbitrium,* and that moral choice cannot exist without a moral polarity."[36] Or, as Hammer Films' less high-falutin *Blood from the Mummy's Tomb* expressed it, "You can't only have good things, beautiful things, holy things. They're worthless without their opposites." (Seth Holt's mummy movie, incidentally, was released in the same year as Kubrick's *A Clockwork Orange.*) But is music actually capable of a moral framework? Is it not in fact "ambiguity made a science" (as one of the characters in Visconti's adaptation of Thomas Mann's *Death in Venice* insists)? Mann's other novel, *Doctor Faustus,* has its main character, the composer Adrian Leverkühn, discuss the idea of music's basic ambiguity in much more detail:

> He played a chord: all the black keys, F-sharp, A-sharp, C-sharp, added an E, and so unmasked the chord, which had looked like F-sharp major, as belonging to B major, as its dominant. "Such a chord," he said, "has of itself no tonality. Everything is relation, and the relation forms the circle.... Relationship is everything. And if you want to give it a more precise name, it is ambiguity."[37]

One may extend the analogy. Would we have any conception of pleasure if we had not felt pain? The pleasure we anticipate before eating a meal would have no meaning for us if we never felt the pangs of hunger. Is Margaret Fuchs in *Blood from the Mummy's Tomb* right when she suggests that nothing can have meaning or value without its opposite? If this is so, might it suggest a way of explaining the problem of evil in the world? Is it somehow necessary? This is certainly one way of interpreting the idea of original sin. If Eve had not eaten the apple from the tree of knowledge, human history would never have happened. She needed to commit this *felix culpa* (or fortunate crime) if life was to have any purpose or meaning. We need the opportunity of free will.

That Burgess and Kubrick use Beethoven's music to illustrate the counterpoint of this argument suggests that the ambivalent quality of such music is much greater than that of other composers whom Alex also enjoys, such as Mozart and Bach. Alex, the futuristic thug who revels in violence, does so to the strains of Beethoven's Ninth Symphony. Alex's interpretation of Beethoven's setting of the "Ode to Joy" implies the orgiastic joy of sex and violence. Allied to different words in praise of these dubious activities, the music would indeed serve them well. As Burgess put it, "There were still musicologists around who alleged that Beethoven opened up a vision of divinity. Alex gets something very much opposed to that out of the scherzo of the Ninth."[38] If Alex is inspired to ultra-violence by the great Ludwig van Beethoven, what does this say about the esoteric element apparently embedded within his music? Surely that it is no more than an *intention* on the part of the composer. The music itself remains amoral, ambivalent. Like Lucifer's light or Prometheus' fire, it can illuminate, warm, blind or burn depending on how we use it. Burgess and Kubrick's thesis is really a kind of commentary on those propaganda films of German orchestras playing the Ninth Symphony to workers in Nazi factories. Who is to say that the Nazi authorities were any less committed in their response to Beethoven than Alex? It would appear that Beethoven's *intentions* are probably irrelevant, and the music is in fact incapable of expressing them by itself.

# Chapter Three
## *The Birth of the Demonic*

Music has always been required in magical and religious ritual as a means of creating a numinous state of mind. Goethe, in his conversations with Eckermann, suggested that religious worship "cannot dispense with it; it is one of the chief means of working upon men miraculously." For Goethe, this daemonic quality of music "stands so high that no understanding can reach it, and an influence flows from it which masters all, and for which none can account."[1] Similarly, in opera, theater and film, music is a vital ingredient when these art forms attempt to make magical effects convincing. Music is a particularly important element in many occult movies because it is the most effective way to express forces that lie beyond the merely phenomenal world. As Schopenhauer expresses it, music is a direct expression of the Will. "For this reason," he continues, "the effect of music is so very much more powerful and penetrating than is that of the other arts, for these others speak only of the shadow, but music of the essence."[2] If a film decides to suggest rather than show an action or event, music fills in what might, for very good reasons, be missing visually. For example, we never actually see more than the shoes of the Devil in *The Mephisto Waltz* (dir. Paul Wendkos, 1971). When he is summoned to appear toward the end of the film, we see only Jacqueline Bisset's reaction, and quite rightly so, for to show the Devil would be much less convincing than relying on a human reaction to his presence. It is therefore up to the music to perform this largely invisible role, just as, in Hitchcock's *Rebecca* (1940), Franz Waxman's music becomes the "presence" of the unseen (because already deceased) title role. From James Bernard's classic scores for Hammer's *The Devil Rides Out* (dir. Terence Fisher, 1968) and the black magic scenes of *The Kiss of the Vampire* (dir. Don Sharp, 1963), through the interpolation of Mike Oldfield's *Tubular Bells* and avant-garde music in *The Exorcist* (dir. William Friedkin, 1973), to Jerry Goldsmith's pastiche of a Black Mass for the *Omen* films in the 1970s and 1980s, movie composers and film directors have manipulated a collection of "demonic" effects to create atmosphere and dramatic tension — not least to aid in the suspension of the audience's disbelief.

The Finnish semiotician Eero Tarasti has isolated several ways in which various types of magical activity have been expressed in musical terms. He refers to these as "semes," suggesting that the musical signs form part of a vocabulary of music and myth. The two most "occult" semes he lists are "the demonic" and "the mystic," which he opposes with "the sacred" (though he also mentions "the primitivistic," "the fantastic" and "the nature-mythical," each of which might be said to be related to some of occultism's concerns). To demonstrate "the demonic," Tarasti immediately draws our attention to the music associated with the evil magician Klingsor in Wagner's *Parsifal* (1882). He points out that in Wagner's music, "the demonic" is associated with chromaticism, diminished seventh chords and augmented triads, as are all made evident in the prelude to Act II of that work, which introduces us to Klingsor's magical domain. Wagner had used diminished sevenths as a signifier of the demonic in his earlier Grail opera, *Lohengrin* (1850), the music associated with the sorceress Ortrud (particularly in the Act II prelude) being largely based on them, but the demonic diminished seventh was inherited by him from Carl Maria von Weber (1786–1836), who used it to particularly demonic effect in *Der Freischütz* (1821). Indeed, diminished seventh chords consist of two interlocked tritones, so they are doubly demonic in their effect, as well as being harmonically disorienting, belonging, as they do, to no particular key of their own. This tonally disruptive aspect makes them singularly appropriate symbols of Goethe's definition of the demonic. It was for this reason that Nicolay Rimsky-Korsakov (1844–1908) used the diminished seventh to describe the magician in his opera *Katschei the Immortal* (1902), which was based on the same folktale that inspired Stravinsky's later ballet, *The Firebird*. Rimsky-Korsakov was rather proud of an astonishing passage in *Katschei* that he "succeeded in plotting almost entirely on the sustained diminished chord of the seventh."[3]

Franz Liszt (1811–1886) also exploited four augmented triads in the opening theme of his *Eine Faust Symphonie* (1857). Arpeggiated as they are, they coincidentally formed one of the world's first twelve-tone themes, but their demonic quality, reflecting Faust's difference from other men and his questing, questioning temperament, is entirely due to the associations of this particular harmonic effect. (Interestingly, Goethe himself denied his Mephistopheles any "daemonic" traits, arguing that "Mephistopheles is much too negative a being. The Daemonic manifests itself in a thoroughly active power."[4] But writers and composers who followed in Goethe's wake did not, of course, always agree with him.) Wagner similarly employed augmented triads at moments of extreme tension and energy, such as at the end of *Göt-*

*terdämmerung* (1876), when Brünnhilde's "Valkyrie" motif is changed from a major to an augmented triad as she leaps into the flames on her horse Grane. Such "daemonic" energy is ideally expressed by this harmonic effect.

The avant-garde techniques of composers such as Krzysztof Penderecki (born 1933) have been applied to more visceral occult shockers such as *The Exorcist* and *The Shining* (dir. Stanley Kubrick, 1980), but the advanced note clusters and sonic experiments of this music are employed in much the same way as more traditional musical signifiers of the demonic. Avant-garde techniques are "demonic" (as Thomas Mann had labeled Schoenberg's serialism) because they are, in Goethe's terms, "separate" and "different" from the prevailing tonal environment of the film's general audience. For Goethe, "the Daemonic loves to throw itself into significant individuals, especially when they are in high places."[5] The demonic is, therefore, in Tarasti's reference to Karl Jaspers' observation, "everything which is individual and separates one from the others."[6]

Satanism is sinister in much the same way that being left-handed was once regarded with uneasiness as being an indication of difference — of "the other." Indeed, this is where the word "sinister" originated, meaning, as it does, "left-handed," along with all that is implied in magical terms by being a follower of the so-called "left-hand path," so different from those who sit obediently at the right hand of God. Faust makes a pact with the Devil to increase his knowledge, while Klingsor has castrated himself to gain a sinister power over others. In addition, Mocata, the black magician of *The Devil Rides Out,* casts no shadow, is a master of hypnosis, and is in simple terms a villain whose daemonic power, as Goethe put it, "cannot be explained by Reason or Understanding [... and is] full of unlimited power of action and unrest, so that his own dominion was too little for him, and the greatest would have been too little."[7]

James Bernard's music for *The Devil Rides Out* also makes use of that other demonic quality of syncopation. In the magic circle scenes of the film, in which Christopher Lee's Duc de Richlieu defends his friends against the magical attack of Mocata, Bernard uses a syncopated figure that could, on a superficial level, be interpreted as an imitation of a heartbeat, but it also signifies something more demonic because it threatens to disrupt the sense of an established order. It was for this reason that the English composer Cyril Scott (1879–1970) was of the opinion that jazz "was definitely 'put through' by the Dark Forces" and resulted in "a very marked decline in sexual morals."[8] Indeed, a little later in this section of his book *Music — Its Secret Influence Throughout the Ages,* which would warm the heart of any guardian of conventional morality, he spells out the problem, as he saw it, in no uncertain terms:

> The orgiastic element about its syncopated rhythm, entirely divorced from any more exalted musical content, produced a hyper-excitement of the nerves and loosened the powers of self-control. It gave rise to a false exhilaration, a fictitious endurance, an insatiability resulting in a deleterious *moral* and physical reaction. Whereas the old-fashioned melodious dance-music inspired the gentler sentiments, Jazz, with its array of harsh, ear-splitting percussion-instruments inflamed, intoxicated and brutalized, thus causing a set-back in Man's nature towards the instincts of his racial childhood. For Jazz-music at its height very closely resembled the music of primitive savages.[9]

This was a problem the Nazis shared with regard to jazz, which they too (albeit principally for racial reasons) regarded as dangerous music of "the other." As Erik Levi points out, jazz was too popular to ban outright in Nazi Germany, but German jazz was promoted as having taken "a step away from exaggerated syncopation," thus achieving a style that would "blend together equalised rhythm and melody."[10] What is equalized is therefore "good," and what is syncopated is consequently "bad." (Ironically, the Nazis appear to have overlooked the considerable amount of syncopation in the music of the racially acceptable Robert Schumann [1810–1856]. In some passages, this reaches such extremes that the syncopation begins to interfere with the listeners' sense of pulse, as is particularly the case in the first movement of Schumann's *Faschingswank aus Wien*, and such a rhythmically disruptive tendency might have had some connection with Schumann's unstable mental condition.)

Instinctively following Scott's program (and unwittingly endorsing the Nazis' prejudice), James Bernard employed a vigorous syncopated beat for the orgy scene in *The Devil Rides Out*, in which a slightly modified version of the motif associated with Mocata is subjected to effectively "demonic" syncopation above furious African-style drumming, the tuned percussion of which hammers out tritone intervals with savage abandon. Sadly, censorship at the time prevented the orgy from being performed naked, as was originally intended, so Bernard's uninhibited rhythms are interpreted by devil-worshippers in diaphanously wafting, less offending robes.

Tarasti argues that "the mystic" is a more recent seme, derived from the nineteenth century's infatuation with "the demonic" and "the fantastic." Myth differs from mysticism, he points out, because mysticism suggests "a decline of the genuine aspects and original mythical quality, lapsing from a direct connection with various aspects of life into mere secret societies and occultism."[11] He cites the music of Alexander Scriabin (1872–1915) as the most important example of this development, and, indeed, Scriabin's reliance on more complex tritone relationships rather than the (by then) more hackneyed diminished seventh chord suggests both the connection and the development.

His most mystical and demonic music (such as the Ninth Piano Sonata, nicknamed the "Black Mass" by Scriabin's friend, Nikolay Podgayetsky) also relies on the ambivalent effect of trills. Trills, because of their ambiguity of pitch, evoke the unpredictable energies of occult forces. Scriabin himself equated them with luminosity, and the archetypal Bringer of Light is, as we have seen, Lucifer, the fallen angel, whose fall was the result of challenging divine authority. Like Prometheus, he brought fire and the wisdom it symbolizes to mankind.

For Scriabin, trills also represented "palpitation ... trembling ... the vibration in the atmosphere."[12] When playing the Ninth Sonata himself, Scriabin confessed that he was "practicing sorcery."[13] Scriabin's trills bear some relation to the effect of string tremolos in this respect, and string tremolos are also often used both as a signifier of the demonic and as a musical metaphor of physiological trembling. In Don Banks' music for Hammer Films' historically inaccurate account of *Rasputin the Mad Monk* (dir. Don Sharp, 1966), for example, string tremolos graphically reflect the agitated trembling of Christopher Lee's hands when, as the Mad Monk of the title, he draws an illness from the body of a sick woman at the beginning of the film. Here, not only is the act of physical trembling reflected in the music, but the mystical forces being summoned are also embodied in and amplified by the music. In the real Russia of Rasputin's time, genuine Black Masses were indeed practiced. As Faubion Bowers, Scriabin's first biographer, points out, Scriabin was ghoulishly fascinated by the stories of painter Nikolai Sherpling, who confessed to drinking the blood of wounded soldiers and eating the flesh of those just killed in action during the First World War.[14] But on a more esoteric level, Scriabin's interest in the "left-hand path" was part of a well-established occult tradition that aims at wholeness. The true magician (and Scriabin certainly thought of himself in these terms) embraces all that there is, and that includes the Devil as well as God. As Richard Cavendish puts it, "All things are grist to the magician's mill."[15] The complete, fully integrated and magical man has embraced everything, both good and evil, and aims to become God — indeed, to supersede God. This is the Great Work, and accordingly, on many occasions, Scriabin pronounced, "I am God":

> I will ignite your imagination with the delight of my promise. I will bedeck you in the excellence of my dreams. I will veil the sky of your wishes with the sparkling stars of my creation.
> I bring not truth, but freedom.[16]

Occultists do not see the story of the Garden of Eden as a tragedy, but rather as a kind of triumph. There is, however, a heavy price to pay for such a triumph. In his essay "On the Marionette Theatre," Heinrich von Kleist

# Three. The Birth of the Demonic 49

(1777–1811) argues that consciousness, which is the result of eating the fruit from the tree of knowledge, has dislocated us from ourselves—we are neither animals nor gods—but if we were to increase our knowledge, wisdom, understanding and intelligence, we might be able to get back into Eden as aware and mature but also intuitive beings, free of the debilitating self-consciousness that so often hampers what Kleist calls our "Grace." Philip Pullman's fantasy trilogy, *His Dark Materials* (1995–2000), takes Kleist as its starting point. Pullman goes against the dogma of institutionalized religion, which he sees as opposing the spread of "Dust," his metaphor for awareness, knowledge, intelligence and all that makes us human. The final novel in the trilogy, *The Amber Spyglass*, depicts, in Miltonic terms, a war on heaven, which is, however, only a war on God's *kingdom* of heaven. Pullman wants to transform it into the *republic* of heaven. The God he calls "The Authority" is the enemy because He wants humanity to remain in the childlike state of the Garden of Eden. The "Magisterium," Pullman's equivalent of institutionalized religion, regards knowledge as original sin, but Pullman, following in the footsteps of Percy Bysshe Shelley, regards God as the ultimate tyrant. Shelley (1792–1822) had encapsulated this interpretation at the end of his 1820 verse drama *Prometheus Unbound*:

> To defy Power, which seems omnipotent;
> To love, and bear; to hope till Hope creates
> From its own wreck the thing it contemplates;
> Neither to change, nor falter, nor repent;
> This, like thy glory, Titan, is to be
> Good, great and joyous, beautiful and free;
> This is alone Life, Joy, Empire, and Victory.[17]

By overthrowing God with the aid of Lucifer, we can reclaim heaven for ourselves. This program makes Pullman's trilogy one of the most powerful occult texts of the twentieth century, and the film adaptation of *The Golden Compass* (dir. Chris Weitz, 2007) the most "occult" movie, far more radical in its implications than *The Exorcist* or *The Omen*, which toe the traditional Catholic party line, as did Hammer Films with its conservative and strictly dualistic adaptation of *The Devil Rides Out*.

Scriabin's occult music is very much in this trajectory. But Tarasti's "sacred" seme also plays its part in demonic music. Secure triadic harmonies (either major or minor) play an important role in such a musical seme, and Tarasti refers to Anton Bruckner's Third Symphony as a particularly successful example of it. Its "triad on the tonic in D minor and played by a lonely trumpet against the strings' mystically rippling D minor tonal field convey a particularly sacred effect."[18] Similarly, Bernard's score for *The Devil Rides Out* makes eloquent use of minor and major triads in juxtaposition with the chromatic diabolism of its demonic sections. At the end of that film, when evil has been vanquished by the forces of good, the main theme, based on the syllables of the title (one of Bernard's characteristic fingerprints), is presented in major tonality, preceded by a sequence of consecutive triads, which have previously been associated with the sacred powers of good. They have accompanied de Richlieu's mystical ability to hypnotize the hero, Simon Aaron, but unlike Mocata, de Richlieu uses hypnosis for purely benevolent ends. Triadic harmony is also much at the forefront in the earlier scene in which de Richlieu summons the spirit of the dead Tanith to guide their next move in the war against evil. Bernard introduces the "sacred" timbre of hand bells here. Together, they form a major chord, under which trilling strings rise up through an exotic, otherworldly whole tone scale. Such "sacred" triads owe much of their effect to Wagner's *Parsifal*, which Tarasti rightly describes as "one of the most important expressions of the sacred seme in the Western music tradition."[19]

Central to Wagner's repertoire of sacred effects in *Parsifal* are the Grail bells, which resonate to such dramatic effect in the ritual scenes of the first and third acts. Originally hammered out backstage by means of gigantic metal canisters mounted on wheels, the effect is nowadays often created or manipulated electronically, with varying degrees of success. (Herbert von Karajan's classic 1981 recording has by far the most compelling and atmospheric bells anyone is likely to hear.) More importantly, the bell motif is based on perfect fourths (two descending fourths a third apart: C–G, A–E), and fourths also form the basis of Scriabin's later "mystic chord," which permeates so much of his later music. Scriabin's chord is a composite of perfect, augmented and diminished fourths, but Wagner's bell motif led the way toward it by equating perfect fourths with the sacred and mystic semes identified by Tarasti.

Bells, of course, have their own sacred connotation. In J. K. Huysmans' occult novel, *Là-bas* (1891), we are introduced to a bell-ringer who knows all about the satanic underworld of *fin de siècle* Paris. He also knows about the sacred nature of bells:

> It is baptized like a Christian, anointed with sacramental oil....
>
> It is the herald of the Church, the voice from without as the priest is the voice from within. So, you see it isn't a mere piece of bronze, a reversed mortar to be swung at a rope's end. Add that bells, like fine wines, ripen with age, that their tone becomes more ample and mellow, that they lose their sharp bouquet, their raw flavour.[20]

For Scriabin (as, indeed, for Russians in general), the sound of bells acts like incense to create a sense of heaven on earth. Scriabin even went so far as to

## Three. The Birth of the Demonic

dream of suspending bells from the clouds above the Himalayas during his mystical *Mystery,* a work he was prevented from completing due to his premature death. The many overtones of bells, which underlie and resonate over the fundamental tone, symbolized for Scriabin the mystical oneness that lies at the heart of the universe's multiplicity — the relationship between the microcosm of mankind and the macrocosm of the universe. Indeed, they embody what we learn from Robert Fludd's engraving of the Great Monochord: "The One is all things and all things are One."

In medieval times, bells were central to everyday life. They not only told the time and called the faithful to prayer but also protected vulnerable Christian souls from attacks by demons. Bells can be both joyful and funereal; they sound alarms and celebrate victory. Given their special appeal to the Russian soul, it is not surprising that Sergei Rachmaninoff (1873–1943), who was also fascinated by their sound, should have set Edgar Allan Poe's poem "The Bells" to music. The poem moves from the sound of silvery, joyful sleigh bells and the mellow warmth of wedding bells through the crash of brazen alarum bells ("What a tale of terror, now their turbulency tells!") before concluding with the tolling iron bells of death ("In the silence of the night,/How we shiver with affright/At the melancholy menace of their tone!"). Given such significations, it was inevitable that Jerry Goldsmith would include tubular bells in his resonant score for the main title of *The Omen,* for they work in the same way as John Cacavas' organ music underlying the Black Mass scenes of *The Satanic Rites of Dracula* (dir. Alan Gibson, 1973) and John Cameron's organ and electric guitar mix for the satanic "temple" with its magic mirror in *Psychomania* (dir. Don Sharp, 1973). One might also include the use of Bach's Adagio from the Toccata, Adagio and Fugue in C-minor BWV 564 in *The Black Cat* (dir. Edgar G. Ulmer, 1934), for these musical symbols of orthodox Christianity become, in such contexts, the sonic equivalents of an inverted crucifix.

Incantations also feature in occult entertainment, reflecting, as they do, the traditional method of raising demons, as instructed by countless grimoires throughout the ages, but few dramatic incantations work without musical support. In opera, of course, the music is inevitable; in film, an underscore is usually considered vital to suspend disbelief and provide magical momentum. There are exceptions to this general rule, such as the marvelously resonant incantation performed by Hazel Court in *The Masque of the Red Death* (dir. Roger Corman, 1964), in which she begins a demonic invocation entirely unaccompanied by music: "Lord Satan, he who is known as Belial by the ancients, Demon Lover, of all those who wish to live in your eternal night, here in your hour of deepest dark, in your temple and before your altar, I twice bind myself to thee, as your handmaiden and your betrothed." However, music does appear beneath her words as she picks up the red-hot branding iron of an inverted crucifix. "And with this symbol of your lasting victory, I inscribe the final mark and offer myself to thee." As the branding iron touches her well-exposed cleavage, a cymbal suggests the pain she feels, which then turns to ecstasy as she utters the final lines. Composer David Lee punctuates these lines in the manner of a traditional operatic recitative: "Oh Lord Satan, send me a demon so I may know I'm to be your wife."

Hammer's *Twins of Evil* (dir. John Hough, 1971) showcases Peter Cushing as a Puritan witch hunter (apparently on the side of God, though he burns and stakes his way through the film in a particularly sadistic manner). During the prologue sequence, he invokes the Almighty before burning the first of his unfortunate victims at the stake. He is aided in this by Harry Robinson's music, which loosely echoes the imposing plainsong sequence of the *Dies Irae* (of which more later). He also summons echoes of Wagner's music for Loge, the fire god of the *Ring,* as the flames burn into the pyre, as well as evoking the terrifying sound world of Sibelius' last orchestral work, *Tapiola* (1926), during the impressive Black Mass sequences early in the film. Having dismissed the charlatan performers of a "fake" invocation to the Devil in his castle, Count Karnstein (played with cynical relish by Damien Thomas) decides to raise the Devil himself. He sacrifices a decorously draped virgin, her blood trickles into the tomb beneath her body, and Carmilla Karnstein materializes from it, suitably enshrouded. As she advances upon the count in Hough's magisterially directed sequence, Robinson almost directly quotes Sibelius' tremolo string writing from his final tone poem. Tapio was the Finnish forest god — a terrifying force of nature; Carmilla proves to be an equally terrifying supernatural force of vampiric evil.

Early in the history of musical Romanticism, one of the most famous Parisian grand operas, *Robert le diable* (1831), by Giacomo Meyerbeer (1791–1861), featured a particularly impressive incantation, in which Bertram (in fact the fiend incarnate) summons the spirits of nuns who had been unfaithful to their vows in a ruined abbey. Diminished sevenths inevitably add their demonic allure here, but pale by comparison with Weber's more sonorously orchestrated diminished sevenths in Caspar's incantation in the celebrated Wolf's Glen scene of *Der Freischütz.* Weber also uses the very simple but even more effective incantatory device of a rising chromatic scale in the low register of cellos and basses in which Caspar's spoken rhyming couplets summon the assistance of Zamiel, the Devil, in the forging of magic bullets, vital to the development of the plot. The fact that Caspar speaks rather than sings these lines is due to *Der Freischütz* belonging, like Mozart's *Magic Flute,* to that peculiarly Germanic form of the *Singspiel,* but it also points the way forward

## Three. The Birth of the Demonic
### 53

to cinematic underscoring, and we will be returning to both *Der Freischütz* and *Robert* from this perspective in chapter seven.

Though music is now so frequently used to evoke timeless occult forces, "demonic" music is, in fact, a relatively recent invention, which basically began with Weber and one of his most ardent admirers, Hector Berlioz (1803–1869). We can go a little further back to Mozart, whose use of trombones in the finale of *Don Giovanni* (1787) brought a demonic quality to a timbre until then regarded only as sombre and funereal. Later commentators on this work, particularly the arch-Romantic theorist E. T. A. Hoffmann (1776–1822), spoke of this music, which also appears in the Overture, with particular relish:

> During the *andante,* my spirit was seized with premonitions of horror. I shuddered in awe of the infernal *regno del pianto.* The seventh bar of the *allegro,* with its jubilant fanfare, became the voice of crime itself, exulting. Out of the dark night I saw demons stretch their fiery claws and loom menacingly over the lives of carefree mortals dancing merrily on the thin lid of a bottomless pit. The conflict between human nature and the unknown, the terrible powers that confront man on every side and lie in wait for his ruin, took on a visionary intensity with the music.[21]

If Mozart was the John the Baptist of demonic music, Berlioz was without doubt its high priest. In his *Treatise on Orchestration,* Berlioz described the trombone as "formidable" and suitable, among other things, "for the awakening of the dead or the death of the living," both of which are central to occult entertainment. But Berlioz was much more instrumental in the birth of demonic music than merely as the identifier of Mozart's demonization of the trombone. One of the most effective clichés so often used in horror films is the *Dies Irae* sequence, which, in its original medieval presentation, was quite the opposite of demonic, its frightening text notwithstanding. We do not know who wrote the music, but the text is attributed to one Thomas of Celano (who died around 1250) and it soon became incorporated into the Requiem Mass:

> Dies irae, dies illa,
> solvet saeculum in favilla,
> teste David cum Sibylla.
>
> Quantus tremor est futurus,
> quando iudex est venturus,
> cuncta stricte discussurus!
>
> Tuba mirum spargens sonum
> per sepulcra regionum,
> coget omnes ante thronum.

Mors stupebit et natura,
cum resurget creatura,
iudicanti responsura.

(That day of wrath, that dreadful day,
shall heaven and earth in ashes lay,
as David and the Sybil say.

What horror must invade the mind
when the approaching Judge shall find
and sift the deeds of all mankind!

The mighty trumpet's wondrous tone
shall rend each tomb's sepulchral stone
and summon all before the Throne.

Now death and nature with surprise
behold the trembling sinners rise
to meet the Judge's searching eyes.)

Haydn had used the opening four notes of the *Dies Irae* melody in his Symphony 103 in E-flat major (the "Drumroll"), composed in 1794–1795, but though its appearance there is somber, it was not meant to be demonic. The theme is not quoted in full, but it is the semitone intervals of the opening three notes that provide the sense of unease, which was always present in the plainchant. That unease was eventually amplified into demonic terror by Berlioz in the last and most nightmarish movement of his *Symphonie fantastique* of 1830. As the program of the work explains, the *Symphonie fantastique* is a musical response to the emotions felt by a composer (presumably Berlioz himself) who, unlucky in love, has taken a near-fatal opium overdose. His subsequent visions form the basis of the symphony's five movements. The whole thing is, indeed, one of the first musical "trips," and, as such, is a direct forerunner of the LSD-inspired psychedelia of The Beatles' "Lucy in the Sky with Diamonds" and "Strawberry Fields," and films like *Sebastian* (dir. David Greene, 1968), in which Dirk Bogarde is almost persuaded to leap off a tower-block while under the influence of drugs. Even the section "Neptune and Beyond" from Kubrick's *2001: A Space Odyssey,* with its avant-garde music by György Ligeti (1923–2006), can trace its lineage to Berlioz.

Appropriately, Tarasti classifies the *Symphonie fantastique* as an example of his "fantastic" seme, which he describes as being characterized by "a succession of different elements opposed to each other," adding that "the demonic quality approaches the fantastic in that, as the antithesis of the commonplace and the usual, the fantastic style requires its strongest contrasts and finally a transition to an irrational sphere."[22]

## Three. The Birth of the Demonic

Throughout the five movements of Berlioz's symphony, a musical *idée fixe* represents the unattainable beloved, but in the final movement, subtitled "Songe d'une nuit du Sabbat" (Dream of a Witch's Sabbat), with the hero having imagined his own decapitation, we enter upon a demonic scene of witches exulting over the hero's death. The *idée fixe* is here transformed into a grotesque Irish jig (presumably because the object of Berlioz's passion in real life at the time was the Irish actress Harriet Smithson — surely a somewhat cruel jest). It is followed by a sepulchral scoring of the *Dies Irae* melody (first for bassoons, tuba and bells, then repeated by horns and trombones), before being interrupted by more metamorphosed statements of the *idée fixe*. This Romantic demonization of what had previously been a sacred melody changed the signification of the *Dies Irae* forever, and other Romantic composers inevitably followed Berlioz's example. Liszt's *Totentanz* (a series of variations on the *Dies Irae* for piano and orchestra) combines virtuosity with the demonic, and provided the ideal piece for Roger Daltry's Liszt to destroy Paul Nicholas' Wagner by means of a flame-throwing piano in Ken Russell's *Lisztomania* (1975). The *Dies Irae* also appears in many subsequent pieces with either demonic or less specifically unsettling connotations. We hear it in Ottorino Respighi's *Impressioni brasiliane* (Brazilian Impressions) of 1928, where it suggests the poisonous and predatory dangers of the jungle. It also forms an integral element of Rachmaninov's symphonic poem of 1908 inspired by Arnold Böcklin's painting, *The Isle of the Dead*, as well as his *Rhapsody on a Theme of Paganini* (1934), to which it bears a thematic resemblance. In 1912, Nikolai Myaskovsky based his Piano Sonata No. 2 in F-sharp minor on the chant, and Tchaikovsky also incorporated it into his Suite No. 3, not to mention his song "Dark Hell." Shostakovitch likewise satirized it in one of the movements of his experimental piano collection, *Aphorisms* (1927). These are just a few of many other examples, all of which followed the original example of Berlioz. It is therefore to be expected that Erik, the Phantom of the Opera in Gaston Leroux's 1910 novel of that name, should also perform his own version of the *Dies Irae*. Erik is the grotesque amalgam of demonic Romanticism, a cross between Don Giovanni, Dr. Faustus, Liszt, E. T. A. Hoffmann and the ghoulish specter in Gottfried Bürger's famous poem, "Lenore" (1773). Along with the many movie makeovers of this famous story, Erik was also the prototype of horror film characters like Dr. Phibes and the piano-playing vampire Carl Ravna in *The Kiss of the Vampire*: "Erik sang like the god of thunder, sang a *Dies Irae* that enveloped us as in a storm. The elements seemed to rage around us. Suddenly, the organ and the voice ceased so suddenly that M. de Chagny sprang back, on the other side of the wall, with emotion."[23]

Film composers similarly take their cue from Berlioz, not necessarily quoting the whole melody and often only using the opening four notes, as

Haydn had done before them. It is a very useful cliché when pressed for time (or inspiration), but when used more creatively it provides a powerful resonance. Harry Robinson provided a long sequence based on the melody to accompany a singularly uninspired sequence of Hammer's generally lackluster *Lust for a Vampire* (dir. Jimmy Sangster, 1971). James Bernard also incorporated it into his score for the much more vibrant *Dracula Has Risen from the Grave* (dir. Freddie Francis, 1968). It even briefly appears in Dimitri Tiomkin's music for the Christmas ghost story, *It's a Wonderful Life* (dir. Frank Capra, 1946). *The Exorcist,* as we have seen, exploited Mike Oldfield's *Tubular Bells,* a piece that more subtly interpolates the melody into its main theme. Disguised though it may be, it is nonetheless present, and it duly contributes its effect. Ennio Morricone even turned the *Dies Irae* into a dance track for the 1968 movie *Escalation* (dir. Robert Faenza), which became known as "Dies Irae Psychedelico." It was an appropriate musical response to a story about the corrupting effect of wealth and power. It seems that everywhere one looks, the *Dies Irae* has informed our idea of demonic music.

Walt Disney created one of his most compellingly demonic sequences when interpreting Mussorgsky's musical depiction of a witches' sabbath in *Night on the Bare Mountain* for *Fantasia* in 1940, and, sure enough, the opening three notes of the piece are no more than a rearrangement of the opening three notes of the *Dies Irae:* in this instance, a falling semitone followed by a drop of a tone. (The *Dies Irae* itself consists of a falling semitone, which then returns to the original note before falling a tone, covering the syllables "Di-es Ir-ae.")

The most significant of all musical devices to suggest the demonic is the tritone, which the opening phrase of Mussorgsky's piece also implies. Otherwise known as the augmented fourth, it has been more colorfully dubbed "Diabolus in music" (the Devil in music). This interval is ubiquitous in the music written for the Gothic horror genre, as it is in much Romantic music concerned with evil. We have already mentioned its fundamental importance to the musical palette of Scriabin. More contemporary occult movies often rely on the far more extreme harmonic techniques of avant-garde twentieth-century music, to which we shall be returning later, but tritones, along with augmented triads, play a crucial role in James Bernard's score for *The Devil Rides Out,* which is appropriate for a story set in a fantasized 1930s, rather than the more up-to-date setting of *The Exorcist* and *The Shining.* The tritone is a highly appropriate musical short-hand for the Devil in Bernard's score, but its appearance in occult cinema is by no means limited to this particular film.

Rejected in earlier ages as an unstable interval, the tritone came into its own in the nineteenth century, when, due to crises of faith, not to mention

## Three. The Birth of the Demonic    57

the cult of individualism, industrialism and the consequent fascination with the past, the demonic became a major theme of the Romantic movement. This is not to say that the tritone was never used until this time. It appears in some Gregorian chants, and J. S. Bach famously exploited it in his chorale *Es ist genug* ("It is enough")— a singularly unsettling and disturbing setting of a text concerned with suffering and death. Mozart and Beethoven also employed tritones but in nowhere near as prolific (and certainly not as exposed and demonic) a manner as composers in the nineteenth century. Anthony Burgess concisely summed up the emotional effect of the tritone in his short story "1889 and the Devil's Mode," in which the character of Debussy explains, "It stands for something faulty. Something shaky in the iron structure, a rivet missing or something.... The interval's a perfect image of the breakdown of the moral order."[24]

One of the nineteenth century's most impressive and influential manipulators of the tritone was Franz Liszt. Part Lothario, part abbé, part pop star, and part musical genius, Liszt was dubbed "Mephistopheles disguised as a priest" by Ferdinand Gregorovius.[25] James Bernard's "Vampire Rhapsody" from *The Kiss of the Vampire,* which depends almost entirely for its demonic effect upon the tritone, was consciously modeled on the idiom of Liszt. Liszt was the ultimate demonic pianist, often painted wearing black against a dark background (most famously in the portrait by Henri Lehmann, from 1839). Carl Ravna (played by Barry Warren), who "performs" Bernard's hypnotic pastiche, is similarly not at all what he at first appears to be. Disguised as a very charming young man, he is in fact a very nasty vampire, and his piano recital soon begins to hypnotize the unwitting Marianne (played by Jennifer Daniel). The effect bears some resemblance to that of Liszt's recitals, which similarly overwhelmed his besotted audiences. Similarly, the celebrated scene in Hammer's *The Reptile* (dir. John Gilling, 1966), in which Anna Franklin (played by Jacqueline Pearce) performs an unnerving sitar solo, expresses the repressed contempt Anna feels for her father, whose meddling with an obscure Malayan sect caused her to be turned into a hideous shape-shifting snake-woman. Anna's expression becomes increasingly impudent and provocative, even going so far as to suggest that some kind of Elektra complex is also at work here, and just as the "Vampire Rhapsody" is rudely interrupted by Marianne's concerned husband (played by Edward de Souza), Anna Franklin's display of sinister Oriental virtuosity is peremptorily shattered by her father (Noel Willman), who snatches the instrument from her hands and smashes it to pieces against the fireplace.

The sitar brings with it colonial fears of the exotic East, but the piano is even more demonic in its connotation, especially since it became coffin black. It was not always so, however. Indeed, the grand piano in *The Kiss of the Vam-*

*pire* is a very ornate object in rococo style, and much more the kind of thing that Liszt would have been familiar with, but Liszt had nonetheless made the instrument satanic, just as Niccolò Paganini (1782–1849) had sent the violin to the devil. Without Liszt, we would never have had the murderous piano in the "Mr. Steinway" episode of Freddie Francis' *Torture Garden* (1967), which pushes the unfortunate Barbara Ewing out of a window, punishing her for distracting John Standing's Leo Winston from his musical devotions. In this astonishing sequence, in which the keyboard of the instrument is photographed in a way that makes it resemble a row of teeth, the piano is transformed into a terrifying juggernaut of satanic malevolence.

The demonic power of music is fully expressed in each of these imaginative scenes from Hammer and Amicus horror films, but its power to hypnotize is also reminiscent of other nineteenth-century literary models, particularly Svengali, the anti-hero of George Du Maurier's novel *Trilby* (1895). Svengali was partly modeled on Paganini, the most "demonic" of all nineteenth-century virtuosi. Du Maurier describes Svengali as having "bold, brilliant black eyes, with long heavy lids, a thin sallow face, and a beard of burnt-up black."[26] The obvious element of antisemitic caricature here made the combination of musical virtuosity and hypnotism all the more unsettling for Du Maurier's original readers. The previously unmusical Trilby is transformed into a virtuoso singer by Svengali's demonic power over her: "She could keep on one note and make it go through all the colours in the rainbow — according to the way Svengali looked at her.... That was Svengali ... he was a magician! ... Svengali could turn her into the other Trilby, *his* Trilby — and make her do whatever he liked ... you might have run a red-hot needle into her and she would not have felt it."[27] Even more naturalistic fiction indulges in this demonic (or at least daemonic) aspect of music. In George Moore's 1898 novel *Evelyn Innes*, the eponymous heroine, a soprano, is influenced by her own Svengali in the form of Sir Owen Asher, who persuades her to perform the great Wagnerian roles. Sir Owen performs the hypnotic "Liebestod" from Wagner's *Tristan und Isolde* (curiously, on the harpsichord) and Evelyn succumbs:

> The gnawing, creeping sensuality of the phrase brought little shudders into her flesh; all life seemed dissolved into a dim tremor and rushing of blood; vague colour floated into her eyes, and there were moments when she could hardly restrain herself from jumping to her feet and begging him to stop.... The servant brought in the tea, and she thought she would feel better when the music ceased. But neither did the silence nor the tea help her. He sat opposite her, his eyes fixed upon her, that half-kindly, half-cynical face of his showing through the gold of his moustache.[28]

Liszt's fascination with the demonic was shared by the British actor Sir

## Three. The Birth of the Demonic    59

Henry Irving (1838–1905), whom Liszt met at one of the famous Beefsteak Room banquets organized by Irving at the Lyceum Theatre in London, where his manager was Bram Stoker, the author of *Dracula*. Stoker commented on the similarity of the two men, both of whom were closely associated with the character of Mephistopheles. Irving played the role with great success at the Lyceum, dressed from head to toe in scarlet, while Liszt (always dressed in more sober fashion as an abbé) composed not only a *Faust* symphony but also four "Mephisto" waltzes. The first of these (1859–1862) later informed the "occult" music of Scriabin and was itself inspired by Nikolaus Lenau's demonic poem, "The Dance of the Village Inn," in which the Devil strikes up on the violin and inspires an amorous dance. (A similar thing happens in Saint-Saëns' *Danse macabre* [1874], though in that case the violinist is Death rather than Mephisto. Significantly, Saint-Saëns also quotes the *Dies Irae* in that piece.)

The *Mephisto Waltz* opens in a breathtakingly adventurous manner by imitating the sound of a fiddle player tuning up. The piano piles open fifths on top of each other, which, combined with a driving rhythm in 3/8, creates a suitably unnerving effect. Open fifths (along with their even more suspect relatives, consecutive fifths) had always been problematic to musical theorists. Because this sonority was largely "forbidden," it acquired a connotation of the demonic when composers dared to use it. (Liszt combined them in one of his most terrifying pieces, the *Czárdás macabre* of 1881–1882.) We similarly find the open fifth, albeit sometimes sequenced through consecutive movement, in many an occult movie soundtrack. Open fifths also sound "hollow," as they lack the defining third (which makes the tonality either major or minor). This hollowness suggests an ambivalence that is also easily equated with the diabolic; the Devil, after all, traffics in illusions. This sense of hollowness also explains why Wagner used an open fifth to symbolize the magical Tarnhelm, with its power of invisibility and shape-shifting, in his *Ring* cycle.

But the tritone is far more ambivalent than the open fifth because it does not conform to any particular tonality. No major or minor scale includes the two notes that comprise this interval, and having been prohibited for centuries by church authorities, it became the most unsettling interval of all. The *Mephisto Waltz* is the apotheosis of the tritone, particularly in its central erotic section when the tempo slows down somewhat and the mood becomes lugubriously amorous. Via Scriabin, these passages ultimately paved the way for the harmonic basis of Harry Robinson's music in *Countess Dracula* (dir. Peter Sasdy, 1971), a horror film loosely based on historical fact, which takes seriously the idea that a virgin's blood can restore youth and beauty. The love scene between Ingrid Pitt's Countess Elisabeth and Sandor Eles' Imre Toth is

Alan Alda as Myles Clarkson, at the piano, watched by Curt Jurgens as Duncan Ely in *The Mephisto Waltz* (dir. Paul Wendkos, 1971).

accompanied by passionate love music, the harmonic basis of which is a sequence of tritone relationships.

The most overt impact of Liszt's *Mephisto Waltz* on the movies, however, occurred when Paul Wendkos adapted Fred Mustard Stewart's novel of the same name for the screen in 1971. The entire movie is structured around Liszt's famous composition, which is the party piece of a demonic pianist by the name of Duncan Ely, played by Curt Jurgens. Ely, who is dying of leukemia, aims, with the help of his daughter Roxanne (with whom he is involved in an incestuous affair) to transfer his soul into the body of Myles Clarkson, a young music journalist, played by Alan Alda. Ely is fascinated by Clarkson's hands, which he describes as "Rachmaninov hands"—the perfect vehicles for his genius. The occult transfer complete, Myles' wife (played by Jacqueline Bisset) is disconcerted to find her husband far sexier but much meaner, more ambitious and also insufferably arrogant. Jealous of Ely's daughter, who is responsible for the death of her daughter, she eventually murders Roxanne and, having summoned the Devil, transfers herself into Roxanne's body, so that she can enjoy Myles' body and torment Ely's soul for ever.

## Three. The Birth of the Demonic 61

The film's occult premise is an engaging and ultimately quite accurate allegory of how unpleasant highly successful people in the art world (or any other world, for that matter) can be. The various party scenes demonstrate all too realistically the kind of back-biting and sniping indulged in by the cognoscenti, regardless of the fact that, here, they are all meant to be devil worshippers. The real star of the film, however, is the composer, Jerry Goldsmith (1929–2004), whose score adapts Liszt's demonic war-horse and filters it through a series of avant-garde techniques, virtually reinventing the piece in the process. He uses the stock in trade of 1960s composers such as Penderecki and Witold Lutoslawski (1913–1994), employing dramatic string glissandi, tone clusters, electronic instruments and other special effects. Goldsmith also often distorts the sound by means of reverberation, distortion or even playing the music backward, all such manipulations being added during the mixing process. *The Mephisto Waltz* was released two years before *The Exorcist* and five years before *The Omen*, for which Goldsmith won an Oscar for Best Score. Goldsmith's score for *The Mephisto Waltz* was therefore among the first to ally such extreme avant-garde techniques with the emerging new wave of occult shockers.

The main title introduces the initial open fifths of Liszt's piece and juxtaposes them with the celebrated *Dies Irae* chant, which is first presented by "ecclesiastic" tubular bells against a disorientating string glissando. Phill Norman's vividly colored psychedelic title design also adds an element of the synesthetic to the proceedings here, which Scriabin would no doubt have appreciated. Goldsmith's approach differed vastly from previous occult thrillers such as Hammer's *The Devil Rides Out* or even *Eye of the Devil* (dir. J. Lee Thompson, 1966), with its contemporary setting and Gary McFarland's jazz-influenced symphonic score. *Eye of the Devil*, however, does use occasional open fifths, sung by a wordless choir, which combines the idea of a Black Mass with the sound of plainchant. This is highly suitable for a story (ultimately derived from Sir James Frazer's *The Golden Bough*) in which an aristocrat sacrifices himself to save the grape harvest of his ancestral chateau. Tragically, though perhaps appropriately given its 1960s context, McFarland died from an overdose of methadone in 1971, and one of the stars of the movie, Sharon Tate, was murdered by Charles Manson three years after the film's original British release, a subject I will be dealing with in more detail in chapter ten.

*The Mephisto Waltz* also emphasizes Fred Mustard Stewart's Romantic equation of virtuosity with the demonic, which derives from the "demonic" legends about Paganini, on whom Liszt modeled his own persona. Paganini was the ancestor of Lovecraft's Erich Zann, just as Carl Ravna is the offspring of Liszt, and Paganini was well aware of the publicity value of his demonic reputation. He later tired of it, however, complaining in a letter to the press shortly before his death, "My mind was disturbed for a long time by these reports, and I sought every means to prove their absurdity."[29] Earlier in his career, however, his reputation had been greatly enhanced by such gossip. A story by Peter Lichtenthal for a Leipzig newspaper, reporting on Paganini's Milan debut, was in no doubt regarding the importance of Paganini's persona:

> Everyone wanted to see and hear this phenomenal wizard and everyone was really staggered. It fairly took one's breath away. In a sense, he is without question the foremost and greatest violinist in the world. His playing is truly inexplicable.[30]

Duncan Ely is described in similar terms by Fred Mustard Stewart:

> Duncan knew how to coax every effect out of the piano. His sensuous legato in the dolce amoroso passage; his pyrotechnical brilliance in the vivace section; his hammering power in the brutalimente octaves seemed to conjure Mephistopheles himself out of the strings.[31]

When Myles becomes Duncan Ely, he becomes more amorous, just as the dancers in Lenau's poem become increasingly lascivious under the influence of the Devil's playing, and Liszt's *amoroso* section is the perfect accompaniment to this development. So too is the repeated use of the *Dies Irae,* which is either played by bells or punctuated by bells during Duncan's funeral (in a ceremony replete with peacock feathers and devil-worshipping mourners). The *Dies Irae* also accompanies the various nightmare dream sequences and grisly deaths that occur later. None of this symbolism would have been possible without Berlioz's demonization of the *Dies Irae*, but most important of all is the cult of the Mephistopholean hero that Liszt's piece celebrates. The film simply wouldn't work if it had been called *The Moonlight Sonata,* still less if it had been based on a Mozart piano sonata or a Bach fugue. The film is a post–Romantic offering, despite its contemporary setting and the avant-garde musical techniques Goldsmith brings to bear upon it.

Stewart's novel also belongs to a literary tradition that was inspired by the myths of Romantic music. Most famous of these stories is John Meade Falkner's *The Lost Stradivarius* (1895). Falkner (1858–1932) is perhaps better known for his novel *Moonfleet,* but his day job was chairman of the arms manufacturer Armstrong Whitworth Co. *The Lost Stradivarius* is deeply indebted to the demonic aura of Paganini. In this story, an Oxford undergraduate, John Maltravers, discovers an unknown Stradivarius in a cupboard in his rooms. It turns out to have been owned by one Adrian Temple, an occultist who was murdered by his best friend after that friend had discovered that Temple had seduced his bride to be. Temple was a thoroughly bad egg

# Three. The Birth of the Demonic    63

who seems to have sold his soul to the Devil, though this is only suggested in the text. The violin itself is also spiritually unwholesome, having been made for another follower of the black arts by Stradivarius himself. At the conclusion of this tale, by which time Maltravers has been morally corrupted by the instrument and the spirit of Temple that has haunted him for so long, the violin shatters under the strain of the strings:

> As the strings slackened, the last note became an unearthly discord. If I were superstitious I should say that some evil spirit then went out of the violin, and broke in his parting throes the wooden tabernacle which had so long sheltered him. It was the last time the instrument was ever used, and that hideous chord was the last that Maltravers ever played.[32]

There are two labels inside the instrument, the second of which gives the clue that "Stradivarius had made the instrument for some Neo-Platonist enthusiast who had dedicated it to his master Porphyrius."[33]

As well as providing the basis for an occult ghost story in the manner of M. R. James, the subject matter of *The Lost Stradivarius* gave Falkner an opportunity to discuss aspects of musical philosophy, which are relatively rare in fiction of this type. For example in the fourth chapter of the novella, he writes the following:

> For we must remember that the influence of music, though always powerful, is not always for good. We can scarcely doubt that as certain forms of music tend to raise us above the sensuality of the animal, or the more degrading passion of material gain, and to transport us into the ether of higher thought, so other forms are directly calculated to awaken in us luxurious emotions, and to whet those sensual appetites which it is the business of a philosopher not indeed to annihilate or to be ashamed of, but to keep rigidly in check. This possibility of music to effect evil as well as good I have seen recognized, and very aptly expressed in some beautiful verses by Mr. Keble which I have just read:
>
>> Cease, stranger, cease those witching notes,
>> The art of syren choirs;
>> Hush the seductive voice that floats
>> Across the trembling wires.
>> Music's ethereal power was given
>>  Not to dissolve our clay,
>> But draw Promethean beams from heaven
>>  To purge the dross away.[34]

Music (ironically, the most physical of the arts, being wholly dependent upon vibration and atmosphere) is revealed as the gateway to a world beyond the merely physical:

> The tone of the violin, and also, I may say with no undue partiality, my brother's performance, were so marvelously fine that though our thoughts were elsewhere

when the music commenced, in a few seconds they were wholly engrossed in the melody, and we sat spellbound. It was as if the violin had become suddenly endowed with life, and was singing to us in a mystical language more deep and awful than any human words.[35]

But music is also capable of being a *bad* influence, a channel through which evil may find its way into the human soul. The music that first summons the spirit of Adrian Temple is a galliard, played by Maltravers and his college chum before the former discovers the fatal Stradivarius. Later the same college chum informs us that

it is curious that Michael Praetorius in the *Syntagma musicum* should speak of the Galliard generally as an "invention of the devil, full of shameful and licentious gestures and immodest movements," and the singular melody of the gagliarda in the "Areopagita" suite certainly exercised from the first a strange influence over me.

He adds, "I say this advisedly, because I am sure that if some music is good for man and elevates him, other melodies are equally bad and enervating."[36]

It is intriguing that H. P. Lovecraft failed to mention Falkner's tale in his otherwise extremely thorough essay on "Supernatural Horror in Literature." Though he was obviously fully aware of his debt to the likes of Arthur Machen (1863–1947) for his own Cthulhu mythos, there are so many similarities of theme between *The Lost Stradivarius* and "The Music of Erich Zann" that he might have wished to give the impression that the idea was entirely his own. There is no doubt, however, that Falkner's novel strongly foreshadows Lovecraft's style in this passage:

As I opened my bedroom door the violin ceased suddenly in the middle of a bar. Its last sound was not a musical note, but rather a horrible scream, such as I pray I may never hear again. It was a sound such as a wounded beast might utter. There is a picture I have seen of Blake's, showing the soul of a strong wicked man leaving his body at death. The spirit is flying out through the window with awful staring eyes, aghast at the desolation into which it is going. If in the agony of dissolution such a lost soul could utter a cry, it would, I think, sound like the wail which I heard from the violin that night.[37]

Sax Rohmer (1883–1959) also exploited the Paganini persona in his story "Tchériapin," from the collection *Tales of Chinatown* (1922). In it, Tchériapin, another demonic violinist, is killed by an artist whose wife Tchériapin has seduced and destroyed. The violinist is then reduced in size and petrified by a process perfected by a mad scientist. The tale is an odd combination of science fiction, music and horror, but its most powerful passages are those derived from nineteenth-century Romanticism at its most demonic. Tchériapin is described as having "something of the personality of Paganini"[38] at the outset, with "long, gaunt, yellowish hands and the face of a haggard Mephistopheles."

> There were stories, too, that were never published — not only about Tchériapin, but concerning the Strad upon which he played. If all this atmosphere of mystery which surrounded the man had truly been the work of a press agent, then the agent must have been as great a genius as his client.[39]

Tchériapin has an "almost emaciated figure, with slow, sinuous movements, and a trick of glancing sideways with those dark, unfathomable, slightly oblique eyes. He could take up his bow in such a way as to create an atmosphere of electrical suspense. He was loathsome, yet fascinating."[40]

Tchériapin's most loathsome composition is a piece called "The Black Mass"—a title whose only parallel in the annals of Western art music is Scriabin's Ninth Piano Sonata (and even in that case the subtitle wasn't actually Scriabin's). Jerry Goldsmith, however, couldn't resist the allusion when marketing his score for *Damien: Omen II* (dir. Don Taylor, 1978), which probably makes it the first use of such a term as a selling point for a film soundtrack. There had, however, been David Vorhaus and Delia Derbyshire's album *An Electric Storm* (1969), which contained a track called "The Black Mass: An Electric Storm in Hell," and this eventually found its way onto the soundtrack of *Dracula A.D. 1972* (dir. Alan Gibson, 1972). Rohmer informs us that Tchériapin's "Black Mass" was never published. "But had it been we should rarely hear it. Like Locke's music to 'Macbeth' it bears an unpleasant reputation; to include it in any concert programme would be to court disaster."[41] However, Tchériapin's music, with its "eerie sweetness" and "evil, hellish beauty[,] indescribably" survives his death: "Listen! It is 'The Black Mass.'" The narrator adds, "My soul rose up in revolt."[42]

Like the music of Erich Zann and the demonic galliard of Falkner's tale, Rohmer can offer nothing more specific about Tchériapin's demonic music, but it seems likely that it might have contained tritones and augmented triads—certainly trills, as there is, after all, that famous piece by Giuseppe Tartini (1692–1770) known as "The Devil's Trill" (and Falkner significantly informs us that Adrian Temple apparently studied with Tartini). Tartini himself claimed to have dreamed that the Devil appeared to him and asked to be his servant. Tartini then gave the Devil his own violin to test his skill, and the Devil played with such virtuosity that Tartini was overwhelmed. He tried to write down what he had heard, but sadly, by his own account, he failed to capture the Devil's genius, and claimed that the resulting sonata was inferior to what he had actually heard.[43] The legend, incidentally, also inspired Madame Blavatsky to pen her own short story, titled "The Ensouled Violin" (from her 1892 collection of *Nightmare Tales*), in which a crazed violinist

# The Occult Arts of Music

challenges Paganini himself to a musical duel and, with the help of his magical violin, the strings of which are made from the tissue of his teacher's intestines, wins the day. The effect of the concert is electric:

> Under the pressure of the long muscular fingers of Franz, the chords shivered like the palpitating intestines of a disembowelled victim under the vivisector's knife. They moaned melodiously, like a dying child. The large blue eye of the artist, fixed with a satanic expression upon the sounding-board, seemed to summon forth Orpheus himself from the infernal regions, rather than the musical notes supposed to be generated in the depths of the violin. Sounds seemed to transform themselves into objective shapes, thickly and precipitately gathering as at the evocation of a mighty magician, and to be whirling around him, like a host of fantastic, infernal figures, dancing the witches' "goat dance." In the empty depths of the shadowy background of the stage, behind the artist, a nameless phantasmagoria, produced by the concussion of unearthly vibrations, seemed to form pictures of shameless orgies, of the voluptuous hymens of a real witches' Sabbat.... A collective hallucination took hold of the public. Panting for breath, ghastly, and trickling with the icy perspiration of an inexpressible horror, they sat spellbound, and unable to break the spell of the music by the slightest motion. They experienced all the illicit enervating delights of the paradise of Mahommed, that come into the disordered fancy of an opium-eating Mussulman, and felt at the same time the abject terror, the agony of one who struggles against an attack of delirium tremens.... Many ladies shrieked aloud, others fainted, and strong men gnashed their teeth in a state of utter helplessness.[44]

Another "demonic" effect frequently used in occult movie scores, which we have already briefly mentioned with regard to Strysik's film version of "The Music of Erich Zann," is the repeated rhythmic or motivic device known as the ostinato. It is one of the most effective methods for creating anticipation and anxiety, as John Williams' theme for *Jaws* (dir. Steven Spielberg, 1975) demonstrates so powerfully. Williams' ostinato consists of only two notes, but it conveys the same intensity and dread when filtered through a crescendo as Anthony Hopkins simply staring at the camera in the Hannibal Lechter films. One of the masters of the ostinato was Maurice Ravel (1875–1937), whose most famous piece, the *Boléro* (1928), is based on an unchanging rhythmic ostinato, while the melody is also continually repeated in differing orchestrations. The sparseness of its actual content (as opposed to its brilliant orchestration) did, however, lead Ravel to confess to the Swiss composer Arthur Honegger that "I've written only one masterpiece—*Boléro*. Unfortunately, there's no music in it."[45] Earlier, he had used various ostinati to suggest demonic obsession in "Scarbo," the third piece of his piano collection, *Gaspard de la Nuit* (1909). Scarbo is a small but malevolent demon who casts immense, terrifying shadows on the walls before suddenly vanishing and then reappearing again. The terrifying climaxes of this virtuosic nightmare are

## Three. The Birth of the Demonic 67

interspersed with passages of brooding expectation created by often *pianissimo* ostinati.

Ravel's example here led the way toward similar moments of demonic expectation in the movies. James Bernard used a similar device for the black magic scenes in *The Kiss of the Vampire*, as does Goldsmith in the accompaniment to the main "Ave Satani" theme of *The Omen*. Ostinati somewhat after the manner of those in Stravinsky's *Rite of Spring* (1913) also provide a very effective sense of tension during the scene in which young Damien, the Devil incarnate, is taken to church by his parents (Gregory Peck and Lee Remick). Damien's increasing discomfort is eloquently mirrored by Goldsmith's ingenuity here, and there are also some impressive ostinati in Goldsmith's follow-up score for *Damien: Omen II*, particularly during the scene featuring a runaway train. In fact, most of the oppressive sense of gathering doom in the *Omen* films is due to ostinati, as is the climax of *Eye of the Devil*, which, unusually in that case, employs seven beats in the bar, and builds to a tremendous climax. David Lee also covered Hazel Court's Freudian dream sequence in *The Masque of the Red Death* with a particularly percussive ostinato. There is, of course, an element of the primitivistic in such a musical device, highly suitable for such a regressive activity as devil worship, but there are also ecclesiastical precedents that suggest these composers are evoking a sacred model. The "Kyrie" from Haydn's "Nelson" Mass, for example, begins with a rhythmic ostinato, which provides an appropriately threatening texture for what Haydn himself subtitled "Mass in Augustilis"—"A Mass in Troubled Times" (i.e., the Napoleonic wars).

More significantly, the opening bars of the "Requiem" from Mozart's *Requiem Mass* provided the model for the underlying ostinato accompaniment of Goldsmith's celebrated "Ave Satane" theme for *The Omen*. Mozart employs a consistent quaver rhythm of four beats in the bar, as does Goldsmith, and if one isolates the first three bass notes of Mozart's accompaniment in the first bar of the "Requiem," we actually find the same pitch relationships as we find in the opening of Goldsmith's ostinato.

If we compare the base line of Mozart here with Goldsmith, we see that the ostinato of *The Omen* begins the same way, but after D, F, and E it returns to F rather than Mozart's movement to G. By using this Mozartian model and combining it with his own setting of the Satanic text —"Sanguis bibimus, corpus edimus, tolle corpus Satani, Ave Satani! Ave Versus Christus!" ("Drink the blood, eat the flesh, raise the body of Satan, Hail Satan! Hail the Antichrist!")—Goldsmith powerfully inverts the sacred connotations of the Requiem Mass to create a musical *Black* Mass.

The modern idea of music suitable for a Black Mass, like the Black Mass itself, is invariably based on such sacred models, but there simply was no

Example 1: The opening bars of the "Requiem" from Mozart's *Requiem*.

"demonic" music before the nineteenth century. The witches in Purcell's *Dido and Aeneas* (1688), for example, are admittedly introduced with dramatically effective music, but it belongs to the tradition of the funeral march. Indeed, the opening "Lento" of this scene has much in common with Purcell's funeral music for Queen Mary. Both feature slowness, minor tonality, dotted rhythms, suspensions, and so forth, but this is not "demonic" in the sense we think of today.

Even more than tritones, open fifths, the *Dies Irae*, and ostinati, what we have now come to regard as the music representative of, and indeed conducive to facilitating, occult experiences are the experimental textures of twentieth-century avant-garde composers. Such a development also has its precedent, this time in literature. Thomas Mann was perhaps the first person to equate early twentieth-century musical modernism with devil worship in his novel *Doctor Faustus* (1947). His model was the music of Arnold Schoenberg (1874–1951), whose serial technique notoriously rejected the traditions of major and minor tonality in favor of what became known as the twelve-tone note row, which now formed the basis of the entire composition. Such a row, consisting of the twelve notes of a chromatic scale, could be varied by reversing it, inverting its pitch relationships and finally reversing the inverted row, thus providing the composer with four related note rows, which could be superimposed and used to form chords and melodies, thus ensuring overall unity. Thomas Mann was not at all convinced by this approach, regarding Schoenberg's theory and practice as chaos made rational. For Mann, the chaos of the content was "justified" by the form, in much the same way that the Nazis "justified" their barbarism by means of ruthlessly organized bureaucracy. The narrator of the novel describes *The Lamentation of Dr. Faustus*, the final masterpiece of its composer-hero, Adrian Leverkühn, as

> a Utopia in form, of terrifying ingenuity, which in the *Faust* cantata becomes universal, seizes upon the whole work and, if I may so put it, causes it to be completely swallowed up by thematic thinking. This giant "lamento" (it lasts an

hour and a quarter) is very certainly non-dynamic, lacking in development, without drama, in the same way that concentric rings made by a stone thrown into water spread ever farther, without drama and always the same. A mammoth variation-piece of lamentation — as such negatively related to the finale of the Ninth Symphony [of Beethoven] with its variations of exultation — broadens out in circles, each of which draws the other resistless after it: movement, large-scale variations, which are nothing else than series of variations.[46]

Needless to say, Schoenberg was outraged by Mann's equation of serialism with totalitarian fascism, especially since he was a Jew. However, in the popular imagination (an imagination in which tonality, through the dominance of popular music, is still very much alive and kicking), serialism and atonality are still regarded as "chaotic," "soulless," "empty," and consequently indicative of the Devil.

Leaving aside their royalty payments, avant-garde composers would be justified in sharing Schoenberg's outrage upon realizing just how much of their music, let alone its influence, has been put to demonic use in movies, which the composers themselves certainly did not have in mind when composing it. Six of Penderecki's pieces, including *Polymorphia*, appeared in *The Shining,* and *Polymorphia* returned for another demonic date in *The Exorcist.* The director of *The Exorcist,* William Friedkin, invited Penderecki to compose original music for the film, but Penderecki declined, deeming it demeaning for a serious composer to write "mere" film music. Ironically, this led Friedkin to interpolate already-existing works by Penderecki into the soundtrack, bringing Penderecki's music to a far wider audience than the composer had ever reached before. A similar fate awaited Ligeti's music when Kubrick applied it to *2001: A Space Odyssey.* It wasn't really until Paul Glass was commissioned by Hammer Films for their third (and final) Dennis Wheatley adaptation, *To the Devil a Daughter...* (dir. Peter Sykes, 1976), that the techniques of avant-garde composition were exclusively used for an occult shocker in an original, specially composed score.[47] Not even Jerry Goldsmith's pioneering work on *The Mephisto Waltz* was as consistently uncompromising as Glass' music for this film; Goldsmith's score was, of course, based on Liszt's music, but *The Mephisto Waltz* anyway required more lyricism than *To the Devil a Daughter...* (and Goldsmith wasn't as self-consciously avant-garde as Glass, despite Glass' many Hollywood film scores).

There is, therefore, a case for arguing that the way in which occult movies have hijacked the avant-garde is just another aspect of their post–Romantic agenda. Occult movies *use* musical modernism but in fact reject its aesthetic by equating it, along Thomas Mann's lines, with what is morally evil. Under these circumstances, such music has no hope of freeing itself from the shackles of Romanticism. Indeed, one might well say that modernism has been defeated by twentieth-century popular culture (which, in many ways, is no more than popular Romanticism). There is, however, another way of looking at the situation, which will become clearer when we deal with Schoenberg's interest in the occult in the next chapter. Briefly, this alternative view argues that Schoenberg used atonality and his later serial style to express a spiritual reality that lies beyond the merely physical universe. Once one has accepted that, the use of atonal music in films such as *The Exorcist* becomes even more appropriate, and in sympathy with Schoenberg's mystical vision.

# Chapter Four

## *Wagner's Racial Mysticism and Schoenberg's Numerical Superstition*

Richard Wagner's music drama, *Tristan und Isolde* is also, by a circuitous route, a descendent of the Pythagorean doctrine of the music of the spheres. It was largely inspired by Schopenhauer's philosophy, which was, in turn, indebted to Pythagorean ideas. After reading Schopenhauer's major work, *Die Welt als Wille und Vorstellung* (*The World as Will and Representation*), Wagner was most impressed by what Schopenhauer had to say about music. According to Schopenhauer, the other arts, such as painting and poetry, "merely" copy the phenomenal world, which itself is only a *representation* of what Immanuel Kant had termed the "Ding an sich," or "Thing in Itself," and which Schopenhauer termed the Will. Music, however, is a direct copy of the Will, cutting out the phenomenal world altogether: "For this reason, the effect of music is so very much more powerful and penetrating than is that of the other arts, for the others speak only of the shadow, but music of the essence."[1]

Schopenhauer's argument is very much in the manner of one of Fludd's monochord metaphors:

> I recognize the whole gradation of those Ideas in which the will objectifies itself. Those nearer to the bass are the lower of those grades, namely the still inorganic bodies manifesting themselves, however, in many ways. Those that are higher represent to me the plant and animal worlds. The definite intervals of the scale are parallel to the definite grades of the will's objectification, the definite species of nature. The departure from the arithmetical correctness of the intervals through some temperament, or produced by the selected key, is analogous to the departure of the individual from the type of the species. In fact, the impure discords, giving no definite interval, can be compared to the monstrous abortions between two species of animals, or between man and animal.... Finally, in the

*melody,* in the high, singing, principal voice, leading the whole and progressing with unrestrained freedom ... I recognize the highest grade of the will's objectification, the intellectual life and endeavor of man.[2]

Schopenhauer replaces the hand of God, which turned the tuning peg of Fludd's monochord, with man's intelligence. He denies the existence of God. There is not even the possibility of being absorbed, at the moment of death, into cosmic harmony. He warns us against dressing up the reality of nothingness with what he called "myths and meaningless words, such as reabsorption in *Brahman,* or the *Nirvana* of the Buddhists."[3] Having said that, he was profoundly influenced by Buddhist philosophy, and in his essay "On the Suffering of the World" he discusses the Buddhist explanation of how the world was created and why it is such a place of suffering:

> Brahma is supposed to have created the world by a kind of fall into sin, or by an error, and has to atone for this sin or error by remaining in it himself until he has redeemed himself out of it. Very good! In Buddhism the world arises as a consequence of an inexplicable clouding of the heavenly clarity of the blessed state of Nirvana after a long period of quietude.[4]

Wagner glossed this passage in the Venetian Diary of 1858, which he wrote for the muse of *Tristan und Isolde,* Mathilde Wesendonck:

> I often turn my gaze towards the land of Nirvana. But for me Nirvana turns rapidly to Tristan; you know the Buddhist theory of the Creation. A breath clouds the clear heavens:

> this swells, becomes denser, and finally the whole universe stands once more before me in impenetrable solidity. This is my fate, as of old, so long as I still have such unredeemed spirits about me![5]

Wagner was also inspired by an orchestral fantasy by Hans von Bülow (1830–

## Four. Wagner's Mysticism and Schoenberg's Superstition      73

1894) titled *Nirwana*, from which he appropriated several ideas for *Tristan*. Later he also stole Bülow's wife, Cosima, and her children by Bülow, which is, of course, another story. *Nirwana* was in turn inspired by a tragedy of the same name by Karl Ritter (1830–1891), whom Wagner also knew. Nicknamed the "suicide fantasy"[6] by members of Bülow's private circle, Wagner wrote of it as a masterful portrayal of "suicidal madness" with a "quite dreadful atmosphere."[7] Wagner thus makes clear the Buddhist connotation of the famous opening bars of *Tristan und Isolde*, which he himself described as an musical expression of yearning:

> Yearning, insatiable longing ever reborn, thirsting and repining! The only release was to die, to perish, to fade away, nevermore to awaken! ... The swooning heart sinks back again to enter the sea of love's endless delight. In vain! The swooning heart sinks back again, to pine away in yearning desire, a yearning that never achieves its goal, since each attainment of such a goal brings only renewed desire — until, in final weariness, a glimpse of the haven of boundless joy transfigures the eye that grows dim in death. This is the joy of dying, the joy of non-being, of final redemption felt by all who enter that wondrous realm from which we wander furthest away whenever we strive to enter it with all the tempest's fury. Are we to call it death? Or is it, rather, that wondrous world of night from which, so the legend tells us, tendrils of ivy and vine grew up, in intimate entwinement, over Tristan's and Isolde's grave?[8]

The influence of Buddhism, via Schopenhauer is clear here, but so are the differences between Wagner and his philosophical inspiration. Clearly, the ambiguity he throws over the word "death" is crucial: "Are we to call it death? Or is it, rather, that wondrous world of night...?" This suggests that Wagner is using the word "death" metaphorically, as a symbol of imaginative and emotional freedom. He concludes his program note with words that seem to confirm this interpretation: "Over Tristan's body the dying Isolde perceives the blessed fulfillment of that yearning which consumes her with its flames, eternal union in measureless space, without barriers, without bonds, but one and indissoluable!"[9] The old yearning for union and integration with the universe is part of the metaphor here as well.

These quotations demonstrate that Wagner took from Schopenhauer only what he required, and, what is more, for Isolde there is, at the moment of death, the possibility of reabsorption into the "Welt-Atems" — the World's Spirit. Through music we are released into the reality that lies beyond the illusory, merely phenomenal world. Some kind of afterlife (or *heightened* life, to put an atheistical gloss on it) is implied here. The text of Isolde's culminating "Liebestod" does not imply the "nothingness" with which Schopenhauer brings the first volume of *The World as Will and Representation* to a close. There he wrote, "We freely acknowledge that what remains after the

74 The Occult Arts of Music

complete abolition of the will is, for all who are still full of the will, assuredly nothing. But also conversely, to those in whom the will has turned and denied itself, this very real world of ours with all its suns and galaxies, is—nothing."[10] Isolde's "Liebestod," however, suggests some kind of reunion with, or absorption *in*, the dead Tristan, whose spirit she can see "stern-umstrahlet/hoch sich hebt" ("borne on high amid the stars"). Absorption in the "wehendem All" ("the blowing All") is not sheer Schopenhaurian "nothingness" for her, but represents the emotional freedom as well as the sexual consummation for which both lovers have yearned and which has been denied them throughout the entire opera.

To be absorbed into Wagner's version of the music of the spheres is not to be united with God but with one's lover — and, perhaps even more significantly, with one's own imagination. Wagner's music is "oceanic" in the sense that it overwhelms, but it does not so much represent the cosmos as use cosmic imagery to convey the act and physiological effect of sexual orgasm. Through such an orgasm we enter the timeless world of emotional and imaginative fulfillment, seemingly as vast and full of possibilities as the cosmos itself. Ironically, Schopenhauer regarded sex as the great illusion, the focus of the Will and the cause of all unhappiness, which was why he advocated chastity. Wagner inverts this and offers sex as the ultimate gateway through which we may escape the Will's tyranny. Whatever Isolde's "Liebestod" really means (and the jury is still out with regard to the precise meaning of the deliberately mystical and vague words Wagner gives Isolde to sing), we are a long way from the classical idea of a music of the spheres. However, the imagery nonetheless derives from the Pythagorean tradition.

The same might be said of many science fiction films (and their scores). Frequently, these do not regard the universe as the handiwork of God, but instead present it as a sublime spectacle that has its own metaphorical "music." James Horner's score for *Star Trek: The Wrath of Khan* (dir. Nicholas Meyer, 1982) provides a good example of what I mean here, as it uses the idiom of nineteenth-century Romanticism in association with oceanic cosmic imagery. The particular musical device Horner uses at the end of the film is very similar to a moment in Richard Strauss' tone poem *Tod und Verklärung (Death and Transfiguration*, 1889), itself a work deeply indebted to Wagner's example and, with its detailed scenario, a kind of prototypical film music. Strauss' composition describes an artist on his deathbed who is given courage to face the end by the faith he has in his artistic ideal, and it ends with a suggestion of eternity by means of lengthily sustained chords. Horner's cue for the final scenes of the *Star Trek* film begins in a contemplative manner that is similar in tone and orchestration to the opening of Strauss' piece. As the camera pans across the universe of stars, Leonard Nimoy intones the famous tagline of the

## Four. Wagner's Mysticism and Schoenberg's Superstition     75

series ("Space: the final frontier..."), under which the *Star Trek* theme is brought in. When he reaches the celebrated split infinitive of "to boldly go where no man has gone before," we are drawn into hyperspace as stars hurtle past our point of view. Then, just before the end title credits, Horner employs a simple motif of two adjacent tones, one falling to the other, which resembles the last two tones of the motif Strauss had used to suggest the artist's ideology. Even though Horner's harmonization differs from that Strauss, the overall effect is similar. In fact, Horner juxtaposes two unrelated triads here, which Wagner had used at the end of *Parsifal* to suggest transcendence and release. This *Star Trek* moment, then, is Wagnerian cosmic mysticism, via Straussian idealism, in the guise of science fiction!

Wagner's interest in Buddhism inspired other aspects of his oeuvre. A long-standing but ultimately never composed project was based on an Indian legend. Wagner grew acquainted with the story through reading Eugène Burnouf's *Introduction à l'histoire du buddhisme indien* (1844), which included the story of Prakriti, a Chandala girl who desperately loves the noble Ananda, who is of a different caste and therefore rejects her. Buddha intervenes and explains that Prakriti is a reincarnation of the daughter of a proud Brahmin. Through pride and haughtiness she denied the love of another young man, and must atone for her previous sin in her present life so that she may understand the pain of unrequited love. Her redemption lies in accepting Buddha's teaching of chastity and entering his community. This she willingly agrees to do and Ananda welcomes her there as a sister.

Wagner never progressed beyond the stage of writing out a prose sketch for this drama. The reason for this is that many of its themes were absorbed into *Tristan* and, even more significantly, into *Parsifal,* where Prakriti is transformed into the character of Kundry, who similarly atones for the sins of her own previous incarnations. Her greatest sin in those past lives was laughing at Christ on his way to Calvary, and in *Parsifal* she has a decidedly schizophrenic character. One half of her personality aims to help the Grail Knights find a cure for their sick leader, Amfortas. The other half of her complex nature, which is revealed in the second act, is under the control of the wicked magician, Klingsor, who wishes to destroy the Grail community and use the Holy Grail for his own selfish purposes. He has already stolen the lance from Amfortas, who was seduced by the femme fatale version of Kundry, and wounded him in the genitals. The Grail and the lance are, among other things, sexual symbols, and it is their proper use with which *Parsifal* is concerned. Klingsor has castrated himself to gain a sinister power over others, in much the same way that Alberich in *The Ring* has renounced love to gain power. Klingsor's misuse of these sexual symbols contrasts starkly with how Parsifal uses them, for, like Prakriti, Parsifal devotes himself to a life of chastity and

"Herauf! Hieher! Zu mir! Dein Meister ruft dich, Namenlose: Ur-Teufelin! Höllenrose!" Illustration by Franz Stassen (1869-1949) for Act II of Wagner's *Parsifal* (Berlin: Fischer & Franke, 1901).

sexual renunciation. (That Parsifal later fathers Lohengrin, the subject of an earlier Wagner opera, proves, as Nietzsche cynically put it, that chastity can work miracles,[11] but the chastity element is perhaps not meant to be taken literally. Wagner seems rather to be advocating genuine love over selfish lust, but with his own trail of illegitimate children and abandoned mistresses, not

## Four. Wagner's Mysticism and Schoenberg's Superstition 77

to mention two wives, he was hardly the man to preach that particular sermon.) Sexual love, as Tristan and Isolde demonstrate, is a singularly self-absorbed expression of love. It is about physical sensation, whereas *Parsifal* seems to be suggesting that the platonic variety is potentially more meaningful and certainly more selfless.

Kundry attempts to seduce Parsifal, the pure fool, who is resistant to her charms, and, having destroyed Klingsor's magic garden with its worryingly ambivalent flower maidens, Parsifal redeems Kundry by forgiving her. At the end of the work she "falls lifeless," which is not quite the same thing as dying. Wagner's stage direction here suggests that her death is a transformative one, though other commentators have (with some reason) seen her death as the fulfillment of the antisemitic program outlined in Wagner's essay "Judaism in Music" (1869). Unfortunately, Wagner believed that only through annihilation could the Jews themselves be redeemed. Indeed, Klingsor tells us that Kundry was a Jew in one of her previous incarnations, but it should be stressed that she was also Germanic and a variety of other racial types in subsequent incarnations. Even so, compassion, in Wagner's understanding of the word, is a rather more selective conception than the one Lord Buddha had in mind, and this raises the troubling aspect of racial mysticism in Wagner's music dramas.

Though it is going too far to suggest, as Robert Gutman would have it, that *Parsifal*, in all its ambiguous complexity, represents "the gospel of National Socialism,"[12] there is absolutely no doubt that Wagner was antisemitic, and that the writings he was working on at the time of composing *Parsifal* were deeply antisemitic as well. As "Know Thyself" (1881), the most worrying of all the supplements to his previous year's essay "Religion and Art," put it, "Even commixture of blood does not hurt him; let a Jew or a Jewess intermarry with the most distinct of races, a Jew will always come to birth."[13] This suggests that Kundry's multiracial reincarnations are not able to purge her of her Jewish interlude as Herodias. (Klingsor refers to her by this name when summoning her in Act II.) Wagner anticipates a state of society when there will "be no longer — any Jews," which he regards as "this great solution within reach of us Germans, rather than of any other nation, if only we would boldly take that 'Know thyself' and apply it to the inmost quick of our existence."[14]

Because Wagner was deliberately non-specific in his text for *Parsifal*, it is quite possible to approach it as a work that has nothing to do with antisemitism, but such an approach in fact "diminishes" the work, in the sense that it strips from the opera an important layer of meaning — albeit an extremely distasteful one. For a start, much of the imagery of *Parsifal* is about blood. As Gutman put it, "'Much too much blood' was Nietzsche's pro-

78 The Occult Arts of Music

Semitic comment on the new Wagnerian Communion."[15] There are, in fact, twenty-one specific references to bleeding and blood (divine or otherwise) in the text of *Parsifal,* to say nothing of the frequent talk of wounds. The blood mostly belongs to Christ, and it flows miraculously into the Holy Grail, rejuvenating the Grail Knights who look after the holy relic in their castle.

The ways in which the text and music might be regarded as antisemitic have been exhaustively analyzed by the likes of Paul Lawrence Rose and Marc A. Weiner,[16] and there is no need to repeat them here, but what is pertinent to the relation of Wagner's ideas to the occult is their similarity to the racial theories of Madame Blavatsky, who founded the Theosophical Society in 1875, the year before the premiere of the *Ring* cycle at Bayreuth. Her first work, the mammoth two-volume study of comparative religion, *Isis Unveiled,* was published in 1877, but her racial theories weren't developed until the publication of *The Secret Doctrine* in 1888, five years after Wagner's death. Blavatsky claimed that humanity is evolving through seven evolutionary cycles or "Root Races." The individuals of the first Root Race were astral and had dwelt in an invisible land, reproducing rather like amoebas. The second were the Hyperboreans, who dwelt and ultimately perished in the Arctic. The third was a Lemurian Root Race, which flourished on a continent in the Indian ocean. The fourth was represented by the Atlanteans, who were annihilated by the destruction of Atlantis, a disaster caused by their misuse of the psychic forces they had developed. Present-day humanity constitutes the fifth Root Race, which Blavatsky termed "Aryan." Eventually, in the 28th century, the sixth race will appear in California (a suitable location for such a fantasy evolutionary scenario) and the seventh, millions of years from now, will eventually inhabit an island in the Pacific ocean called Pushkara.

There is no evidence that Wagner ever read a word of Blavatsky's earlier writings, but his own theories were later blended with her racial fantasies by proto-Nazi theorists such as Guido von List (1848–1919) and Lanz von Liebenfels (1874–1959). Blavatsky was not antisemitic, but was more generally racialist, regarding certain races as being more evolved than others. While insisting in *The Secret Doctrine* that "the occult doctrine admits of no such divisions as the Aryan and the Semite" and that "the Semites, especially the Arabs, are later Aryans,"[17] Blavatsky does point out that

> the Secret Doctrine teaches that the *specific unity of mankind* is not without exceptions even now. For there are, or rather still were a few years ago, descendants of these half-animal tribes or races, both of remote Lemurian and Lemuro-Atlantean origin. The world knows them as Tasmanians (now extinct), Australians, Andaman Islanders, etc.[18]

The whole idea of evolution along racial lines unfortunately lends itself to

# Four. Wagner's Mysticism and Schoenberg's Superstition 79

nationalist and ethnic exploitation, and Blavatsky's use of the term "sub-Race" proved, of course, to be a particularly dangerous one in the wrong hands.

Wagner was of the opinion that non-Jewish man was degenerating due to his rejection of what he believed to be humanity's basic vegetarian nature. Whereas "beasts are only distinguished from man by the grade of their mental faculties"[19] (and, indeed, even panthers and tigers were once vegetarian), "the Jewish God found Abel's fatted lamb more savoury than Cain's offering of the produce of the field. From such suspicious evidences of the characters of the Jewish tribal god we see a religion arise against whose direct employment for regeneration of the human race we fancy that a convinced vegetarian of nowadays might have serious complaint to lodge."[20] Wagner contrasts such a state of affairs with "the Brahminic doctrine of the sinfulness of killing living creatures, or feeding on the carcasses of murdered beasts."[21] Equating Buddhism and Christianity as "the two sublimest religions," Wagner found it necessary to suggest that it was "doubtful if Jesus himself was of Jewish extraction, since the dwellers in Galilee were despised by the Jews on account of their impure origin."[22]

Of course, these views would not be worth considering if they did not hover behind the sublimely beautiful and emotionally persuasive art of *Parsifal*. Wagner's racism is admittedly more spiteful than mystical but, in combination with the occult atmosphere of Blavatsky's theosophy, it proved to be dynamite when the whole complex of Bayreuth Idealism, promoted by the likes of Houston Stewart Chamberlain (1855–1927) and theosophically derived Ariosophy, was exploited by the Third Reich. Theosophy lent Wagner's racism a mystical "authority," as did the context of Wagner's racism within the magical setting of *Parsifal*.

Many theosophical interpretations of Wagner's works followed in the wake of Rudolf Steiner's breakaway anthroposophical movement. Steiner (1861–1925) had at one time been a committed theosophist, but eventually felt the need to found his own mystical movement more firmly based on the Western Christian tradition than theosophy had been. The American offshoot of anthroposophy was run by one-time engineer and scion of a noble German family, Max Heindel (1865–1919). Like Steiner's anthroposophical Goetheanum building in Dornach, Switzerland, Heindel's Rosicrucian Fellowship also had its own temple, the Ecclesia Healing Temple at Mount Ecclesia in Oceanside, California, and his magnum opus was *The Rosicrucian Cosmo-Conception* (1911), which was largely indebted to Steiner's ideas on esoteric Christianity. The racial views expressed within this Rosicrucian Bible were very much of their time and fully in accord with Wagner's, referring to "the Indian and the Negro" who, "because of the duller nervous system, are much less sensitive to lacerations. An Indian will continue to fight after receiving wounds the shock of which would prostrate or kill a white man, whereas the Indian man would quickly recover."[23] Similarly, "the Negros and the savage races with curly hair, are the last remnant of the Lemurians."[24] Heindel also points out that "the sixteen Races are called the 'sixteen paths to destruction' because there is always, in each Race, a danger that the soul may become too much attached to the Race; that it may become so enmeshed in Race-characteristics it cannot rise above the *race*-idea, and will therefore fail to advance; that it may, so to speak, crystalize into that Race and consequently be confided to the Race-bodies when they start to degenerate, as happened to the Jews."[25] Worse, "as the present Aryan Races are reasoning human beings, capable of profiting by past experience, the logical means of helping them is by telling them of past stages of growth and the fate that overtook the disobedient Jews." However, in an artful piece of special pleading, "the American-born Jew is different from the Jew of other countries. The very fact that he has incarnated in the Western World shows that he is becoming emancipated from the Race-spirit, and is consequently in advance of the crystallized Old World orthodox Jew."[26]

Heindel also wrote a lesser-known book titled *Mysteries of the Great Operas* (1921). The first chapter is devoted to Gounod's *Faust,* though, in fact, he doesn't address the opera so much as Goethe's play, on which the libretto was somewhat loosely based. This gives him ample opportunities to expound some of Steiner's Goethean theories (Steiner had begun his own career as a Goethe scholar), but after this make-weight chapter, the rest of the book is devoted to Wagner. Heindel covers *Tannhäuser* in chapter 15, arguing that the goings-on in the Venusburg are "not entirely founded upon fancy. There are Spirits in the air, in the water, and in the fire; and under certain conditions they are contacted by man. Not so much perhaps in the electric atmosphere of America, but over all of Europe, particularly in the north, there broods a mystic atmosphere, which has somewhat attuned the people to the seeing of these elementals. The goddess of beauty, or Venus, here spoken of, is really one of the etheric entities who feed upon the fumes of low desire."[27]

One might be tempted to dismiss the book as a whole on the strength of such passages, were it not for the revealing parallels it offers to Wagner's own racial theories and the synchronicity of Heindel's book with the emerging fascist ideology in Germany around the time of its publication in America. Heindel also discusses reincarnation with regard to *Tannhäuser* — a subject Wagner never believed in as literally as Heindel but that nonetheless interested him as an idea and that he incorporated into *Parsifal.* Heindel argues that Tannhäuser, like Kundry in *Parsifal,* is concerned with "the problem of the spiritual life of the Disciple who aims to follow the path to the higher life and seeks, like Kundry, to undo the deeds of ill of former lives by a present life

## Four. Wagner's Mysticism and Schoenberg's Superstition    81

of service to the higher self."[28] Rather like one of Wagner's rambling "regeneration" essays from the end of his life, Heindel then wanders off into cogitations about humanity's apparently hermaphroditic past and argues that the message of *Tannhäuser* is this: "Passion is poison. Abuse of generation under the sway of Lucifer has been the means of leading us downward into the gloom of degeneration, but the same power turned into the opposite direction and used for purposes of regeneration is capable of lifting us out of the gloom and elevating us to a heavenly state.... Only in chastity can the fetters be loosed, for *heaven is the home of the virgin*."[29] All this is rather reminiscent of Carlos Schwabe's famous 1897 poster for the Rosicrucian *Rose et Croix* art exhibitions organized by Joséphin ("Sâr") Péledan (1858–1915), which used much the same imagery of a soul drowning in the mire of materialism while another soul is being encouraged to ascend the steps of initiation.

Heindel describes *Lohengrin* as an initiation drama, the swan imagery being symbolic of the initiate's ability to elevate himself to higher realms and plunge into the depths of his soul-body. The soul is like a swan that can "fly in the air with great swiftness," swim "majestically upon the water" and "by means of its long neck even explore the depths and investigate whatever may be found upon the bottom of a not too deep pond."[30] Elsa, the opera's heroine, is apparently an old soul, reincarnated many times, and being "high born" she is able to claim the services of a spiritual knight to initiate her: "The true Teacher always comes in response to the earnest prayers of the aspirant, but not till he has forsaken the world and been forsaken by it. He offers to take care of one who is thus anxious for guidance, and forthwith conquers untruth with the sword of truth, but having given this proof, henceforth he requires an absolute unquestioning faith."[31] And this, Heindel argues, is why Lohengrin insists that Elsa not ask his name.

The Truth, by which Heindel presumably means some kind of spiritual insight or absorption into a metaphysical state, is very much at the fore in his analysis of Wagner's *Ring* cycle. Brünnhilde represents "Truth" and, as "Truth is ever on the side of the truth-seeker in his battle against the conventionalities of the Church and social custom," this is why the Valkyrie maiden attempts to intervene in the battle between Siegmund and Hunding in *Die Walküre*. Like Wagner, Heindel's approach to Christianity, viewed as it was through the occult binoculars of Steiner and Blavatsky, was hardly orthodox. Orthodox religion may take care of "a great majority of mankind" but "there are always a few pioneers—some whose faculty of intuition tells them of greater heights unscaled, who see the sunlight of truth beyond the wall of creed."[32] The inherent social elitism of occultism is expressed in a nutshell here, and so too, in the overall context of his thought, is Heindel's inherently racial perspective. Spiritual truth is not for everyone.

Siegfried's discovery of Brünnhilde in the third act of *Siegfried* is interpreted as the attainment of enlightenment: "There are no words adequate to convey a conception of what the soul feels when it stands in that presence, far above the world," Heindel rhapsodizes, before applying Blavatskian evolutionary principles to the dramaturgy of the cycle as a whole:

> The early Atlantean Epoch, when mankind lived as guileless "Children of the Mist" (Niebelung) in the foggy basins of the Earth, is represented in the Rheingold. The later Atlantean time is an age of savagery, where mankind has forsworn love, as Alberich did, and forms "the Ring" of egoism, where it devotes its energies to material acquisitions symbolized by "the hoard" of the Nibelung, over which giants, gods, and men fight with savage brutality and low cunning, as set forth in "The Valkuerie [sic]."
>
> The early Aryan Epoch marks the birth of the idealist, symbolized by the "Walsungs" (Siegmund, Sieglinda, and Siegfried), a new race which aspires with a sacred ardor to new and higher things....
>
> We are now in the latter part of the Aryan Epoch. The truth seekers of the past have again left the fire girt rock of Brunhilde [sic]. We have again assumed the veil of flesh and partaken of the lethal drink, and we are today actually playing the last part of the great epic drama, "The Twilight of the Gods," which is identical in its import with our Christian Apocalypse.[33]

From such an interpretation, it is not hard to see how much Heindel's ideas have in common with Wagner's racial theories, especially in light of his comments on *Parsifal,* which argue that "only those who have the most perfect unselfishness, coupled with the nicest discrimination, are fit to have the spiritual power symbolized by the spear."[34] For Wagner, Jews were the embodiment of selfishness and completely without discrimination, and a Freudian interpretation of Heindel's critique here would also suggest a eugenicist's program. Only the pure in heart (i.e., the racially cleansed) have the right to reproduce and ultimately attain spiritual truth.

Heindel equates the Grail with the flowering staff of the pope mentioned in *Tannhäuser* along with Aaron's rod and the staff of Moses. His account of the creation of the Holy Grail concerns the story of how Lucifer and the Archangel Michael fought over the body of Moses. Lucifer lost a precious emerald from his crown in the contest, which later formed the basis of the Grail. Heindel stresses that green (the color of emerald) is the complementary color of red:

> In the Physical World red has the tendency to excite and energize, whereas green has a cooling and a soothing effect, but the opposite is true when we look at the matter from the viewpoint of the Desire World. There the complementary color is active, and has the effect upon our desires and emotions which we ascribe to the physical color. Thus the green color of the gem lost by Lucifer shows the

## Four. Wagner's Mysticism and Schoenberg's Superstition    83

nature and effect thereof. This stone is the antithesis of the Philosopher's Stone. It has the power to attract passion and generate love of sex for sex, which is the very opposite to the chaste and pure love, symbolized by the apocalyptic white stone, which latter is the love of soul for soul.[35]

Whatever Heindel meant by this typically cloudy and confusing passage, it is good introduction to the next aspect of *Parsifal* I would like to address: the alchemical subtext of Wagner's last work.

Wagner's text unequivocally describes the Grail as "the Cup used at the Last Supper,"[36] and in a letter to the muse of *Tristan*, Mathilde Wesendonck, he explained, "The Grail, according to my own interpretation is the goblet used at the Last supper in which Joseph of Arimathea caught the Savior's blood on the Cross."[37] But Wagner was also fully aware of the other interpretations of the Grail:

> That this miraculous object should be a precious stone is a feature which, admittedly, can be traced back to the earliest sources, namely the Arabic texts of the Spanish Moors. One notices, unfortunately, that all our Christian legends have a foreign, pagan origin. As they gazed on in amazement, the early Christians learned, namely, that the Moors in the Caaba at Mecca (deriving from the pre–Mohammedan religion) venerated a miraculous stone (a sunstone — or meteoric stone — but at all events one that had fallen from heaven). However, the legends of its miraculous power were soon interpreted by the Christians after their *own* fashion, by their associating the sacred object with Christian myth, a process which, in turn, was made easier by the fact that an old legend existed in southern France, telling how Joseph of Arimathea had once fled there with the sacred chalice that had been used at the Last Supper, a version entirely consonant with the early Christian Church's enthusiasm for relics.... I feel a very real admiration and sense of rapture at this splendid feature of Christian mythogenesis, which invented the most profound symbol that could ever have been invented as the content of the physical-spiritual kernel of any religion.[38]

Though Wagner chose to represent the Grail as a cup with Christian symbolism, there are also subliminal echoes of its other interpretations at work in Wagner's conception. His medieval source for *Parsifal,* Wolfram von Eschenbach (1170–1220), said this about the Grail:

> If you have never heard of it I shall name it for you here. It is called "lapsit exillis." By virtue of this Stone the Phoenix is burned to ashes, in which he is reborn.— Thus does the Phoenix moult its feathers! Which done, it shines dazzling bright and lovely as before! Such powers does the Stone confer on mortal men that their flesh and bones are soon made young again. This Stone is called "The Gral."[39]

But what did Wolfram mean by "lapsit exillis"? Did he mean "lapis exilis" — meaning a small stone — or, as others have suggested, "lapis lapsus ex caelis" —

a "stone fallen from heaven"? If so, why a stone? Wagner suggested that it might have been a sunstone or a meteoric stone. It could also, as Heindel suggests, have been the emerald that fell from the forehead of Lucifer during the war between God and Satan. Such an interpretation would also link it with the fabled pearl of Siva: a magical third eye with the power of self-knowledge.

The concept of a magical stone is central to the symbolism of medieval alchemy, and the quest to transmute base metal into gold by means of the *lapis philosophorum* was symbolic of a religious (or, more aptly, a *psychological*) quest to attain integration with the self. As Jung observed, the Renaissance alchemist Romanus Morienus seemed to understand that the philosopher's stone, like the Grail, was only something that can be found in the psyche. In discussing the nature of the philosopher's stone, he explained:

> Haec enim res a te extrahitur: cuius etiam minera tu existis, apud te namque illam inveniunt, et us verius confitear, a te accipiunt: quod cum probaveris, amor eius et dilectio in te augebitus. Et scias hoc verum et indubitabile permanere.
>
> (This thing is extracted from thee, and thou art its ore [raw material]; in thee they find it, and that I may speak more plainly, from thee they take it; and when thou hast experienced this, the love and desire for it will be increased in thee. And know that this remains true and indubitable.)[40]

In *Lohengrin*, Wagner wanted to demonstrate the opposition between the old pagan world, represented by the sorceress Ortrud, and the new civilizing influence of Christianity, obviously symbolized by Lohengrin himself. The Lohengrin story had a huge significance for Wagner, who, at the time of his conception of the opera, felt utterly alone as a man and artist. As he explained in "A Communication to My Friends" (1851), Lohengrin sought the woman who would believe in him, who would not ask who he was or whence he came, but who would love him as he was and because he was what he appeared to be. He sought the woman to whom he would not have to explain or justify himself but who would love him unconditionally. He had, therefore, to hide his higher nature, for only by concealing that higher (or, more correctly, *heightened*) nature could he be sure that he was not being merely admired or adored because of that nature or that he was not humbly and reverentially worshipped as a being past all understanding. He longed not for admiration and worship but for the only thing that could redeem him from his loneliness and still his longing for love — *to be loved* and to be understood through love.

Part of Wagner identified wholeheartedly with Lohengrin. Unlike his hero, however, he eventually found the ideal woman of his dreams in his second wife, Cosima. Wagner succeeded where Lohengrin had failed because he

### *Four. Wagner's Mysticism and Schoenberg's Superstition* 85

understood the perfectly human need of a wife for a complete, loving experience. Discussing Lohengrin's wife, Elsa, he anticipated the psychology of Jung:

> *Elsa* is the Unconscious, the Undeliberate (*Unwillkürliche*), into which Lohengrin's conscious, deliberate (*willkürliche*) being yearns to be redeemed.... This woman, who with clear foreknowledge rushes on her doom, for sake of Love's imperative behest ... I had found her *now*.[41]

In Jung's terminology, Elsa represents Lohengrin's anima, the feminine principle within the male psyche, and it is only when anima and animus are integrated that true creativity can be achieved. More importantly, it is the only basis of a truly loving relationship. In this sense, one must marry oneself, love oneself, before one can love anyone else. Lohengrin is unable to reveal his anima to his animus. He remains a conscious, voluntary male — only half a man — and here the imagery of the Grail is central, representing, as it does in both *Lohengrin* and *Parsifal*, the creative union with oneself that is necessary before union with another can be realistically and fruitfully contemplated. Elsa, both as a loving woman and as a personification of the anima, is, in fact, the real Holy Grail of *Lohengrin*. She is the subject of the orchestral prelude of the opera, which Wagner typically described in the most extravagant of terms:

> From a world of hatred and discord it seemed as though love had vanished: no longer was there a single human community in which it still showed itself clearly, dispensing beneficent laws. Yet amidst the bleak concern for profit and possessions, a concern which regulates all our worldly dealings to the exclusion of all else, the human heart's unquenchable longing for love was finally rekindled by the urge to assuage a need ... longed for and sought after under the name of the "holy Grail."...
> The vision becomes yet more distinct as it wings its way downwards, ever more visible, to this earthly vale of ours, till perfumes of ravishing sweetness well forth from its womb: entrancing fragrance wafts from within it like clouds of gold, usurping the onlooker's startled senses and filling the innermost depths of his quivering heart with wondrously hallowed emotion.... [The] Grail sends forth the sunbeams of this sublimest love like the steady flame of a heavenly fire, so that every heart begins to beat in the fiery glow of eternal ardour.[42]

As we have already discussed, Wagner did not necessarily preach literal chastity in *Parsifal*, nor did he recommend it in *Lohengrin*. Wagner's concern is with love and the dangers of mere lust. The reintegration of the psyche through compassion and the *ideals* of chastity are more to the point. Even though Wagner insisted that *Parsifal* was not a "postludial prelude" to *Lohengrin*, with which it "has nothing whatsoever to do,"[43] the imagery of the Grail,

## The Occult Arts of Music

and Wagner's interpretation of what the Grail actually is, obviously connects them. The point of *Parsifal* is not only the quest for self-knowledge and a complete loving relationship, as was the case in *Lohengrin,* but also achieving a higher form of knowledge about the reality of existence that such self-knowledge brings. The reality proposed by Wagner's idol, Schopenhauer, is that in a meaningless universe, suffering can only be overcome by a denial of the will-to-live, the ultimate cause of all suffering: "He who has reached this point ... resorts to fasting, and even to self-castigation and self-torture, in order that, by constant privation and suffering, he may more and more break down and kill the will that he recognizes and abhors as the source of his own suffering existence and of the world's."[44] Wagner adapted this deeply pessimistic teaching to express his own program of salvation. Though Kundry in the last act of *Parsifal* is indeed released from her cursed existence of suffering (both enduring and inflicting it), her death could be seen as a symbol of renewal: "Durch Mitleid wissend." ("Through Compassion, enlightenment.") Suffering *with* mankind brings self-knowledge and, more importantly, knowledge of the ultimate reality of existence, the only meaning of which is to be found in compassionate love. Fellow suffering, not merely pity, gives Parsifal the insight with which to redeem Kundry and, indeed, the world, and it is the Grail that symbolizes this knowledge.

"Who is the Grail?" Parsifal asks at the end of Act I. Now we are better equipped to understand Gurnemanz's answer:

> Das sagt sich nicht;
> doch, du selbst zu ihm erkoren,
> bleibt dir die Kunde unverloren.
>     Und sieh!
> Mich dünkt, dass ich dich recht erkannt:
> kein Weg führt zu ihm durch das Land,
> und niemand könnte ihn beschreiten,
> den er nicht selber möcht geleiten.

> (That cannot be said;
> but if you yourself are called to its service
> that knowledge will not remain withheld.
>     And see!
> I think I know you aright;
> no earthly path leads to it,
> and none could tread it
> whom the Grail itself had not guided.)

The alchemists used to say that the philosopher's stone was all around us, yet no one prizes it. The Grail, then, lies within us, if only we can find it: this is

## Four. Wagner's Mysticism and Schoenberg's Superstition        87

the meaning of the quest. For all the Christian symbolism of *Lohengrin* and *Parsifal*, Wagner's approach to Grail symbolism was more alchemical and psychological. As he put it in *Religion and Art*, the purpose of art is to breathe fresh life into the symbols of traditional belief:

> One might say that where religion becomes artificial, it is for Art to save the essence of religion by recognising the figurative value of its mythic symbols, which the former would have us believe in their literal sense, and revealing their deep and hidden truth through an ideal representation.[45]

Wagner's alchemical/psychological interpretation of the Grail was given a visual realization by Hans-Jürgen Syberberg in his 1983 film of *Parsifal*, in which the anima and animus of Parsifal himself were represented by two actors—one male, the other female (Michael Kutter and Karin Krick). When Parsifal's compassion is awakened after his encounter with Kundry (Edith Clever), his female aspect emerges, but at the end of the work, both aspects reappear, symbolizing total integration. Syberberg also uses a giant model of Wagner's death mask to imply the psychological aspect of the Grail. When the command is given to "uncover the Grail," the death mask splits open and light pours forth from within, suggesting in no uncertain terms that the Grail is as Romanus Morienus described it: that each one of us is his own Grail, and that the quest we all follow is complete integration of our individual psyche.

Wagner also called *Parsifal* a "Buhnenweifestspiel"—"a stage festival play with which to consecrate a stage." He wished his last work to be performed only at Bayreuth, suggesting that the Festspielhaus itself was a kind of Grail temple for his new proto-psychoanalytical, racial and synesthetic religion of music-drama. At the end of Syberberg's film, we see Kundry embracing a model of the theater beneath a glass dome, rather like a large snowglobe, though without the snow, suggesting what Bayreuth represented for Wagner (and, alas, for his National Socialist disciples) in symbolic terms. Similarly, Stefan Herheim's 2011 Bayreuth production of *Parsifal* used the back of Wagner's villa, "Wahnfried," as one of its stage settings, implying that the Grail was very much a personal symbol for Wagner, and very much tied up with his own psyche, but it is also, by implication, a personal goal for each one of us, in which our own families and domestic arrangements play just as crucial a role.

Arnold Schoenberg (1874–1951) regarded himself very much as Wagner's heir, and Jamie James calls him "the most mystical musician since Pythagoras."[46] Like Wagner, Schoenberg was also fascinated by the philosophy of Schopenhauer, in particular Schopenhauer's belief that music expresses the

88 The Occult Arts of Music

"Thing in Itself"—the noumenon beyond the phenomenon. He may also have been familiar with Rudolf Steiner's conviction that there is an aspect to reality that cannot be perceived by the senses. This has specific relevance to Goethe's theory of the so-called *Urpflanzen*, or "original plant." Steiner, who edited Goethe's scientific writings when a young man, wrote:

> Goethe's basic conviction was that something can be seen in the plant and in the animal that is not accessible to mere sense observation. What the bodily eye can observe about the organism seems to Goethe to be only the result of the living whole of developmental laws working through one another and accessible to the spiritual eye alone. What he saw in the plant and the animal with his spiritual eye is what he described.[47]

Steiner's esoteric Mystery Dramas, which were performed in pre–First World War Vienna and later at Steiner's purpose-built Goetheanum, may also have influenced the libretto of Schoenberg's opera *Die glückliche Hand* (1910–1913), which similarly takes place in a non-specific, symbolic setting. This is usually thought of as an Expressionist landscape, but it might equally well be a rather more "occult" world beyond reality. The same could be said of Schoenberg's oratorio *Die Jakobsleiter* (1917–1922). The angels who ascend and descend the Jacob's ladder in that work must go forth on their respective journeys without asking what lies in front of or behind them. As Jamie James points out, "Such an annihilation of the individual will is, of course, a fundamental aspect of mysticism."[48] Indeed, in Steiner's play titled *The Soul's Probation* (1911), the character of the Grand Master says much the same thing:

> The separate life and being must be sacrificed
> by him who would set eyes on spirit goals
> through sense-world revelation;
> who would, with courage, dare
> to pour into his individual will
> the spirit's power of will.[49]

James adds, "In the second part [of *Jakobsleiter*], the angels are the souls of the dead, who are 'either accepted into higher spheres or sent back to earth in new incarnations.' The conceit of dividing the unjust and just, sending the just to heaven and returning the unjust to earth, is taken directly from Plato's Myth of Er."[50]

Schoenberg was also interested in the mystical ideas of Emanuel Swedenborg (1688–1782), though he accessed most of what he knew about Swedenborg from the work of another of Swedenborg's admirers, Honoré de Balzac (1799–1850). Balzac's novel *Seraphita* (1834) concerns an angel who appears to a male painter as a woman and to the painter's fiancée as a man;

## Four. Wagner's Mysticism and Schoenberg's Superstition    89

the message of the story is that there is a refined, super-physical reality that we cannot access with our normally attuned senses.

> Thus man himself offers sufficient proof of the two world order, — Matter and Spirit. In him culminates a visible finite universe; in him begins a universe invisible and infinite, — two worlds unknown to each other. Have the pebbles of the fiord a perception of their combined being? have they a consciousness of the colors they present to the eye of man? do they hear the music of the waves that lap them? Let us therefore spring over and not attempt to sound the abysmal depths presented to our minds in the union of a Material universe and a Spiritual universe, — a creation visible, ponderable, tangible, terminating in a creation invisible, imponderable, intangible; completely dissimilar, separated by the void, yet united by indisputable bonds and meeting in a being who derives equally from the one and from the other![51]

*Seraphita* also shares Schoenberg's interest in Number:

> You know neither where Number begins, nor where it pauses, nor where it ends. Here you call it time, there you call it Space. Nothing exists except by Number. Without it all would be one and the same substance; for Number alone differentiates and qualifies substance. Number is to your Spirit what it is to Matter, an incomprehensible agent. Will you make a Deity of it? Is it a being? Is it a breath emanating from God to organize the material universe where nothing obtains form except by the Divinity which is an effect of Number?[52]

Two comparisons immediately leap to mind when reading this passage. The first is the phrase uttered by Wagner's Gurnemanz in *Parsifal* when traveling to the Grail temple with Parsifal in Act 1: "Nun Raum wird hier die Zeit." ("Here time becomes space.") The second is Schoenberg's belief that music is an emanation of the soul.

In general terms, these two quotations from Balzac's novel are more than enough to explain why it appealed to Schoenberg. Number, similarly, was the root cause of everything for Schoenberg, who regarded numbers as deeply magical conceptions. The twelveness of Schoenberg's twelve-tone system indeed has magic in it. 1+2 = 3, the trinity. For him, Number expresses that unseen world of which Balzac, Goethe and Steiner speak. Schoenberg was so number sensitive that he went so far as to spell "Aron" with only one "A," so that there would be only 12 letters in the title of his opera, *Moses und Aron*. He loathed the "unlucky" number 13 to such an extent that he would number his musical bars 12, 12A and 14. He was also terrified that he would die in a year of his life that was a multiple of 13. In fact, he died on Friday the 13th in 1951 during his 76th year (7+6 =13!). His wife said to him at a quarter to midnight on the night he died, "You see, the day is almost over. All that worry for nothing." Upon which he gasped, "Harmony," and passed away.[53]

## 90    The Occult Arts of Music

As John Covach points out, Schoenberg even considered setting the Assumption chapter from *Seraphita* as part of his *Die Jakobsleiter,*[54] and Pierre Boulez is in no doubt about the cosmic implications of Schoenberg's obsession with numbers. With twelve-tone music, he explained, "music moved out of the world of Newton and into the world of Einstein. The tonal idea was based on a universe defined by gravity and attraction. The serial idea is based on a universe that finds itself in perpetual expansion."[55]

Covach also suggests that atonality, and later serial technique, was used by Schoenberg to create a musical evocation of a spiritual world beyond the physical. The difference of atonal and serial music from the "normal" world of tonality approximated such a duality, in the same sense that *musica instrumentalis* is an echo of *musica mundana.* As evidence of this intention, one has to look no further than Schoenberg's Second String Quartet, Op. 10, with its atonal last movement setting a Stefan George poem ("Entrueckung") from 1907, which Jamie James calls "a symbolist gloss on Pythagorism."[56]

> Ich fühle luft von anderem planeten.
> Mir blassen durch das dunkel die gesichter
> Die freundlich eben noch sich zu mir drehten.
> Und bäum und wege die ich liebte fahlen
> Dass ich sie kaum mehr kenne und Du lichter
> Geliebter schatten — rufer meiner qualen —
> Bist nun erloschen ganz in tiefern gluten
> Um nach dem taumel streitenden getobes
> Mit einem frommen schauer anzumuten.
> Ich löse mich in tönen kreisend webend
> Ungründigen danks und unbenamten lobes
> Dem grossen atem wunschlos mich ergebend.

(I feel an air from other planets flowing. In darkness I see friendly faces even now turning toward me. Trees and paths that I loved fade, so that I can hardly know them, and your light, beloved shadow, summons my anguish. When the frenzy of chaotic strife is over, deeper blazes blend in tremulous amazement. I lose myself in tones, circling, wreathing. With unfathomable and unbound praise, I surrender to the great breath.)

Intriguingly, the opening line of George's poem was prefigured by Balzac in *Seraphita,* wherein Baron Seraphitus says, after the birth of his child and the mystical appearance to him of Swedenborg's spirit, "I breathe the air of other planets."[57]

Schoenberg also realized that Ferruccio Busoni (1866–1924) was thinking along similar lines, and mysticism indeed played a role throughout Busoni's

## Four. Wagner's Mysticism and Schoenberg's Superstition    91

compositional career. Early in his career he had included a musical portrait of an astrologer in his piano suite, *Macchiette Medioevali*, Op. 33 (1882/1883). This penultimate fifth piece of the suite is mysterious, chromatic, and influenced by the idiom of Bach in its contrapuntal quality. The vast Piano Concerto of 1904, with its five movements and choral finale, also contains mystical elements, which Busoni explained in visual terms by including a symbolic drawing in the score that explained the structure:

> It is the idea of my piano concerto in one picture and it is represented by architecture, landscape and symbolism. The three buildings are the first, third and fifth movements. In between come the two "living" ones; Scherzo and Tarantelle; the first, a nature-play, represented by a miraculous flower and bird; the second by Vesuvius and cypress trees. The sun rises over the entrance; a seal is fastened to the door of the end building. The winged being quite at the end is taken from Oehlenschläger's chorus and represents mysticism in nature.[58]

Adam Oehlenschläger's text, which is sung by a choir in the finale, is as follows:

> Lift up your hearts to the Power Eternal,
> Draw ye to Allah nigh, witness his work.
> Earth has its share of rejoicing and sorrow,
> Firm the foundations that hold up the world.
> Thousands and thousands of years march relentlessly,
> Show forth in silence His glory, His might,
> Flashing immaculate, splendid and fast they stand,
> Time cannot shake them, yea time without end.
>
> Hearts flamed in ecstasy, hearts turned to dust again,
> Playfully life and death staked each his claim,
> Yet in mute readiness patiently tarrying,
> Splendid and mighty both, for evermore.
> Lift up your hearts to the Power Eternal,
> Draw ye to Allah nigh, witness his work.
> Fully regenerate now is the world of yore,
> Praising its Maker e'en unto the end.

Though on a much smaller scale, Busoni's *Sonatina secondo* of 1912 is more adventurous musically, and also without tonality. He also marks it "Lento occulto," thus managing to look forward into new harmonic vistas and backward into a mysterious atmosphere of medieval occultism. Busoni's *Nocturne symphonique*, begun in the same year, in fact started life as a third piano sonata, but evolved rapidly into an orchestral work that, as Busoni's biographer Anthony Beaumont has pointed out, was originally to have included a part for glass harmonica, the instrument E. T. A. Hoffmann believed to be the closest approximation to the music of the spheres.

Busoni met Schoenberg in 1903 and they continued to correspond for many years. Schoenberg was in sympathy with Busoni's harmonic experiments, particularly with quarter tones, explaining that he too had "long been occupied with the removal of all shackles of tonality."[59] And it is perhaps more than a mere coincidence that the year in which Einstein published his special theory of relativity (1906) was the same year in which Busoni completed his *Outline of a New Aesthetic of Music,* a book that Schoenberg found greatly stimulating. In this work, Busoni suggests the possibility of expanding the available twelve tones into micro-intervals (something we shall hear about again when we deal with John Foulds in chapter six). He also discusses electronic instruments and urges pioneers at the frontier of tonality to press on, anticipating Schoenberg's prophecy that what used to be considered discords would eventually be regarded as higher consonances There are also echoes in that short work of Plato's music of the spheres. "Music is a part of the vibrating universe," Busoni suggests at one point.[60] Later, he seems to echo Schoenberg's setting of George's "Entrueckung":

> If Nirvana be the realm "beyond the Good and the Bad," *one* way leading thither is here pointed out. A way to the very portal. To the bars that divide Man from Eternity — or that open to admit that which was temporal. Beyond that portal sounds *music.* Not the strains of "musical art."* — It may be, that we must leave Earth to find that music. But only to the pilgrim who has succeeded on the way in freeing himself from earthly shackles, shall the bars open.
>
> *I think I have read, somewhere, that Liszt confined his Dante Symphony to the two movements, *Inferno* and *Purgatorio,* "because our tone-speech is inadequate to express the felicities of Paradise."[61]

Busoni also attracted the interest and discipleship of another avant-garde composer, Edgar Varèse (1883–1965), whose *Arcana* is framed by images of color and an occult dream world. Varèse agreed wholeheartedly with Busoni's belief that the function of the creative artist consists of creating new rules, not following those already made. Schoenberg similarly saw himself as a lawmaker, like Moses, and regarded his art as a private communion with God, just as Moses communed with the Almighty on Mount Sinai. (Jamie James also points out that Schoenberg's pupils were just as devoted as Pythagoras' students, zealously promulgating the word of the Master.[62])

If Busoni's *Nocturne symphonique* inhabits the unsettling landscape of the sleeping mind, Varèse's *Arcana* (1927) was actually inspired by a dream, and though he was always keen to clarify that his music was about nothing

## Four. Wagner's Mysticism and Schoenberg's Superstition    93

but itself, he nonetheless left us an account of that strange and synesthetic dream vision in a letter to his wife, Louise, in 1925, in which he referred to projectors of different colors and an angel (his wife) playing two trumpets against an incandescent sky. Varèse, the lover of freedom, was bound to enjoy the ultimate freedom of dreaming. For him, Busoni's plea for musical freedom overruled Schoenberg and his obsessive theorizing. Varèse even suggested that Schoenberg was actually frightened by the musical freedom he had pioneered in his atonal period and took refuge in the later system of serialism.

In a dream, the imagination knows no bounds, and it was perhaps to this that Varèse was alluding in his quotation from Paracelsus at the head of the score of *Arcana*: "One star exists, higher than all the rest. This is the apocalyptic star. The second star is that of the ascendent. The third is that of the elements, and of these there are four, so that six stars are established. Besides these there is still another star, imagination, which begets a new star and a new heaven."[63] The text comes from Paracelsus' book *Hermetic Astronomy*. The great physician, alchemist, occultist and astrologer, Phillippus Aureolius Theophrastus Bombastus von Hohenheim (1493–1541), chose the name "Paracelsus" because he thought himself superior to the first-century Roman physician Celsus. A mystic leading a sexless life, one of his greatest achievements was persuading experimenters that the object of alchemy should be the cure of the sick rather than the fruitless search for gold. (As we have seen, Jung drew the attention of modern man to alchemy as more of a psychological than chemical process, concerned with the process of individuation.) For Varèse, Paracelsus' placement of imagination as the highest star in the universe concurred with his belief that our greatest mental health lies in the pursuit of imaginative freedom. *Arcana* is not, however, "about" Paracelsus, but rather a tribute to his ideas.

As we have seen, the equation these composers made between atonality and the spiritual world is shared by certain types of occult films, though avant-garde styles are invariably used in such contexts as signifiers of the demonic rather than the spiritually transfigurative states envisioned by Schoenberg, Busoni and Varèse, and it has been through the cinema that avant-garde music has reached its widest audience. Even so, the connection between such musical styles and an invisible, spiritual world remains. Cinema is also the technological (if not always artistic) fulfillment of the aims of *Gesamtkunstwerk*, providing the most oceanic form of synesthetic experience so far attainable. I shall be exploring synesthesia in more detail in the next chapter, but related to it are Schoenberg's comments at the end of his *Theory of Harmony* (1922), in which he discussed the possibility of what he termed *Klangfarbenmelodie*. These "sound-color melodies" are not strictly speaking synesthetic, in the sense of uniting actual color with music, but Schoenberg uses the German word for color, "Farben," as a metaphor for the characteristic sound-colors (or timbres) produced by different musical instruments, which particular intonations can mute or intensify. (Just as there are many shades of red, there are also many varying "shades" of clarinet or flute — and, of course, an infinite variety of orchestral combinations.) Schoenberg envisioned the possibility of composing pieces around "Farben" rather than "Klang," and essayed this idea in the third of his 5 *Pieces for Orchestra*, Op. 16, which is indeed called "Farben." This emphasis on timbre for its own sake certainly relates to the aesthetic of certain forms of abstract visual art, in which self-contained color is more significant than representation or even form. Schoenberg's argument can usefully be interpreted by comparing the traditional idea of pitch-based melodies, which are then "colored" by orchestration, to the old representational styles of visual art, where the form is "colored in" by pigments. *Klangfarbenmelodie* proposes that sound-color could be the structuring principle of a composition. Instead of using orchestration to "color in" a traditional melody of pitches, the effects of varying orchestral color would now be the melody, and the pitches would take a subservient role. One could, for example, take a single chord and filter its various pitches through different orchestral colors. The play of timbre would therefore be the melody of the piece. Schoenberg described the process as follows:

> The distinction between tone color and pitch, as it is usually expressed, I cannot accept without reservations. I think the tone becomes perceptible by virtue of tone color, of which one dimension is pitch. Tone color is, thus, the main topic, pitch a subdivision. Pitch is nothing else but tone color measured in one direction. Now, if it is possible to create patterns out of tone colors that are differentiated according to pitch, patterns we call "melodies," progressions whose coherence (*Zusammenhag*) evokes an effect analogous to thought processes, then it must also be possible to make such progressions out of the tone colors of the other dimension, out of what we call simply "tone color," progressions whose relations with one another work with a kind of logic entirely equivalent to that logic which satisfies us in the melody of pitches. That has the appearance of a futuristic fantasy and is probably just that. But it is one which, I firmly believe, will be realized. I firmly believe it is capable of heightening in an unprecedented manner the sensory, intellectual, and spiritual pleasures offered by art. I firmly believe that it will bring us closer to the illusory stuff of our dreams; that it will expand our relationships to that which seems to us today inanimate as we give life from our life to that which is temporarily dead for us, but dead only by virtue of the slight connection we have with it.
>
> Tone-color melodies! How acute the senses that would be able to perceive them! How high the development of spirit that could find pleasure in such subtle things!
>
> In such a domain, who dares ask for theory![64]

## Four. Wagner's Mysticism and Schoenberg's Superstition    95

This passage has something in common with Steiner's conviction that there is a super-physical world that spiritual training and art can reveal. "In every man," Steiner writes in *The Way of Initiation* (1912), "there are latent faculties by means of which he can acquire for himself knowledge of the higher worlds. The mystic, theosophist, or gnostic speaks of a soul-world and a spirit-world, which are, for him, just as real as the world which we see with our physical hands."[65]

Schoenberg's ideas about *Klangfarbenmelodie* should also be related to his friendship with Wassily Kandinsky (1866–1944), along with Kandinsky's interest in theosophy, which came about principally through his discovery of C. W. Leadbeater's concept of thought-forms. In 1905, Leadbeater (1854–1934) and his colleague, Annie Besant (1847–1933), president of the Theosophical Society, published a booklet called *Thought-Forms*, in which they stated:

> The mental body is an object of great beauty, the delicacy and rapid motion of its particles giving it an aspect of living iridescent light, and this beauty becomes an extraordinarily radiant and entrancing loveliness as the intellect becomes more highly evolved and is employed chiefly on pure and sublime topics. Every thought gives rise to a set of correlated vibrations in the matter of this body, accompanied with a marvellous play of colour, like that in the spray of a waterfall as the sunlight strikes it, raised to the nth degree of colour and vivid delicacy. The body under this impulse throws off a vibrating portion of itself, shaped by the nature of the vibrations—as figures are made by sand on a disk vibrating to a musical note—and this gathers from the surrounding atmosphere matter like itself in fineness from the elemental essence of the mental world. We have then a thought-form pure and simple, and it is a living entity of intense activity animated by the one idea that generated it. If made of the finer kinds of matter, it will be of great power and energy, and may be used as a most potent agent when directed by a strong and steady will.[66]

But Leadbeater and Besant weren't the first people to suggest that thought could be visualized in this manner. Swedenborg, in his *Arcana Coelestia*, similarly claimed to be able to see thought, and that "in the other life the thoughts of all may be plainly perceived."[67] Leadbeater, however, was the first to offer specific drawings and to provide a key to color symbolism. Popularly, we all associate color with emotion (we can be green with envy or red with rage, we have the blues, cowards are yellow, and so forth), but Leadbeater went further and provided a table that explained the spiritual meanings of all the colors that appeared in the thought-forms.

Kandinsky was not only interested in the purely aesthetic applications of Leadbetter's abstract forms but also deeply involved with occultism himself as a means to explore the inner world. Like Steiner, he was concerned that

# The Occult Arts of Music

materialism was corroding humanity's spiritual reality. And he was not alone in this quest for the inner world. Contemporary with Kandinsky, Rainer Maria Rilke (1875–1926), in the Seventh of his *Duinese Elegien*, declared that "Nirgends, Geliebte, wird Welt sein, als innen." ("No-where will the world exist but within.") The novelist Hermann Hesse (1877–1962) also discussed "der Weg nach innen" (the way within). Indeed, he reissued his stories *Kling-sors Letzer Sommer, Siddhartha* and *Klein und Wagner* under that title in 1931. The phrase derives from a fragment he came across in the *Blütenstaub* of Novalis (1772–1801): "Nach Innen geht der geheimnisvolle Weg" ("Inward lies the secret way").[68] "The Way Within" is a particularly Germanic quest, as the Expressionist painter Ernst Ludwig Kirchner (1880–1938) explained: "The Latin takes his forms from the object as it exists in nature. The German creates his forms in fantasy, from an inner vision peculiar to himself. The forms of visible nature serve him as symbols only, and he seeks beauty not in appearance but in something beyond."[69]

However, it is more useful to strip the nationalist gloss from this aesthetic and place it in the context of early twentieth-century theosophical thought. Kandinsky, in *Concerning the Spiritual in Art,* aimed to express "only internal truths, renouncing in consequence all consideration of external form."

> This all-important spark of inner life today is at present only a spark. Our minds, which are even now only just awakening after years of materialism, are infected with the despair of unbelief, of lack of purpose and ideal. The nightmare of materialism, which has turned the life of the universe into an evil, useless game, is not yet past; it holds the awakening soul still in its grip. Only a feeble light glimmers like a tiny star in a vast gulf of darkness. This feeble light is but a presentiment, and the soul, when it sees it, trembles in doubt whether the light is not a dream, and the gulf of darkness reality. This doubt, and the still harsh tyranny of the materialistic philosophy, divide our soul sharply from that of the Primitives. Our soul rings cracked when we seek to play upon it, as does a costly vase, long buried in the earth, which is found to have a flaw when it is dug up once more. For this reason, the Primitive phase, through which we are now passing, with its temporary similarity of form, can only be of short duration.[70]

Kandinsky's approach to color was profoundly affected by theosophical ideas:

> The eye is strongly attracted by light, clear colours, and still more strongly attracted by those colours which are warm as well as clear; vermilion has the charm of flame, which has always attracted human beings. Keen lemon-yellow hurts the eye in time as a prolonged and shrill trumpet-note the ear, and the gazer turns away to seek relief in blue or green.
>
> But to a more sensitive soul the effect of colours is deeper and intensely moving. And so we come to the second main result of looking at colours: THEIR PSYCHIC EFFECT. They produce a corresponding spiritual vibration, and it is

only as a step towards this spiritual vibration that the elementary physical impression is of importance.

Whether the psychic effect of colour is a direct one, as these last few lines imply, or whether it is the outcome of association, is perhaps open to question. The soul being one with the body, the former may well experience a psychic shock, caused by association acting on the latter. For example, red may cause a sensation analogous to that caused by flame, because red is the colour of flame. A warm red will prove exciting, another shade of red will cause pain or disgust through association with running blood. In these cases colour awakens a corresponding physical sensation, which undoubtedly works upon the soul.[71]

Aiming to find liberation from the material world, Kandinsky saw in music the ultimate non-materialist art form. He also related color to music: "Generally speaking, colour is a power which directly influences the soul. Colour is the keyboard, the eyes are the hammers, the soul is the piano with many strings. The artist is the hand which plays, touching one key or another, to cause vibrations in the soul."[72]

As we shall see in the next chapter, Scriabin, another theosophist, used synesthesia to create the ultimate spiritual art form.

# Chapter Five
## *Synesthesia*

One of the implications of a music of the spheres is that if everything is related to everything else, and if everything is the result of proportion and numbers, then everything must be in some way a version of everything else. The only difference lies in the *form* rather than the *essence*. It is the *essence* that is "hidden" (which is the meaning of the word "occult"). Just as, according to occultism, the spirit resides in matter, and matter is in some way a kind of illusion, so proportion, according to Pythagoras and Plato, lies behind all phenomena and is their essential truth. In his treatise *Musurgia Universalis* of 1650, the seventeenth-century Jesuit priest Athanasius Kircher (1601–1680) called music "the ape of light," arguing that everything visible could be made audible and vice versa. (In the frontispiece of this work Kircher, like Fludd, commemorates Pythagoras' visit to the forge with its four smiths.) Consequently, occult theorists and some composers have attempted to justify a correlation between sound, light and color. Jean-Philippe Rameau (1683–1764), Scriabin and Rimsky-Korsakov each experienced its psychedelic, synesthetic effects, and the impact of it influenced Scriabin's compositions. The fact that Rameau, Rimsky-Korsakov and Scriabin did not entirely agree on the correlation suggests that the experience of seeing colors when hearing pitches is a rather subjective affair. Having said that, there were some intriguing agreements between Rimsky-Korsakov and Scriabin regarding certain pitches: Both felt that D was yellow. Scriabin saw E as "sky Blue," which Rimsky-Korsakov regarded similarly as "sparkling sapphire," but Scriabin saw red when hearing C, which Rimsky-Korsakov interpreted as white.[1] Cyril Scott appended Madame Blavatsky's table of color correspondences to his *Philosophy of Modernism* (1917) and observed that Scriabin "sets a different table of colour-tones to the one I have quoted, which naturally leads one to inquire, before advancing him as an authority, whether he was a reliable psychic or merely an imaginative artist, a question which I am personally unable to answer." Scott also points out that "astral" colors "interpenetrate each other, i.e., one

*Five. Synesthesia*                    99

tint does not obliterate the other. Nevertheless, the colour of the particular key will always preponderate over the others, so to speak, and act as a kind of background, with the difference, however, that what is in the foreground never blots out a portion of it, as it does with the physical-plane landscape, but leaves it perceptible all the time. This is the only lame and inadequate attempt at description I can offer."[2] Needless to say, Scott was a convinced theosophist.

Early in the science of optics, Sir Isaac Newton (1642–1725) deliberately manipulated the spectrum into a series of seven colors so that they would correspond in Pythagorean fashion to the seven intervals of the octave and the seven planets known at the time that were associated with them. The idea was published in Newton's *Optics* of 1704, and one of Newton's aims was to strengthen the concept of a universe in which everything corresponded. The colors of the rainbow, however, are in fact much more complicated than the clearly differentiated hues of red, orange, yellow, green, blue, indigo and violet. Such a designation has a purely occult justification, but it is one that has become a commonly held assumption to this day.

As Joscelyn Godwin has pointed out, similar ideas were developed by the obscure Jesuit theorist, Père Louis-Bertrand Castel (1699–1757), who believed the correspondences were rather more complex, and he published his conclusions in *Optique des couleurs* in 1740. According to Castel, colors emerge from a range that is topped and tailed by black and white. The first color after black is blue, and is associated with the tone C, then comes red, which is the equivalent of the dominant tone G. "Red is certainly the dominant color of nature.... And yellow, whose nature makes it a degree brighter than red, seems to be the exact correspondence to the tone E."[3] Unlike Newton, Castel equated specific pitches, rather than intervals, with different colors, ultimately arriving at twelve colors to correspond with the twelve pitches of the chromatic scale. In 1725, he even set about the construction of a kind of harpsichord that could make colors and music appear simultaneously. The effect wasn't particularly impressive, relying as it did on small pieces of colored paper that popped up as one depressed the keys, but in so doing he anticipated Scriabin's color experiments in *Prometheus — The Poem of Fire* (1910) by nearly two hundred years. Castel's ideas interested Goethe, who quoted him in his own *Farbenlehre* of 1810, but Goethe did not think synesthetically himself. As he put it, "They [music and color] are like two rivers whose sources arise on the same mountain, but which follow their path under conditions and through regions that are entirely different."[4]

Though the arcane details of sound-color correspondences are certainly interesting to explore, as Godwin admirably does, there is no real benefit in doing so from a scientific point of view, as they are obviously all highly subjective ways of manipulating reality to fit a preconceived occult system; even when they are actually experienced psychologically, the correspondences remain subject to the individual consciousness rather than any universal law. The significant thing, from our point of view, is that the idea of synesthetic correspondence has had important aesthetic consequences, as have other theories that expand the argument beyond color to include visual patterns and shapes. With regard to the latter, Godwin draws our attention to Margaret Watts Hughes, an American who invented the "eidophone" in 1890, which aimed to translate sound vibrations into patterns on stretched rubber.[5] (According to the theory concerning crop-circle formation mentioned previously, crop circles are giant eidophones responding to cosmic vibration.) There was also one General Gustave-Auguste Ferrié (1868–1932), who attempted to translate the visible into the audible by means of a microphone and a telephone diaphragm, by which he aimed to convert the sun's rays into sound and actually hear the sun "singing."[6] The Polish philosopher Joseph-Marie Wronski (1776–1853) likewise believed that sound could be transformed into light: "touch, hearing and sight differ only in the different degrees of speed with which they can distinguish instantaneous duration of time." Similarly, colors "depend only on the different durations of the ethereal vibrations that constitute them."[7] For Wronski, light is merely vibration we can no longer hear.

All these ideas, some of which are scientifically proven whereas others are patently not, are nonetheless important as *ideas,* for where there are ideas, art often follows. A significant milestone in the translation of all these theories into aesthetic (and later cinematic) reality is Charles Baudelaire's poem "Correspondance" from *Les fleurs du mal.*

> La Nature est un temple où de vivants piliers
> Laissent parfois sortir de confuses paroles;
> L'homme y passe à travers des forêts de symboles
> Qui l'observent avec des regards familiers.
>
> Comme de longs échos qui de loin se confondent
> Dans une ténébreuse et profonde unité,
> Vaste comme la nuit et comme la clarté,
> Les parfums, les couleurs et les sons se répondent.
>
> Il est des parfums frais comme des chairs d'enfants,
> Doux comme les hautbois, verts comme les prairies,
> — Et d'autres, corrompus, riches et triomphants,
> Ayant l'expansion des choses infinies,
>
> Comme l'ambre, le musc, le benjoin et l'encens,
> Qui chantent les transports de l'esprit et des sens.

(Nature is a temple where living pillars
Sometimes give voice to confused words;
Man passes there through forests of symbols
Which watch him with understanding eyes.

Like long echoes mingling in the distance
In a profound and tenebrous unity,
Vast like the night and the light of day,
Perfumes, sounds, and colors correspond.

There are perfumes as cool as the flesh of children,
Sweet as oboes, green as meadows
— And others are corrupt, and rich, triumphant,

With power to expand into infinity,
Like amber and incense, musk, benzoin,
That sing the ecstasy of the soul and senses.)

The ideas expressed in this poem are more than "merely" aesthetic. They in fact derive from Swedenborg's mystical convictions highlighted in works such as *Heaven and Hell* and *Celestial Arcana*. Balzac quotes from the latter in *Seraphita*:

> "The kingdom of heaven," says Swedenborg ("Celestial Arcana") "is the kingdom of motives. *Action* is born in heaven, thence into the world, and, by degrees, to the infinitely remote parts of earth. Terrestrial effects being thus linked to celestial causes, all things are *correspondent and significant*. Man is the means of union between the Natural and the Spiritual."[8]

A presentation of this idea from within popular culture can be found in the 1970s British science fiction television series *Space: 1999*, in which a space station based on the moon finds itself traveling through the universe after a nuclear explosion has put the moon out of Earth's orbit. In the episode "Black Sun" (dir. Lee H. Katzin, 1975), the moon is pulled through a black hole. During the ordeal, Commander Koenig (Martin Landau) and Professor Bergman (Barry Morse) encounter a spiritual entity, which is perhaps God. At one stage, Koenig says, "Everything is everything else. And the whole universe is living thought.... Every star is just a cell in the brain of the universe." These ideas derive, via Baudelaire, from Swedenborg's mystical vision.

Baudelaire was the first person in France fully to comprehend and, more importantly, emotionally identify with the works of Richard Wagner. Immediately after experiencing Wagner's *Tannhäuser* for the first time in 1861, he wrote his famous pamphlet *Richard Wagner in Paris*, in which he compared Wagner's music to wide spaces and white light. Of course, the aim of *Gesamtkunstwerk* is to unify the arts into a cohesive whole, an aesthetic ideal of which the cinema is the ultimate technological fulfillment, but Baudelaire's response to Wagner in terms of the correlation between light, color and music was truly pioneering. There are, indeed, many effects in Wagner that aim to equate light and sound, such as the descent into Nibelheim and the subsequent return back to Valhalla in *Das Rheingold,* which Wagner achieves by means of contrasting pitch and timbre. Then there is the evocation of a rainbow at the end of that work, the shape of which is imitated by the general arch of the leitmotif's pitch contour, but the glitter and effulgence of which is suggested by the six harps, which took up so many staves that the full score is required to present them as an appendix. There is also the sunrise in the prelude to *Götterdämmerung,* which equates increased rhythmic agitation and *crescendo* with an increase in the intensity of light, as well as the violin writing in *Siegfried* that reaches an excessively high pitch when the hero penetrates the Magic Fire to discover Brünnhilde, thus creating a musical symbol for light, space and altitude.

One of the effects in *Tannhäuser* to which Baudelaire may well have been particularly responsive is the effect of distance created by Wagner in the Venusberg scene, where he holds a note in the horns that blurs the harmony of the choir of Sirens. There is also the sudden change from the Venusberg to the fresh clear light of a mountain pasture, replete with shepherd and sheep, which is again created by music as much as by scenographic means. Perhaps the most famously synesthetic statement in Wagner are Tristan's words "Nun hör' ich das Licht?" ("Do I hear the light?"), which refer to Tristan's delirious confusion as Isolde returns to him in the third Act. Here, Tristan confuses the light from the torch, which had signaled their first amorous encounter in Act II, with the sound of the shepherd's piping, signifying Isolde's return at the end of the drama. We might even see such a line as a premonition not only of later synesthetic experiments but also of the invention of the CD, a technology that indeed uses laser light to create sound. The theosophical occultist Ella Adelia Fletcher's *The Law of the Rhythmic Breath* (1908), which the British composer Cyril Scott included in his *Philosophy of Modernism,* puts Tristan's confusion into terms of a somewhat Frankenstein-like medical experiment:

> In Berlin an operation was performed upon a man's brain which required the severing of both the auditory and the visual nerves. When the nerves were reunited they were mismated, the upper sections of the optic nerves being joined to the under sections of the auditory nerves, and *vice versa.* The result of this distressing blunder is that the man *sees* sounds and *hears* colours. Looking at a red object he heard a deep bass tone, and when blue was shown, the *sound* was like the tinkle of electric bells; but the ringing of an electric call-bell produced a sensation of blue light, and listening to Beethoven's *Pastoral Symphony* caused a vision of green meadows and waving corn.[9]

## Five. Synesthesia                                                103

Fletcher also mentions the case studied by Professor Cesare Lombroso (1835–1909) of a patient who could read with the tip of her ear. "As a test, the rays of the sun were focused upon the ear through a lens, and they dazzled her as if turned upon normal eyes, causing a sensation of being blinded by unbearable light. Still more puzzling to Prof. Lombroso was the fact that her sense of taste was transferred to her knees, and that of smell to her toes."[10]

Wagner never referred to synesthesia in a theoretical sense. His impact on future synesthetes was purely musico-dramatic, but his predecessor, E. T. A. Hoffmann, did discuss synesthesia, even though he did not use that particular designation for the effect. In *Kreisleriana* (1814), the work that so fascinated Robert Schumann that he named one of his most important piano collections after it, Hoffmann has this to say: "It is no empty metaphor, no allegory, when the musician says that colour, fragrance, light appear to him as sounds, and that in their intermingling he perceives an extraordinary concert."[11] Later, in the section titled "Extremely Random Thoughts," Hoffmann adds,

> Not only in dreams, but also in that state of delirium which precedes sleep, especially when I have been listening to music, I discover a congruity of colours, sounds, and fragrances. It seems as though they are all produced by beams of light in the same mysterious manner, and have then to be combined into an extraordinary concert. The fragrance of deep-red carnations exercises a strangely magical power over me; unawares I sink into a dream-like state in which I hear, as though from far away, the dark, alternately swelling and subsiding tones of the bassett-horn.[12]

These words uncannily prefigure the synesthetic experiments of Scriabin in the first years of the twentieth century, with the significant difference that Scriabin was also thinking theosophically (a subject I will deal with later). For the present, it is necessary to see Scriabin's interest in synesthesia as part of his quest for unity, for the ultimate *Gesamtkunstwerk*, which would achieve an integration that would exceed even what Wagner had achieved in Bayreuth. Scriabin aimed for the ultimate psychedelic, holistic experience, which would unite all the senses and all humanity.

Scriabin's aim of pan-sensory integration can be compared to the loss of ego experienced by someone who takes LSD or Ecstasy. A nightclub environment, with its light, music and drug-induced euphoria, creates very much the psychological condition that Scriabin had in mind, as does the cinema, at least potentially, even though one does not expect to find drug use in a cinematic environment. Scriabin's dreams of including perfume in the mix were prefigured by J. K. Huysmans in his novel *À Rebours* (1884), in which the decadent hero, Des Esseintes, loved "to soothe his spirit with harmonies in perfumery."[13]

Scriabin's never-completed *Mysterium,* a religio-dramatic "event," was also to have been instrumental in helping mankind evolve to a higher spiritual level. Scriabin's early death from septicemia in 1915 prevented him from realizing his vision and probably simultaneously saved him from complete insanity. However, irrational and perhaps unrealizable though the project may have been, the aesthetic, sensory and social unity Scriabin sought nonetheless has its roots in nineteenth-century Romantic thought, which, as we have seen, can be traced back via Hoffmann to earlier occult theorists. Many of the ideas take Wagner's theories to their ultimate conclusion. For example, Scriabin wanted to build his own theatrical space, as Wagner had done, but this was not to be a conventional theatre with footlights. There was to be space for the audience to interact and co-create the work while it was being performed. The audience would not be spectators, as they are at the Bayreuth Festspielhaus, but active participants in a mystical-socialistic music drama. Scriabin even went so far as to purchase some land in India in 1914 on which to build this temple to Scriabinism.[14] Surviving sketches for this project show a spherical structure that has certain things in common with Rudolf Steiner's contemporaneous first Goetheanum building. That structure had a comparable mystical purpose and its successor is still the venue for performances of Steiner's interminable anthroposophical mystery plays about the evolution of the soul. The original Goetheanum burned down on New Year's Eve 1922/1923. Steiner was appalled but immediately began to build a second structure out of concrete rather than wood. Scriabin, however, had the destruction of his temple in mind from the very beginning. He thought of opening the roof to let in light and sounds from the natural world during the "action" of his *Mysterium,* and again echoed Wagner's fantasies by suggesting that the performing space should be demolished as the performance progressed. Wagner suggested a similar thing when planning his *Ring* cycle, proposing that after the performance the "rough theatre" should be pulled down and the score burned.[15]

(The general feeling of crazy psychedelia here might well be said to have anticipated the "Happenings" of the 1960s—the kind of thing, indeed, that the film director David Miller evocatively portrayed in the opening title sequence of the James Bond–like spy thriller *Hammerhead* [1968]. This also begins somewhat synesthetically, with David Whitaker's score responding to the three different colored lights that open the sequence, which was filmed in London's Roundhouse, a popular venue for such events at the time. A performance artist by the name of Pietro Vendriani [played by Douglas Wilmer] then shoots a shop mannequin, which turns into Judy Geeson. The no-doubt stoned audience blows bubbles, semi-naked female musicians play various instruments, Vendriani scatters confetti, and Geeson squashes a tomato onto

## Five. Synesthesia

the nose of another mannequin, inspiring a general food fight from the audience. The other mannequins are then hacked and decapitated by the performers, and a naked girl is covered with tomato ketchup from a gigantic bottle before being made into a human hot dog.)

Steiner's Goetheanum also incorporated color in a comparable way to that envisioned by Scriabin. Steiner wrote in 1914:

> We have reached a time in which, if man's living contact with the world is not to atrophy completely, it is essential that we begin to dive down into the spiritual waves of the natural forces, that is the spiritual forces lying behind nature. We must once more gain the ability not merely to look at colours and apply them here and there as external surfaces but rather to live with them, to experience the inner force of colours.... We can only achieve it if with our soul we submerge ourselves in the manner in which red, or blue for instance, flows and streams; we can only achieve it if the flowing and streaming of colour becomes directly alive for us.[16]

Similarly, Scriabin explained his last completed work, *Prometheus — The Poem of Fire*, to his friend Leonid Sabaneev as follows:

> What plans I have, what plans! You know, I have lights in *Prometheus.* [He whispered the words "lights."] I will play it for you. Lights. It's a poem of fire. Here the hall has changing colors. Now they glow; now they turn into tongues of flame. Listen how all this music is really fire.[17]

To achieve this effect, Scriabin composed a line at the top of his musical score for an instrument that did not exist. Called the *tastiera per luce* — or "keyboard of light" — it denoted the changing harmonies (for Scriabin equated colors with chords rather than individual notes). The electrical engineer Alexander Mozer eventually constructed a color organ for performances of *Prometheus,* and there were other experiments taking place around the same time. The Rimington Color Organ, for example, invented by A. Wallace Rimington, actually appeared some years before in 1895. In more recent times, the technology of rock and roll light-shows has been applied to concert performances of Scriabin. In 2010 Anna Gawboy organized a performance of *Prometheus* in collaboration with Toshiyuki Shimada, the conductor of the Yale Symphony Orchestra, and Justin Townsend, an award-winning lighting designer, but by that time, all these theatrical attempts at synesthetic integration had already reached their fullest potential in the cinema, which is entirely an amalgam of light and sound, with no "live" element to interfere with the illusion.

Just as Wagner concealed his distracting orchestra beneath the stage of the Festspielhaus, so cinema now disguises the means of musical production while simultaneously creating the *entire* spectacle by means of light. The cinema has also proved to be the most successful medium for realizing those

## The Occult Arts of Music

attempts by M.W. Hughes, General Ferrié and Wronski to visualize sound. With regard to this idea, one need look no further than the experiments of the Warner Brothers' animator Chuck Jones, the creator of Bugs Bunny and the Road Runner. Roy Prendergast, in his pioneering book about film music, has drawn attention to Jones' attempts to find visual equivalents to particular timbres.[18] Animated film often depends for its effect upon musical equivalents to shapes and movement, as does its three-dimensional ancestor, ballet, in which bodily movement and music achieve a far greater sense of integration than in opera, where the music is much more concerned with matching the word and scenic effect. For this reason, many cartoons require much less dialogue, being primarily about physical movement (one thinks of the dialogueless Road Runner cartoons and the mostly mute Tom and Jerry cartoons).

A pinnacle of animated cinematic success is Disney's *Fantasia*, which similarly contains virtually no dialogue. It also has many synesthetic elements, particularly in the opening of the first section based on Bach's Toccata and Fugue in D minor. Here we see the instruments of the orchestra tuning up, and different colored lights are projected onto the instruments in question. Against a blue screen in the background, we watch the orchestra assemble. As conductor Leopold Stokowski conducts the opening bars, he is illuminated by a disc of pink light during the crescendo. Wind instruments are lit with green and blue, and these are answered by the strings in red and yellow. The overall effect is more powerful than a projection of lights in a concert hall because of the dramatic way in which Disney is able to arrange and present the instruments, using shadows, superimposition and different camera angles in conjunction with the film that, if applied to a performance of *Prometheus*, would fulfill many of Scriabin's dreams. The use of abstract shapes and movements in the subsequent fugue might also be regarded as the realization of Kircher's belief that music is the ape of light (though, in the case of *Fantasia*, it is really the other way around). What Disney achieves here is an abstract ballet, where shapes and colors take the place of the human body in their choreography of the music. There is, of course, nothing occult going on here, though it is significant, I think, that "magical" pieces are often chosen, such as *The Sorcerer's Apprentice* of Dukas and Mussorgsky's *Night on the Bare Mountain,* and this choice does relate to the overall occult context of synesthesia that we have been exploring. The magical aspect indeed adds a half-remembered resonance that certainly contributes to the overall effect of the whole.

Another aspect of cinema that is distinctly synesthetic are the main title sequences of fantasy films that emerged in the wake of the James Bond movies in the 1960s. Maurice Binder's title sequences for Bond were cut to complement the musical form of John Barry's title songs, and, anticipating the pop

# Five. Synesthesia

107

video of later years, they also grew out of the emerging television advertising industry of the time. 1960s psychedelia and drug imagery were even more significant ingredients in the title sequences of some fantasy films. An early example is the imaginatively abstract end title sequence of Roger Corman's *The Pit and the Pendulum* (1961). Les Baxter's accompanying score for this is hardly in Scriabin's league, but the effect of the swirling, multicolored oil paints combined with music does achieve a synesthetic quality that Scriabin might have found intriguing, uncoordinated though the colors are. The extended psychedelic "trip" sequence in Kubrick's *2001: A Space Odyssey,* which introduces "Neptune and Beyond," might have interested him even more, coupled as it is with the disturbingly experimental music of György Ligeti. Taken as a whole — colors, perspectives and variously hued blinking eyes — Kubrick's famous sequence realizes much that Aldous Huxley had to say about the mind's awareness of color while under the influence of mescalin in *The Doors of Perception* (1954):

> Mescalin raises all colours to a higher power and makes the percipient aware of innumerable fine shades of difference, to which, at ordinary times, he is completely blind.... Like mescalin takers, many mystics perceive supernaturally brilliant colours, not only with the inward eye, but even in the objective world around them.[19]

In the same year that Kubrick was taking psychedelia to outer space, Hammer Films made its own reference to the previous year's summer of love with the similarly "trippy" abstractions that introduce *Dracula Has Risen from the Grave.* The palette was confined to two rather Warhole-esque hues of scarlet and purple, which might also have referenced the Whore of Babylon, "arrayed in purple and scarlet," from the Book of Revelations. The imagery itself suggests blood vessels and various internal organs, which drift toward the spectator and dissolve into one another. When combined with James Bernard's astonishingly resonant score, it is perhaps more psychedelic (and certainly more disturbing) than the multicolored visualization of The Beatles' "Lucy in the Sky with Diamonds" in George Dunning's *Yellow Submarine,* which was released in the same synesthetic year.

# Chapter Six
## *Theosophy*

Scriabin's biographer, Faubion Bowers, claimed that "theosophy stimulated Scriabin's overall purpose — that of 'making the impossible possible.'"[1] Another way of looking at *Prometheus — The Poem of Fire,* however, is that it employs cosmic imagery to discuss imaginative freedom. Theosophically speaking, the virtuoso pianoforte part represents the microcosm (humanity), and the orchestra represents the macrocosm (the universe). But one might also say that the work is an apotheosis of the Romantic piano concerto, a form that became popular in the nineteenth century due to the ever-increasing importance of the individual and his conflict with society, convention and, most of all, God. Prometheus defied God in favor of mankind, and in Scriabin's *Poem of Fire* man actually becomes God through sexual and intellectual self-discovery.

Scriabin had explored the darker side of this quest in works such as "Satanic Poem" (actually more of an ironic scherzo than anything more sinister) and the Ninth ("Black Mass") Piano Sonata, a genuinely unnerving piece. When performing it, Scriabin confessed to "practicing sorcery."[2] Podgayetsky, who gave the piece its satanic subtitle, along with the theosophist Alexander Brianchaninov, wanted to canonize Scriabin as a prophet of a new age, an honor that was indeed posthumously awarded him by the Soviet authorities, who saw in Scriabin a prophet not only of socialism but also, because of his cosmic and earth-shattering ideas, of space flight and even the atom bomb. Scriabin made a more subtle distinction. With regard to the 1905 Revolution, he pointed out that "the *political* revolution in Russia in its present phase and the upheaval I want are different.... I don't want to *bring about anything* except the endless soaring of creative activity which my art will bring."[3] His other theosophical piano pieces include "Dark Flames" (the black fire of ignorance) and "Towards the Flame" (the flame here being the center of the World Soul).

Scriabin very much wanted to meet Annie Besant, the successor to

Madame Blavatsky as president of the Theosophical Society. When he was in London he hoped for an opportunity, but Besant was by then at the society's new headquarters in India. Coincidentally, this was the country in which Scriabin hoped eventually to perform his *Mysterium*. He even spent hours working outside in the sunshine to prepare himself for the rigors of the climate there, and he also studied Sanskrit in preparation for the new language he intended to create for the performance.

For Scriabin, the point of music was the expression of an *idea*. This is the thread that connects all the minds in this book: Music as Idea. Indeed, Scriabin said he wished he had been born as an idea, with the power to float through the universe[4]: "People who just write music are like performers who just play an instrument. They become valuable only when they connect with a general idea. The purpose of music is revelation."[5] Scriabin even regarded the explanatory verses for *The Poem of Ecstasy* as just as important as the music — kind of Bible for the new religion of individual creative ecstasy:

The seal of the Theosophical Society.

> Spirit playing
> Spirit fluttering
> By its enduring longing
> Creating Ecstasy
> Gives itself up to Love's thrill
> Mid the flowers of its creations
> It lives in freedom.[6]

Not everyone was convinced. As Faubion Bowers points out, "The sting of serpents and the bite of hyenas ... was ridiculed in some quarters. 'How does he know what *that* feels like?' Muscovites chided."[7] In 1910, the *Boston Daily*

*Advertiser* famously compared the ecstasy of Scriabin's Fourth Symphony, *The Poem of Ecstasy,* to "the kind of ecstasy that is sold in Russia at two roubles a bottle," but it was precisely the intoxication of his audience that Scriabin wished to achieve. Indeed, when he was a young man, Scriabin loved drinking himself stupid, and he often looked intoxicated even when he wasn't. He wanted his music to sound drunk too—by which he meant to attain spiritual heights denied to sober reality. His expression was to "absent" himself from reality.

Certain intervals and musical patterns had a specific meaning for Scriabin. The plunging descent of a minor ninth, for example, signified the "descent of spirit into matter." Whole tone oscillation equated to "the breathing in and out of Brahma, the Creator of the world," whereas a falling semitone "embodied human sorrow."[8] Bells also had deeply mystical connotations for Scriabin. Bowers observes that there is a Russian phrase for being misinformed: "'hearing the bell, he didn't know where he was,' meaning that bells can transport a person until he loses his bearing or takes leave of his senses."[9] *Prometheus* ends with a clamor of tubular bells. Scriabin's dream of hanging bells from clouds over the Himalayas to summon spectators to his *Mysterium* was no madder, perhaps, than Blavatsky's claim to be in telepathic contact with two Tibetan monks, one of whom was called Master Koot Hoomi. (Cyril Scott also believed himself to have been in contact with him.) This was a privileged contact for Blavatsky, as it was Koot Hoomi who had informed her of the Secret Doctrine.

In 1903, Scriabin abandoned his wife for Tatyana Schloezer, the sister of a Russian music critic. The previous year, Tatyana had encouraged Scriabin's interest in Nietzsche's philosophy and she was also largely responsible for the more elaborate French markings in Scriabin's scores, such as "avec une douceur de plus en plus caressante et empoissonnée" ("with a softness more and more poisonous in its sweetness") in the Ninth Sonata, or simply "tres parfumé" in *The Poem of Ecstasy.* Tatyana also fueled the fires of Scriabin's interest in theosophy, which he first encountered in Brussels in 1905. She no doubt shared his private musings, made shamelessly public in the poetic text he wrote to accompany *The Poem of Ecstasy*:

> O waiting world,
> Weary world!
> You art thirsting to be created
> You seek a creator.
> Your tenderly sweet sigh,
> > Calling
> Has been wafted to me.

## Six. Theosophy

I will come.
Already I dwell in you
O world of mine!
...
I will come
To dazzle you
With the marvel
Of enchantment repeated;
I will bring you
The magical thrill
Of scorching love
And unimagined caresses.
Surrender to me in all faith!
I will drown you in oceans of bliss
And beloved kisses
And great heaving waves[10]

When Scriabin encountered the ideas of Madame Blavatsky and Rudolf Steiner, he found a "scientific" justification for his mystical visions. The Third Symphony, subtitled "The Divine Poem," was his first attempt to combine theosophy with symphonic music. The accompanying explanatory text elucidates how the ego is divided into "Man-God" and "Slave-Man," which struggle with each other (the first movement is called "Luttes" or "Struggles"), and how, through sensual play ("Voluptés"), the two aspects achieve unity and divine freedom. (The third movement is called "Jeu Divin"—"Divine Play.") In other words, man becomes God.

Reading Blavatsky also modified Scriabin's color-music associations. He followed her correlations: red for anger, yellow for intellect, grey-green for deceit, black for hatred.[11] Blavatsky herself devoted several pages to color theory in the third volume of *The Secret Doctrine,* which was compiled from notes assembled by Annie Besant, and many of her observations were synesthetic. She believed, for example, that "the best psychics can perceive colours produced by the vibrations of musical instruments."

> As a string vibrates and gives forth an audible note, so the nerves of the human body vibrate and think in correspondence with the various emotions under the general impulse of the circulating vitality of Prana (cosmic energy), thus producing undulations in the psychic aura of the person, which results in chromatic effects.[12]

These ideas about the psychic significance of color, whatever that really means in practice (if it means anything at all), also influenced the modernist artist Piet Mondrian (1872–1944), whose later geometric style emerged out of an earlier, more overtly theosophical phase. His triptych *Evolution* (1910–1911), for example, is a visualization of Blavatsky's theory of spiritual evolution. The color scheme does indeed appear to follow Blavatsky's ideas regarding the seven hierarchies of spiritual evolution. Red is at the bottom of the scale, and somewhat vulva-like flowers of that color flank the neck of the first figure in Mondrian's triptych. (Red is not only the color of anger but also of "Kâma, animal desire."[13]) "Spiritual" stars replace the flowers in the right-hand panel and these are orange, yellow and blue, which are Blavatsky's colors of spiritual ascent. Indigo and violet are higher still, and violet is the color of the figure's head in this panel. The central panel shows the eyes of the figure fully open, surrounded by a corona of "pure" white light (which, ironically, is anything but pure, as Newton famously demonstrated when splitting white light into its spectrum). What is significant here is that Mondrian's interest in theosophy led the way to abstraction. This later style was not the result of reason and logic, as many critics would like to believe, but rather the consequence of attempting to express Blavatsky's occult agenda. In this respect, Mondrian was fully in accord with the famous statement by Constantin Brancusi (1876–1957): "What is real is not the external form, but the essence of things. It is impossible for anyone to express anything essentially real by imitating its exterior surface."

Scriabin's blend of theosophy with music was even more explicit, and his desire to unite music with color along theosophical lines led him to commission the *tastiera per luce* from Alexander Mozer. Scriabin used it on occasion in 1910, when the dancer Alisa Koonen improvised "symbolic gestures" for Scriabin's private piano performance of *Prometheus* in his Moscow apartment, filling the room with changing colored lights.[14]

Blavatsky also assigned colors to vowel sounds. Indeed, page 205 of *The Secret Doctrine* is headed with the *Tristan*-esque phrase "Seeing sound, hearing colours." The page itself contains an analysis of the spurious "Stanzas of Dyzan," on which the whole book is based. The section under examination is this: "Sound is the characteristic of Akâsa (Ether): it generates air, the property of which is Touch; which (by friction) becomes productive of Colour and Light." Blavatsky admits that "perhaps the above will be regarded as archaic nonsense" but is determined to argue that it isn't. More instructive from our point of view, however, is that her correspondence between vowels and color was to be incorporated into Scriabin's *Prometheus*. This relationship had already been of interest to the poet Arthur Rimbaud (1854–1891), who played with the idea in his poem "Les Voyelles" (1872):

A noir, E blanc, I rouge, U vert, O bleu: voyelles,
Je dirai quelque jour vos naissances latentes:

## Six. Theosophy

A, noir corset velu des mouches éclatantes
Qui bombinent autour des puanteurs cruelles,

Golfes d'ombre; E, candeurs des vapeurs et des tentes,
Lances des glaciers fiers, rois blancs, frissons d'ombelles;
I, pourpres, sang craché, rire des lèvres belles
Dans la colère ou les ivresses pénitentes;

U, cycles, vibrements divins des mers virides,
Paix des pâtis semés d'animaux, paix des rides
Que l'alchimie imprime aux grands fronts studieux;

O, suprême Clairon plein des strideurs étranges,
Silences traversés des Mondes et des Anges;
— O l'Oméga, rayon violet de Ses Yeux!

(A black, E white, I red, U green, O blue: vowels,
I shall tell, one day, of your mysterious origins:
A, black velvety jacket of brilliant flies
which buzz around cruel smells,

Gulfs of shadow; E, whiteness of vapours and of tents,
lances of proud glaciers, white kings, shivers of cow-parsley;
I, purples, spat blood, smile of beautiful lips
in anger or in the raptures of penitence;

U, waves, divine shudderings of viridian seas,
the peace of pastures dotted with animals, the peace of the furrows
which alchemy prints on broad studious foreheads;

O, sublime Trumpet full of strange piercing sounds,
silences crossed by Worlds and by Angels:
— O the Omega! the violet ray of His Eyes!)

Vowels and color are indeed united at the end of *Prometheus*. The spirit of reborn humanity sings the vowels as it emerges into the universe, through which it floats rather in the manner of the cosmic fetus at the end of Kubrick's *2001: A Space Odyssey*. Ultimately, Scriabin wanted his music to destroy matter — in other words, destroy the universe completely and release materially confined humanity as pure spirit. In this way, he was hastening the evolutionary process Blavatsky outlined in her *Secret Doctrine*, and it seems he believed his music had the power to achieve this result. "Pure" music was almost irrelevant to him. "I cannot understand how to write *just* music now," he confessed. "How boring! Music, surely, takes on idea and significance when it is linked to a single plan within a whole view of the world."[15] His never-completed *Mysterium* was meant to achieve this process by breeding a new race of men by musical means. Bowers describes the process as follows:

On the seventh day, after the assault of the sense of all the arts battering at man's psyche, and with the music incarnating ectoplasmic visions, all men and all nature would combine to bring the world to its closest possible point of being on "the plane of unity." Mass joy would be like the ocean endlessly shifting and unchanging. Soul and matter would be released from their corporeal bondage one to the other. Male and female polarization would vanish. The divine androgyny of two sexes in one (as Plato envisaged them) would first return and then become a nullity. Everything — man and his world — would plummet into the "ecstatic abyss of sunshine."[16]

In *Prometheus,* the closest Scriabin ever got to realizing the visions he wanted to make manifest in the *Mysterium,* the opening six-note "mystic" chord symbolizes original chaos — a Scriabin-esque version of what Haydn had expressed in a comparably revolutionary manner (for the eighteenth century) in his oratorio *The Creation.* The first theme of *Prometheus* represents the "Creative Principle." Then, four chords made up from fourths in the trumpets signify the fire-giving moment symbolized by the Prometheus myth. A trumpet subsequently announces the theme of Will, followed by "the Dawn of Human Consciousness." The microcosmic piano now takes over the Will theme originally played by the trumpets, and the piano part grows increasingly ecstatic in a "Dance of Self-Discovery." Spirit descends into matter with a plunging minor ninth, and, finally, the chorus enters with its vowel sounds. The whole piece ends in utter affirmation, with a gigantic orchestra of triple woodwinds, eight horns, five trumpets, bells, piano, organ and choir. Bowers colorfully describes the effect as "galactic orgasms of ecstasy."[17]

Prometheus had also inspired earlier Romantic artists. The atheistical Percy Shelley found in the myth of Prometheus a perfect symbol of a political dissident who suffers the oppression of tyranny, for Prometheus was punished for his crime of freedom by being chained to Mount Caucasus, where a vulture daily pecked out his liver. Shelley described the horror of the Titan's predicament in *Prometheus Unbound*:

> The crawling glaciers pierce me with the spears
> Of their moon-freezing crystals, the bright chains
> Eat with their burning cold into my bones.
> Heaven's winged hound, polluting from thy lips
> His beak in poison not his own, tears up
> My heart.[18]

Such highly charged imagery is not so far from the distinctly sadomasochistic vocabulary of Scriabin's own ecstatic poetical style:

> That which frightened
> Is now a pleasure.

And the bight of panther or hyena
Is a new caress.
   Another
   And a serpents sting
Is but a burning kiss.
And the universe resounds
   With a joyful cry
   I am![19]

Mary Shelley subtitled her *Frankenstein* novel "The Modern Prometheus," thus comparing her scientist with the infamous Titan, and it was perhaps due to this Promethean connection that the award-winning British Independent Radio Drama adaptation of the novel in 1989, starring Crawford Logan in the title role, was underscored with Scriabin's piano music, performed by Leo Debono. The piano music itself is not specifically concerned with Prometheus, but the Promethean spirit of Scriabin's oeuvre is certainly appropriate here. The usage of Scriabin's music in film drama is very rare, which is something of a missed opportunity, especially in science fiction subject matter, though he does have an asteroid named after him.[20]

More to the point, perhaps, is the fact that both Scriabin and Percy Shelley equated Prometheus with Satan. In his *Defence of Poetry* (1819), Shelley pointed out that Milton's Satan was really the hero of *Paradise Lost:*

> Nothing can exceed the energy and magnificence of the character of Satan as expressed in "Paradise Lost." It is a mistake to suppose that he could ever have been intended for the popular personification of evil.... Milton's Devil as a moral being is as far superior to his God, as one who perseveres in some purpose which he has conceived to be excellent in spite of adversity and torture, is to one who in the cold security of undoubted triumph inflicts the most horrible revenge upon his enemy, not from any mistaken notion of inducing him to repent of a perseverance in enmity, but with the alleged design of exasperating him to deserve new torments.[21]

Satan is the ultimate embodiment of rebellion against tyranny, but for Scriabin the parallel was a spiritual one. Satan also appealed to the egocentric in Scriabin. Among his many effusions, Scriabin enthused, "I am God! I am freedom, I am a dream, I am weariness, I am unceasing burning desire, I am bliss, I am insane passion. I wish I could possess the world as I possess a woman."[22] Increasingly Messianic, he even tried to imitate Christ by walking on the waters of Lake Geneva with his fisherman friends, and as Alexander Pasternak recalled, he often attempted to fly by flapping his arms in the air.[23]

Scriabin also equated Prometheus with Lucifer. Fire, like knowledge, is an ambivalent force that can be used for good or evil, which is why Steiner (and Blavatsky) did not relegate Lucifer to an entirely demonic status. Indeed, having established her religion and written its Bible, Madame Blavatsky subsequently occupied herself with two rather elaborate parish magazines, one of which was called *Lucifer*. When Dennis Wheatley later provided an introduction to extracts from this publication, he rather predictably failed to understand the symbolism of the title, merely commenting instead that the essays "are replies to questions sent to her as the editor of a magazine which, for some strange reason, she entitled *Lucifer*."[24] Well, Lucifer still shines as the Morning Star — an appropriate planet given Scriabin's penchant for sexual imagery, as it is actually Venus.

Although Scriabin sometimes wished his audiences to respond to his compositions as pure music, he mostly wanted them to understand the meaning behind the music. He even went to the trouble of commissioning his friend, the Belgian symbolist Jean Delville (1867–1953), to provide a frontispiece for *Prometheus*. Delville's design depicts the face of the Titan staring out at the viewer with the kind of androgynous intensity found in the faces of the gods and angels painted by Gustave Moreau. The flame of wisdom burns from his forehead, and the lyre of music surrounds him. At the base of this image are inscribed the interlocking black and white triangles that form the Seal of Solomon. This is the symbol of Lucifer. The sun flares overhead and all is surrounded by spiraling comets and whorls of flame. Delville, who not only painted Wagnerian images but was also an ardent theosophist, wished to revitalize the world by means of the esoteric traditions of the past. His paintings form a visual parallel with Scriabin's music. In *Satan's Treasures* (1894), Satan appears as a dancer leaping over swooning bodies floating on a languid river. In *The Angel of Splendor* (1894), an ecstatic spirit flies with blue wings, a dazzling light radiating from its effulgent crown. Delville even painted his own *Prometheus* in 1907: a striking nude carrying a five-pointed star in upraised hands while striding through an orgasmic cosmos.

The gigantic chord of F-sharp major that brings *Prometheus — The Poem of Fire* to a close was more than just a chord for Scriabin. First of all, it represented to him blazing violet light, and, according to his synesthetic scheme, the key of F-sharp major conveys the conceptual significance of Creativity. Liberated from the tyranny of matter, the spirit of the artist attains the peak of creativity, the summit of ecstasy. When World War I began, Scriabin was initially stunned by the news but then welcomed it as a "world-shaking" metaphysical event, reflecting the battles he thought were already taking place in the astral plane. He (correctly) predicted that after the war enormous socialist changes would take place in society, though his attitude to the Germans was very much of his time: "You can see the bestiality of the Germans when you listen to Richard Strauss' music," he claimed.[25] When he died on April 13,

1915, from blood poisoning, his last words were "But this is a catastrophe! Who's there?" Perhaps the real tragedy was that there was no one there after all.

Scriabin's music was popular among the British intelligentsia during his lifetime. He performed the piano concerto and *Prometheus* under Sir Henry Wood. The general public was not always so supportive, however. Osbert Sitwell recalled in his autobiography how Scriabin "received with equinimity the boos that greeted his work at the end."[26] Earlier, in February 1913, *Prometheus* had been given a "tumultuous and, indeed, rowdy reception."[27] Scriabin himself was self-contradictorily concerned that it had been the mysticism rather than the music that had appealed to his British intellectual supporters,[28] and this might well have been the case given the popularity of theosophy in England at that time. Mysticism was all the rage in some quarters, and theosophy in particular intrigued many notable names in British society (such as, for example, the wives of Bernard Shaw and Sir Edwin Lutyens), while the Order of the Golden Dawn, based in London at the time, included among its members the poet W. B. Yeats, the writer Algernon Blackwood, Constance Wilde (the wife of Oscar), Arthur Machen and, of course, the infamous Aleister Crowley. (In 1995, the film director Ken Russell even put forward the intriguing possibility that Scriabin encountered Crowley in Moscow in Russell's only radio play, *The Death of Alexander Scriabin*, starring Oliver Reed as Crowley, which was broadcast on BBC Radio 4 on June 18. The play has Scriabin playing his Ninth Sonata to accompany Crowley's Black Mass in St. Basil's Cathedral.)

Among the mystically inclined musical figures in England was Gustav Holst. Though never a member of the Order of the Golden Dawn, Holst had also been interested in theosophy, a subject to which he returned when he came across a book on astrology by the theosophist Alan Leo. This, in turn, inspired his most famous work, *The Planets*. The first movement of this suite of seven pieces is a musical evocation of "Mars, the Bringer of War," which appears from our own perspective to have been a terrifying premonition of the unstoppable devastation of the First World War. This, however, was not Holst's intention, as we shall see. Holst was, in fact, far more interested in astrology than astronomy, and despite *The Planets'* originally more abstract title of "Seven Pieces for Large Orchestra," suggesting that the planetary associations are detachable, Holst actually had the planets' astrological significance in mind all along. His aim was to create, in effect, a musical parallel to the idea so beautifully put forward in the "Anatomical Man" of the *Très Riches Heures de Duc de Berry*, which graphically equates the signs of the zodiac with parts of the body. Holst's suite similarly suggests the influence of the seven planets upon human psychology and spiritual development.

Alan Leo's pioneering works on this subject, *How to Judge a Nativity* and *The Art of Synthesis*, were the mystical foundation of Holst's suite. As Raymond Head has observed, Leo even invited Holst to open a occult lodge in Brixton.[29] Head conclusively traces the connections between Leo and *The Planets,* which even affects the ordering of the individual pieces in the suite. He points out, for example, that if the planets had been arranged according to their distance from Earth, the first planet in Holst's suite should have been the Moon, followed by Venus and only then Mars, but Holst, following Leo's plan, put Mars first, which Leo calls "the energiser," and this rampant, self-devouring energy is certainly what Holst's music represents in its most violent manifestation as "the Bringer of War" (Holst's own subtitle, of course).

There is also a link here with Holst's parallel interest in Hindu mythology, an interest that was so consuming he even taught himself to read Sanskrit. The Hindu trinity of Brahma, Vishnu and Siva embodies the acts of creation, preservation and destruction. Siva is, like Mars, the "destroyer" but only in the sense that out of destruction new life arises. Destruction is a necessary (though terrifying) force, heralding creation. Only when the energy of Mars is spent can the harmonizing qualities of Venus take over. Leo calls Venus "the unifier," bringing "harmony out of discord." We see the same process depicted in Botticelli's painting of *Venus and Mars* (c. 1483). Mars lies in a kind of post-coital slumber as Venus awakes, a state of affairs that Fred Gettings analyzes further as a metaphor of the sleeping physical body being guarded by the female etheric body (or body of light): "The emphasis on the physical body as a sort of shell is expressed in the idea of the armour [discarded by the male figure], which is nothing other than a protective metal shell placed around the body — in itself as lifeless as the body." He concludes that "the physical is really nothing more than a heavy extrusion into space and time of the Vital body."[30]

In the third movement of *The Planets,* "Mercury" represents the intellect. Head even suggests that Leo's description of Mercury as "the silver thread of memory" is evoked musically by the use of glockenspiel and celesta. Only in peace can the intellect emerge and create ideas. "Jupiter" is "the uplifter" in Leo's terminology, or "The Bringer of Jollity" in Holst's. But it is also the force of balance, adding maturity and wisdom, which is represented in the middle section of the piece, now associated with the jingoistic hymn "I Vow to Thee My Country." (Sir Cecil Spring-Rice's lyrics for this hymn are a far cry from Holst's original intentions. Indeed, Holst hated the words and everything they stood for.) Saturn "subdues," according to Leo. Holst interprets this as the process of old age and the renunciation of worldly concerns. The process is a painful, even terrifying one, but is nonetheless unavoidable and necessary. The "Saturn" movement is indeed a kind of funeral lament with

## Six. Theosophy 119

its own peal of hard, clamoring bells. In "Uranus—the Magician," Holst includes a musical cipher of his own name. Holst regarded himself as magician, much as had Scriabin, and he used music to cast his emotion-affecting and consciousness-expanding spells. (He represented his name as GuStAvH, which corresponds to the German designations of the pitches G, E flat, A and B.)

The most mystical-sounding of the seven planets, "Neptune," represents the departure of the spirit into the unknown on its lonely journey to self-enlightenment and union with the universe, a program it shares with Scriabin's similarly inspired theosophical vision and Kubrick's *2001: A Space Odyssey.* Though Kubrick did not include any of the music from *The Planets* in the soundtrack of his film, the martial connotations of "Mars" strongly influenced John Williams' *Star Wars* music, while "Neptune," with its heavenly choir and mystical tuned percussion, became the prototype for many of the musical effects that often appear in biblical epics or science fiction films. (There is also a touchingly human aspect regarding the first performance of this most otherworldly of pieces, when Holst asked the choir of female singers to walk further and further away down a backstage corridor into a room whose door was then shut to create the right kind of *diminuendo.* Anyone with squeaking shoes was asked to walk barefooted, and whoever was in charge of the door had instructions to close it without a sound.)

In 1908, Holst took a bicycle tour of the Algerian Sahara Desert. His sister, Imogen, recalls how he heard an Arab musician "playing the same short phrase on his flute for hour after hour,"[31] and the memory of this musical experience later inspired the hypnotic finale of his Oriental suite *Beni Mora* (1909–1910). The title was taken from a setting in Robert Smythe Hichens 1904 novel *The Garden of Allah,* which the female heroine associates with transcendence:

> In coming to Beni-Mora she had had a sort of vague, and almost childish, feeling that she was putting the broad sea between herself and it. Yet before she had started it had been buried in the grave. She never wished to behold such truth again. She wanted to look upon some other truth of life — the truth of beauty, of calm, of freedom.[32]

Later in the novel, a dialogue exchange emphasizes the symbolic quality of the place:

> "I come here to be foolish, Madame, for I come here to think. This is my special thinking place."
> "How strange!" Domini exclaimed impulsively, and leaning forward on the divan.
> "Is it?"

"I only mean that already Beni-Mora has seemed to me the ideal place for that."

"For thought?"

"For finding out interior truth."[33]

The heroine visits Beni-Mora "in search of recovery, of self-knowledge,"[34] and the ostinato in Holst's *Beni-Mora* is consequently related to the idea of a chant or mantra, the repetitions of which induce trance states and what Hindu tradition would call "spiritual transformation." There is also a more disturbing quality to the piece that perhaps reflects Hichens' description of the desert in *The Garden of Allah* as a place "of variety, of mystery, of terror. Was it everything? The garden of God, the great hiding-place of murderers!"[35] But ultimately Holst no doubt felt the same sense of spiritual liberation as Hichens' heroine:

What she had sought in coming to Beni-Mora she was surely finding. Her act was bringing forth its fruit. She had put a gulf, in which rolled the sea, between the land of the old life and the land in which at least the new life was to begin. The completeness of the severance had acted upon her like a blow that does not stun, but wakens. The days went like a dream, but in the dream there was the stir of birth.[36]

Perhaps Holst also felt the same as Hichens' heroine when he returned to England. He had gone on holiday to escape from financial worries and to recover from the nervous exhaustion induced by his heavy teaching commitments at the time. Hichens' heroine "had come out of a sort of death to find life in Beni-Mora, and now she felt that she was going back again to something that would be like death."[37] Certainly Holst's financial situation had not improved. His Hindu opera *Sita* had won only third prize in the Ricordi Competition of 1908. Deprived of the £500 first prize he was rather banking on, his Algerian holiday had consequently been taken on the cheap. Holst later dismissed *Sita* as "good old Wagnerian bawling."[38] It had taken him seven years of hard work, and it told the story of Rama and Sita as related in the Hindu epic *Ramayana*. Rama, which means "one who permeates and who is present in everything and everyone," is the seventh avatar (or earthly incarnation) of the god Vishnu, and Sita is an avatar of Vishnu's consort, Lakshmi. As a young prince Rama performed many heroic acts and eventually won Sita as his wife after succeeding in bending a great war bow. Rama goes into exile after having been cheated from assuming his rightful role as the successor of his father, the king. He is later kidnapped by the ten-headed demon Ravana, but, helped by Hanuman, the god of the monkeys, Rama eventually defeats Ravana and returns to Sita to rule in peace. Holst's *Sita* has sadly never been performed in its entirety.

## Six. Theosophy

In his second opera, *Savitri* (1908), the orchestral forces are reduced to those of a chamber ensemble, allowing the singers a central, and sometimes unaccompanied, role. Savitri loves her husband, Satyavan, but Death comes to claim him. Savitri pleads with Death, who is so impressed by her devotion that he agrees to spare Satyavan. One of the most mystical elements in the score is the choral writing that accompanies Satyavan's explanation of the concept of Maya — the illusion of matter, behind which lies pure spirit. The choral writing anticipates the mystical writing at the end of "Neptune" and simply consists of an alternation between an F minor chord and an A major chord in its second inversion, accompanied almost inaudibly by tremolo strings. The effect, however, is startlingly metaphysical.

> It is Maya!
> Dost thou not know her?
> Illusion, dreams, phantoms.
> But to the wise, Maya is more.
> Look around —
> All that thou seest —
> Trees and shrubs —
> The grass at thy feet,
> All that walks or creeps,
> All that flies from tree to tree,
> All is unreal.
> All is Maya.

Holst returned to Indian mysticism in his setting of hymns from the *Rig-Veda*. The combination of female choir and solo harp accompaniment is particularly ethereal in its effect, and perhaps the harp writing was in Bernard Herrmann's subconscious (Herrmann was a great admirer of British music) when he scored the oceanic harp parts of the otherwise rather more prosaic adventure film, *Beneath the Twelve-Mile Reef* (dir. Robert D. Webb, 1953). Sadly, Max Steiner's score for Richard Boleslawski's sumptuous 1936 Technicolor adaptation of *The Garden of Allah,* starring Marlene Dietrich and Charles Boyer, did not reference *Beni Mora.*

Holst's mysticism also touched on modern science. As Imogen Holst explains:

> He was perpetually chasing the idea of the Space-Time continuum. In the hopes of making it easier to reckon in light-years, he had taken lessons in elementary mathematics. But the effect of the bracket on the minus sign was too much for him. It seemed utterly lacking in logic as well as art. So he gave up algebra, and continued to dream his unscientific dreams of an expanding universe.[39]

One musical result of this interest was his setting of Humbert Woolf's poem

# The Occult Arts of Music

"On Betelgeuse" (1929). The poem describes the ethereal, timeless landscape of that gigantic, distant star. Time stands still there, and nothing stirs the leaves upon its golden avenues."

To convey this surrealistically timeless landscape, Holst employed sustained phrases in the very slow ostinato accompaniment, rather in the manner of Sibelius' cosmos-creation tone poem *Luonnotar* of 1913. The opening leap of a sixth for the first two syllables of the vocal line indeed suggests a leap into outer space.

A rather more overt British follower of theosophy was Cyril Scott. His commitment to the subject resulted in his own book on the history of modern occultism, and another on the influence of the occult on the history of music. Despite all this, Scott's actual music is less specifically mystical than Holst's. He did dedicate his piano suite *Egypt* to "Mrs Marie Russak — That enlightened Seer, who brought back for me the memory of my past Egyptian lives," but the pieces themselves, though written in what would then have been called a "modernist" manner, are really no more than atmospheric Orientalist fantasies describing "The Temple of Memphis," the "Waters of the Nile," an "Egyptian Boat Song," the "Funeral March of the Great Raamses" and the "Song of the Spirits of the Nile." He also wrote an opera called *The Alchemist*, which we will encounter in the next chapter, and composed other pieces with mystically-sounding titles such as "Dagobah" (1904) and *Sphinx* (1908) but they have no specifically mystical program, and are no more than decorative mood pieces, redolent of *fin-de-siècle* decadence (or at least as decadent as Scott was capable of imagining). The ballet suite, *Karma* (1924), perhaps suggests more than it actually delivers on a mystical level, consisting of the attractively theatrical orientalisms of "A Song from the East" (somewhat reminiscent of Albert W. Kètelbey's *In a Persian Market,* which had appeared four years earlier in 1920). "The Piper in the Desert," which follows it, is Scott's less extreme answer to Holst's *Beni Mora.* There is also a somewhat Stravinskyian "Barbaric Dance," surely influenced in part by *The Rite of Spring* (1913). Two other pieces, "Before the Church" and "Souvenier de Vienne," make up the five pictures of the whole, which was originally composed for one of André Charlot's London Revues.

Scott's musical style is often reminiscent of Scriabin and Debussy — indeed, in some cases, he anticipated certain of Scriabin's effects. Some pieces successfully evoke a transcendental state of mind, such as *Rainbow Trout* (1916), for example, which, belying its rather prosaic title, suggests something rather more mystical than an afternoon of fishing on an English riverbank. With its mixtures of fourths and tritones, and slow, obsessive five-in-the-bar ostinato accompaniment, Scott seems to be describing a very theosophical fish, but he is quite content to leave the harmonic effects to speak for them-

## Six. Theosophy

selves in the context of a character piece. (*Karma*'s "The Piper in the Desert" seems to have been a dry run for this more watery harmonic experiment.)

Theoretically speaking, Scott, as we have seen with regard to his interest in color-music theory, was more specific. In *Music—Its Secret Influence Throughout the Ages*, he applied Blavatsky's Root Race theory to the development of Western music, pointing out that in Atlantis, apparently, "Sound was employed to build beautiful and wonder-inspiring forms; but in the later phases of that mighty civilization it came to be employed entirely as a force for destruction. Discordant sounds were deliberately used to shatter and disintegrate." Debussy, however, was "unconsciously used by the Higher Ones to carry over Fourth Race sound-vibrations into the Fifth. To this end he made a study of and absorbed the characteristics of Javanese music, which is a remnant, though mellowed and modified of the Atlantean."[40] Scott also reminds his readers that "so far, with our earthly music we have only been able to imitate the faintest echo of the Music of the Spheres, but in the future it will be given us to swell the great Cosmic Symphony. In that unimaginable Unity-Song is the synthesis of Love, Wisdom, Knowledge and Joy, and when Man shall have heard it upon earth and become imbued with its divine influence he will attain the eternal consciousness of all these attributes."[41] He concludes his overview with a message he apparently received from Master Koot Hoomi, Blavatsky's Tibetan psychic contact: "To-day, as we enter this new Age, we seek, primarily through the medium of *inspired* music, to diffuse the spirit of unification and brotherhood, and thus quicken the vibration of this planet."[42]

Scott's occult life was truly strange. He was not only apparently in contact with Koot Hoomi but also wrote three books about an initiate of apparently Kashmiri origins, who claimed to be over 150 years old, spoke fluent English, and had been Pythagoras in a previous life. This individual, to whom Scott gave the pseudonym of Justin Morewood Haig, features as the Guru of Scott's three "Initiate" books, which read as curious pseudo-novels, replete with gossipy dialogue and deliberately tantalizing hints and suggestions of Haig's occult powers. Scott published this trilogy anonymously and the books were remarkably successful, probably because more is left unsaid than revealed in them, but anyone expecting Dennis Wheatley sensationalism will be sadly disappointed. Haig is presented as being mostly concerned with pointing out the error of people's ways and helping them to help themselves.

"I have been compelled for many reasons to conceal his identity," Scott explained. "And I emphasise the fact of his existence because there are a number of people who may doubt the possibility of attaining to that degree of perfection which he undubitably manifested, thus crediting me with writing romance instead of fact."[43] It has to be said that such a supposition is hard to resist. Other composers, many of whom admired his experimental and distinctively sumptuous musical style, certainly found this aspect of Scott's personality distinctly bemusing, and there is no doubt that it did not help his subsequent reputation. The composer Gerald Finzi regarded him as "a second-rate mind,"[44] and when he was a guest at the home of Elgar's main Edwardian competitor, Sir Granville Bantock, Scott caused bemusement and hilarity when he pinned a note on his bedroom door while taking an afternoon siesta: "Do not disturb. I am in an astral slumber."[45]

More musically influenced by mystical thought was Scott's less-well-known contemporary, John Foulds (1880–1939). A fellow theosophist, Foulds even carved theosophical symbols, such as the swastika and ankh, into an elaborate wooden fireplace on which he worked in the early years of the twentieth century. This extraordinary creation also combined his own initials with the motto "Ho exoriente fos"— an odd mixture of Greek and Latin that translates as "Light from the East."[46] Foulds' wife, Maud Woodcock, was also a theosophist and had traveled in India with Annie Besant, where she collected Indian folk music. Such an interest in Hindu tradition later brought her into contact with Holst, and she was to have a considerable influence on her husband when he turned to Indian mysticism for his inspiration. Before that happened, however, Foulds, like Scott, first came to public attention through light music, of which his *Keltic Suite* (1914) is perhaps the best known. Also like Scott, he was intrigued by Edgar Allan Poe, and composed a melodramatic recitation for voice and orchestra based on Poe's "The Tell-Tale Heart" in 1924. (Scott had written a ballet on "The Masque of the Red Death" for André Charlot in 1932, and the story had also inspired Debussy's protegé, Andre Caplet [1878–1925], not to mention Joseph Holbrooke [1878–1958].) Foulds was also interested in the possibilities of synesthesia, the *Aquarelles* for string quartet (c. 1905) forming one of his so-called "Music Pictures," which attempted to make a correlation between painting and music.

Foulds' marriage to Maud increased his esoteric tendencies. She encouraged his attempts to compose by means of "clairaudience," which his biographer, Malcolm MacDonald, explains as "the ability to hear, and take down as if from dictation, music apparently emanating directly from the world of nature of the spirit."[47] Various pieces inspired by "memories" of ancient Greek music followed, such as the piano suite *Recollections of Ancient Greek Music* (1915) and the orchestral *Hellas: A Suite of Ancient Greece* (1932). Another clairaudient piece was *Gandharva-Music* (1915–1926), a piano piece that is reminiscent of Erik Satie's style in its lack of bar lines and non-developing minimalist repetitions. (Gandharvas are male nature spirits with exceptional musical abilities.)

Foulds' most public success was his *World Requiem* (1923), which inau-

## Six. Theosophy

gurated the Festivals of Remembrance in memory of the fallen of the First World War. Anticipating Benjamin Britten's use of disparate texts in his own *War Requiem* (1961), Foulds juxtaposed texts by, among others, John Bunyan and a sixteenth-century Hindu poet in this extended and monumental poem in praise of pacifism. As with his later *Dynamic Triptych* (1927–1929) for piano and orchestra, Foulds also exploited the sound of quarter-tones, another idea gleaned from Hindu tradition (Maud could apparently sing the Hindu scale of 23 microtones[48]), and he experimented with what he called "counterpoint of timbres"—a similar idea to Schoenberg's *Klangfarbenmelodie*.

The *Requiem*, despite its initial success, failed to grasp a permanent hold on the repertoire, and performances of it are now very rare, but Foulds' aim to form a multi-racial "Union of East and West" continued.[49] Celtic pieces, inspired by the general mood of the Celtic Twilight movement of Yeats and Fiona MacLeod, followed, but Fould's most mystical pieces are undoubtedly the *Three Mantras* (1919–1930), which are widely regarded as his orchestral masterpiece. They began life as interludes in a now lost opera called *Avatara* (a word related to that of "avatar," as discussed above). We know nothing about the action of the opera, but Foulds did explain that each mantra related to the "basic vibration-type of the whole act" that it preceded. In his book *Music Today* (1934), Foulds suggests that certain music is of a more spiritually evolved kind than others. (The evolution element is perhaps derived from Blavatsky's Root Race theory in *The Secret Doctrine* and is comparable to Scott's occult categorization of various Western composers in *Music—Its Secret Influence Throughout the Ages*.) Foulds' categories range from the "Physical" to the "Divine," passing through "Emotional" (lower) and "Spiritual" (higher). These evolutionary characteristics consequently relate to the meaning of each of the *Mantras*: "The first — Mantra of Activity — appertains to the 'higher' third plane (Manas); the second — Mantra of Bliss— to the fourth plane (Buddhi); the third — Mantra of Will — to the fifth plane (Atma)."[50] Foulds also seems to have believed that his *Mantras* would have the same sort of definite physical and spiritual effects that Scriabin (whose music Foulds greatly admired) believed would be achieved by his *Mysterium*. Foulds described a mantra similar to the way that Jill Purce describes the process of chanting — as an arrangement of words or musical sounds "which, when constantly repeated — in conformity with laws not generally known but as definite as a mathematical formula — set going causes which produce predictable results."[51]

Of course, the *Three Mantras* can be enjoyed as orchestral showpieces in their own right, but that was not Foulds' intention. For him, they had a definite mystical purpose. His interest in Indian mysticism was not only very much a part of his time (as we have seen in the case of Holst and Scott and their shared interest in Indian-derived theosophy) but also predicted the revival of interest in Indian thought and other aspects of the "occult" in the 1960s. Foulds, like The Beatles after him, went to India. There, he learned to play the vina, the traditional string instrument that later gave way in popularity to the sitar, an instrument that George Harrison learned to play. Redolent of "mystic India," the evocative timbre of the sitar soon found its way into some of The Beatles' later transcendental tracks, such as "Within You, Without You" from *Sgt. Pepper's Lonely Hearts Club Band* in 1967. Perhaps not so coincidentally, in the previous year, Hammer Films had released John Gillings' *The Reptile*, with the unnerving sitar solo we discussed in chapter three. Hammer was also very much of its time, but whereas The Beatles were searching for alternative means of expression and spiritual salvation, *The Reptile* was responding to repressed colonial guilt. The "occult" signification of the music in the film, however, grew directly from the efforts of Foulds earlier in the century, which ultimately derived from his interest in theosophy.

Finally, a brief word about Debussy's interest in the occult. Debussy was not a theosophist, but his tenuous connection with the occult underworld of Paris was similarly indicative of the times. Along with Erik Satie (1866–1925), he was associated with various members of Joséphin Péladan's Order of the Rose + Croix. A prolific novelist and publicist, Péladan had organized the first salon in March 1892, and commissioned Satie to write suitable music for its gatherings and private views, such as the fanfares for trumpet and harp known as *Trois Sonneries de la Rose + Croix* (1892). Other "mystical" works include the *Première Pensée Rose + Croix* (1891) and his celebrated mediation on boredom, *Vexations* (1893), which is only three lines long but is intended to be repeated 840 times. (This well-nigh impossible instruction must surely rank *Vexations* as the world's longest musical chant and it would certainly induce a trance state in both performer and audience if each were able to endure it.) Satie's greatest influence on mystical movie-making is Allan Gray's groundbreaking minimalist score for *A Matter of Life and Death* (dir. Michael Powell and Emeric Pressburger, 1946). The scenes in heaven, filmed in monochrome against the technicolor of the real-life scenes on earth, are accompanied by Gray's understated yet persistent two-chord ostinato for piano, which, despite (or perhaps *because* of) its "tick-tock" quality, suggests the timelessness of the afterlife. A World War II drama echoing the *fin de siècle* world of the Rose + Croix might seem to be a curious state of affairs, but, given the metaphysical interests of both parties, perhaps not so odd after all.

The list of visual subjects forbidden by Péladan's salon is rather more revealing about the type of work permitted to pass through its esoteric portals

## Six. Theosophy

than its suggestions for suitable subjects. The following subjects were prohibited:

1. historical painting, prosaic and illustrative
2. patriotic and military painting
3. any representation of contemporary life
4. portraits, except iconic ones
5. all rural subjects
6. all landscapes except in the style of Poussin
7. ships and sailors
8. anything humorous
9. anything at all picturesque, including animals
10. flowers, baubles, fruit and knick-knacks[52]

According to Robert Orledge, the character of Bihn in Péladan's novel, *Le panthée,* "may be modelled on either Satie or Debussy."[53] More contentiously, Debussy has been claimed as the Thirty-Third Grand Master of the Prieuré de Sion, that notorious organization made world-famous by Dan Brown's novel *The Da Vinci Code* (2003), which is supposed to be the guardian of the Blood Line of the House of David — in other words, the descendants of Jesus Christ himself. Orledge lists the role of honor of this organization, but the connection was first brought to the attention of most people in Michael Baigent, Richard Leigh and Henry Lincoln's bestseller, *The Holy Blood and the Holy Grail* (1982). There, Debussy is said to have succeeded Victor Hugo and been succeeded by Jean Cocteau. Other Grand Masters included Sir Isaac Newton and Robert Fludd. Subsequent investigation has exposed much of this speculation as a deliberate hoax.

Orledge also reports that Maggie Teyte believed Debussy to be interested in Egyptology and the works of the magician Éliphas Lévi (1810–1875).[54] Debussy certainly flirted with Egyptology in musical terms when scoring the ballet *Khamma* for the Canadian dancer Maud Allan in 1912, though in fact he didn't bother to orchestrate it, a job he left to Charles Koechlin. There is much that is vaguely "occult" in this work, which concerns an Egyptian priestess (Khamma) who dances herself to death before the statue of Amon-Râ to save her city from fire, but Debussy maintained an ambivalent attitude to this piece. Frustrated by the inconsiderate personality of Miss Allan, and resentful of the fact that he was forced to compose the piece for money, he nonetheless wrote some of his most compelling music for this ballet, and, as he put it himself in a letter to his publisher, "She has paid, she can therefore do anything she likes with it. An arrangement for piccolo and bass drum might please her perhaps? In any case, it will be *most* Egyptian!"[55]

Debussy also used tarot cards and attended séances.[56] He was friendly with the poet Gabriel Mourey, who knew the novelist J. K. Huysmans along with the occultist Jules Bois (1868–1943). Bois, who was a member of an off-shoot of the Order of the Golden Dawn (the dubious Ahathoor Temple, founded in Paris in 1890), wrote, among other things, *Le Satanisme et la Magie* (1895), which had an introduction by Huysmans and also provided detailed descriptions of the Black Mass. Debussy considered writing music for Bois' play *Les Noces de Sathan* (1890), but the project failed to materialize. Later, however, Bois collaborated with Satie, who wrote music for his *La Porte héroïque du ciel* (1894), in which a poet is sent on a mission to replace the Virgin Mary with the Isis cult.

However, one does begin to wonder how seriously Satie approached this commission when reading the words inscribed over the staves of his *Prélude de la porte héroïque du ciel*, which include "Avec déférence," "Très sincèrement silencieux," "Eviter toute exaltation sacrilèdge" and, perhaps most tellingly, "Superstisieusement." It seems likely that it was Debussy who introduced Satie to the esoteric world of Sâr Péladan rather than the other way around, and the introductions may well have taken place at the famous bookshop of Edmond Bailly, the man who published Debussy's setting of *La Damoiselle élue* and of Pierre Louÿs' *Chanson de Bilitis*.

The characters of *Les Noces de Sathan* include Satan, of course, as well as Psyche, Adam, Eve, Cain, Mephistopheles, Faust and various demons. Like D'Annunzio, whose *Le Martyre de Saint-Sébastien* Debussy also set to music in 1911, Bois indulges in very exotic stage directions and props, such as, for example, stormy skies and purple lilies. Debussy unfortunately lost confidence in the project and pulled out[57] (the music was eventually composed by Henry Quittard, a pupil of César Franck), but the evidence that he was commissioned by Bois certainly helps us place him in the occult milieu of *fin de siècle* Paris. Debussy was always attracted to the mysterious, as his sketches for an unfinished opera on Poe's "The Fall of the House of Usher" demonstrate. He labored for nine years over this project, from 1908 until his death, obsessed by the character of Roderick Usher, with whom he closely identified.

Orledge points out that Debussy used tarot card references in conjunction with his musical sketches for the evil doctor in *Usher*. The line from the libretto, "Le scorpion oblique et le Sagittaire rétrograde ont paru sur le ciel nocturne," has perhaps an occult significance, especially as Debussy wrote the libretto himself. The Golden Dawn (to which Bois belonged) was the only occult organization to associate astrological signs with the tarot alphabet, so it was probably through Bois that Debussy got to know about such symbolism. Orledge paraphrases the meaning as follows:

Le Scorpion oblique = Tarot trump XIII: Death
et le Sagittaire rétrograde = Tarot trump XIV: Temperance

## Six. Theosophy                                                             129

Orledge glosses this as follows:

> The reverse position of Sagittarius implies opposition created by ineptitude (the friend blocking the doctor's plans?), also frustration and the wastage of creative energy: the evil of prejudice founded on narrow, constricting rules of life (both apply to the doctor and to Roderick Usher).
>
> ont paru sur le ciel nocturne = "The night sky is found only on the cards of the eight of cups (disillusion) and the seven of swords (danger, opposition)."[58]

Orledge also includes an intriguing footnote in which he explains that the Prieuré de Sion "had an extra sign *between* Scorpio and Sagittarius, called Ophiuchus (The Serpent Holder).... Scorpio and Sagittarius also played a substantial part in the initiation rites for novices in certain occult sects."[59]

But whatever esoteric secrets Debussy had, he took them with him to the grave. Vladimir Jankélévitch's *Debussy et le Mystère* (1949) is in no doubt about the connection, though, and the following passage from it was quoted by Léon Guichard in his 1958 article "Debussy and the Occultists." Guichard's article in turn it found its way into the second volume of Edward Lockspeiser's *Debussy — His Life and Mind* (1965):

> "His attraction to the mysterious ... derived from the occult ideas of the Rosicrucians in Paris in the 1880s [rather than the 1890s], from the frequenters of the Chat Noir, and from the Sar Péladan in whose entourage mysticism would sometimes degenerate into hypocrisy or a mere hoax. Debussy became intoxicated with the Eleusinian mysteries of the *fin-de-siècle* but neither more nor less than Ravel or Satie." However this may be, the abortive collaboration with Jules Bois adds greatly to our evidence of Debussy's leanings in this direction.[60]

The mysticism of Debussy's disciple, Olivier Messiaen (1908–1992), is rather more orthodox. There is nothing really "occult" about his Catholic inspiration and musical mission. For Messiaen, birdsong was the music of God, and the thrust of his mission (which included transcribing birdsong and incorporating it into his works) was to worship God rather than raise the occult veil of His mysteries, let alone encourage man to become a god himself. The gigantic *Turangalîla Symphony* (1949), however, does contain elements of Indian music. The title is derived from two Sanskrit words: "Turanga," meaning "time" or "rhythm," and "Lîla," meaning "divine play." Messiaen referred to this work as a hymn to joy. There are male and female themes, which Messiaen called the "statue" and "flower" themes (Freudians might be tempted to label them rather more explicitly), and the idea of mystical union through physical love relates the work to the Wagnerian metaphysics of *Tristan und Isolde,* itself influenced, as we have seen, by Indian mysticism. However, instead of a "Liebestod," the *Turangalîla Symphony* evokes the death of time through love — a similar thing but not quite the same.

The so-called isorhythmic structures of the *Turangalîla Symphony* and other Messiaen works are based on Indian talas—those rhythmic motifs that signify times of day, concepts and states of mind, which Messiaen first discovered in an encyclopedia where he learned that the 120 rhythms had been arranged and collated in the thirteenth century by the Indian scholar Sharngadeva. Messaien's rhythmic structures therefore have a life of their own, independent of the melodic element (hence the term "isorhythm," itself a technique formerly associated with medieval music). In Messiaen's *Quartet for the End of Time* (1941), isorhythmic structures are employed to evoke timelessness, which is an impossibility for a medium that can only exist in time, but Messiaen was fascinated by the charm of impossibilities, such as the fact that the whole tone scale cannot transpose itself into another key, and that some talas cannot be played backward without having the same rhythm. The self-contained nature of these rhythms (forms of rhythmic palindromes) consequently makes them incapable of organic relationships with each other. He rarely used the whole tone scale himself, as he felt that Debussy had exhausted its possibilities, but he often used talas as structuring devices. He also exploited Hindu ragas (or scales), folk songs, medieval plainchant, jazz elements, synesthesia and the textures of the Balinese Gamelan Orchestra — but all for the greater glory of God. The thrust of such mysticism is theological and not in the tradition of "occult science" and magic that I have been exploring in this book. The emphasis is quite different and really belongs to the corpus of Christian music that forms its own venerable tradition.

# Chapter Seven
## *Phantoms at the Opera*

The occult has always played a role in the history of opera. Among the very first operas in the seventeenth century were several adaptations of the Orpheus and Euridice legend. Jacopo Peri (1561–1633), credited with having composed the world's first opera, set Ottavio Rinuccini's *Euridice* in 1600. This was followed two years later by another musical treatment of the same text by Guilio Caccini (1554–1618) and the *Orfeo* of Claudio Monteverdi (1567–1643) in 1607. So grief-stricken is Orpheus when Euridice dies that he is allowed to descend to the Kingdom of the Dead to persuade Pluto and Proserpina to return her to him. This is agreed to on the condition that Orpheus will not look at Euridice before they return to the surface of the earth, which, of course, he fails to do.

The Orpheus story is one of the earliest manifestations of that aspect of occultism known as necromancy, or the raising of the dead. Richard Cavendish quotes the Catholic Encyclopedia at the head of his chapter on necromancy in *The Black Arts*:

> The Church does not deny that, with a special permission of God, the souls of the departed may appear to the living, and even manifest things unknown to the latter. But, understood as the art or science of evoking the dead, necromancy is held by theologians to be due to the agency of evil spirits.[1]

A form of necromancy occurs in Hammer's screen adaptation of Dennis Wheatley's *The Devil Rides Out,* when Christopher Lee's Duc de Richlieu uses Egyptian magic to raise the spirit of Tanith, who then takes possession of Sarah Lawson's Marie Eaton. The composer, James Bernard, accompanies this magical moment with the delicate sound of hand bells in different pitches to create a suitably ethereal effect. Bernard's music for Hammer's earlier *The Plague of the Zombies* (dir. John Gilling, 1966) was less subtle, as the zombies in question were soulless reanimated corpses, but perhaps even more the product of necromancy. Aleister Crowley describes a necromantic operation

131

132

# The Occult Arts of Music

in his novel *Moonchild* (1917). The ritual does not achieve its aim, but it is gruesome, to say the least, involving the ritual slaughter of a goat and the death, by impaling, of four black cats. Nothing so bloody occurs in the Orpheus and Euridice operas, but this doesn't alter the fact that necromancy is what Orpheus practices.

Witches have long been associated with necromancy. If we are to believe the Roman writer Lucan (39–65 A.D.), the Thessalian witch Erichtho, a contemporary of Nero, revived a corpse at the request of Sextus Pompey, who was keen to learn the outcome of the Battle of Pharsalus. Dante mentions her in *The Divine Comedy* ("Erictho, sorceress, who compelled the shades/Back to their bodies"[2]) and she also appears at the beginning of the Classical Walpurgisnacht scene in the second part of Goethe's *Faust,* where she describes herself as "not quite the hideous hag o'erslandering poets picture."[3] Witches are also popular figures in opera, and Henry Purcell (1659–1695) was one of the first composers to give witches a dramatic impact in his 1689 opera, *Dido and Aeneas.* The witches dwell in a cave in the second scene of Act I, and are introduced with funereal dotted rhythms in F minor — an appropriate key, according to the nineteenth-century theoretician, Christian Schubart (1739–1791), who defined that key as expressing "deep depression, funereal lament, groans of misery and longing for the grave."[4] Nahum Tate's text for *Dido* is fully in accord with all that:

> Wayward sisters, you that fright
> The lonely traveller by night,
> Who like dismal ravens crying
> Beat the windows of the dying.

These witches have a rather jolly, laughing, contrapuntal chorus consisting of "Ho ho ho," but their intention is far from that of Santa Claus. They take pleasure in malicious destruction, and plan to separate Dido from her lover Aeneas for the sheer pleasure of such mischief: "Harm's our delight and mischief all our skill." They conjure a storm, and in so doing they inspire Purcell to compose one of his most inspired passages in the famous echo chorus, "In our deep vaulted cell." This is in the more tranquil key of F major, which Schubart would have regarded as a suitably ironic key, being representative of "naive, womanly innocent declaration of love, lament without grumbling; sighs accompanied by few tears; this key speaks of the imminent hope of resolving in the pure happiness of C major."[5]

George Frideric Handel (1685–1759) created another impressive witch in *Rinaldo* (1711). She is Armida, and she uses her magic arts to bewitch the hero Rinaldo, making him fall in love with her rather than Almirena, the woman he really loves. Armida flies through the air on a chariot drawn by

## Seven. Phantoms at the Opera

two fire-breathing dragons and, this being a magical opera, Handel obliges with the use of special sound effects and spectacular staging, though Sir Richard Steele, writing an account of the first production in *The Spectator*, obviously felt there could have been more in that department: "We had also but a very short Allowance of Thunder and Lightning; th' I cannot in this Place omit doing Justice to the Boy who had the Direction of the Two painted dragons, and made them spit Fire and Smoke."[6]

Witches also appear in two operas by Giuseppe Verdi (1813–1901). In *Macbeth* (1847), they follow the example of Purcell's witches and are somewhat grotesquely upbeat. There are, for a start, rather more witches on stage at the beginning of the opera than there are in Shakespeare's play. Instead of three individuals, Verdi presents us with three covens to provide a noisy chorus, but the dialogue is at least closely modeled on Shakespeare's original. For the Paris production of 1865, a ballet was inserted in the first scene of Act III, in which the witches conjure apparitions in their cave (the same accommodation of Purcell's crones). They are dancing around their cauldron to thunder and lightning when Macbeth appears and asks what they are up to. "Un' opra senza nome," they reply (meaning "a piece of work without a name"). When Macbeth demands that they show him the future, they summon a helmeted head, which brings Macbeth the famous warning to "beware Macduff." Then the vision of a child, drenched in blood, materializes with the other famous prophecy that no child born of woman shall harm Macbeth. Macbeth wants to know still more and the witches oblige by summoning the phantoms of seven kings, with the ghost of Banquo indicating that they are his descendants. Macbeth collapses in a faint and the witches go back from whence they came. Of course, by this stage in the proceedings the ghost of Banquo has already appeared at the banquet scene, Shakespeare and Verdi giving the audience every opportunity to sup full of horrors.

In Verdi's later *Un ballo in maschera (A Masked Ball,* 1859) there is another witch, Ulrico, who is a negro fortune-teller. The original libretto of the opera by Eugène Scribe (1791–1861) was based on the historical assassination of King Gustavus III of Sweden, but the censor of the time insisted that the names of the characters and the place of the action be changed, as the assassination of a monarch on the stage was considered quite unacceptable, so the action was moved, rather implausibly, to seventeenth-century Boston. Originally, Ulrica was called Madame Arvedson, and her purpose is to introduce an element of the supernatural into the plot's political intrigue. She lives in a hut and is visited by Riccardo, the governor of Boston, who is in love with his best friend's wife, Amelia. This is made even more painful because that best friend has recently uncovered a plot against Riccardo's life. Amelia is disturbed by Riccardo's feelings, as they inspire similar feelings in her. She

134         The Occult Arts of Music

visits Ulrica to ask for a cure for this disturbing emotion, and Ulrica obliges by telling her how to make a potion from a herb that grows near a hangman's scaffold, which must be picked during the hours of darkness. Ulrica also predicts that Riccardo will die by the hand of a friend, and this is indeed what happens. Verdi's music creates a distinctly eerie atmosphere at the beginning of Ulrica's scene in Act I by starting off with three *fortissimo* chords and then exploiting the low, chalumeau register of the clarinet, a timbre subsequently much loved by horror film composers.

More ghosts followed in 1868 in the operatic adaptation of *Hamlet* by Ambroise Thomas (1811–1896). This work is nowadays perhaps most famous for its note in the score that "To be or not to be" should be regarded as "Optional," but the graveyard scene broke new ground with its use of the newly invented saxophone, which had not yet acquired its current jazz connotations. Thomas regarded the instruments as a new, strange and consequently ideal timbre to represent the macabre, much as Mozart had exploited the trombone for the infernal statue come to life in *Don Giovanni*.

It should now be clear how much horror films have in common with operas, which in so many ways were the theatrical equivalent of the cinema in their blend of spectacular settings, music, sound effects and star performers. Indeed, Christopher Lee, that most reluctant but prolific of Draculas, has always regretted that he never became an opera singer, but in a way the Dracula films he starred in for Hammer Films required a rather operatic performance style, even though he spoke rather than sang what few lines he was given. Given his operatic ambitions, it is ironic that Lee so resented Hammer's increasingly operatic presentation of the character, with scarlet linings for his cape and blood-shot contact lenses (both of which were significantly resisted in the first version); James Bernard's accompanying music for Hammer's Dracula series, however, was always operatic in its general approach. In *Taste the Blood of Dracula* (dir. Peter Sasdy, 1970) for example, Dracula says, "He has destroyed my servant.... He will be destroyed," and Bernard's music punctuates the phrases in a way that isn't so far removed from the approach of Verdi, whose music Bernard greatly admired. The ride to the ruined church in that film is also comparable to the moment at the end of Act I of Verdi's *Rigoletto* when the eponymous hunchback jester realizes with utter panic that his beloved daughter has been abducted right before his admittedly blindfolded eyes. Like Verdi, Bernard raises the tension of the scene in question by sequencing his little motif through successively higher pitches to create a very operatic sense of dramatic tension. A ghastly gong then reverberantly shudders as we cut to the interior of the church, lit by flaming torches, and the succeeding silence provides a stark contrast to the melodrama of hooting owls and squeaking cemetery gates that preceded it.

## Seven. Phantoms at the Opera

A particularly important date in the ancestry of the horror film was 1821, when Carl Maria von Weber first unleashed *Der Freischütz* on an unsuspecting but delighted audience. This is a rather difficult title to translate, literally meaning "the free shot," which is why it is usually left in the original German, but "The Magic Bullet" is a fairly close approximation of its meaning. When the opera was put on in Paris after its Berlin premiere, it suffered the indignity of being called *Robin des Bois* — the French appellation for Robin Hood. This, and the appalling production it was given, so outraged Hector Berlioz (1803–1869), himself the composer of one of the world's most supernatural symphonies (*Symphonie fantastique*), that he never forgot it. In his *Memoirs* he referred to the production as "a gross travesty, hacked and mutilated in the most wanton fashion,"[7] but he was so enthusiastic about *Der Freischütz* that he composed music for all the dialogue, which in Germany was merely spoken, this being a Singspiel rather than an opera. However, if a work was to be produced at the Paris Opéra at that time, it was necessary that every word be sung rather than spoken, so Berlioz duly obliged. He also orchestrated Weber's concert waltz, *Invitation to the Dance,* to supply the equally required ballet scene. In his collection of stories about music, assembled together under the title of *Evenings in the Orchestra,* Berlioz tells an amusingly macabre tale about how a real skeleton found its way on stage as one of the ghoulish props. It so happened that a grocer's assistant — "a big red-headed lout" — had hissed at Weber's music and been thrown out of the theater by Weber's enthusiastic champions. Six months later the grocer's assistant died from overeating, and when the prop master in charge of the current production of *Der Freischütz* paid a visit to a doctor friend of his in search of gruesome props, the doctor presented him with the prepared skeleton of the offending red-headed philistine:

"You see that young man?" [the prop master explains when he returns to the theater with his prize.]

"Yes, sir."

"He is making his debut at the Opéra tomorrow. Make him a nice little box where he can stretch his legs in comfort."

"Yes, sir."

"As for his costume, take an iron rod and stick it in his backbone, so that he stands as straight as M. Petitpa when he is about to do a pirouette."

"Yes, sir."

"Then you must fasten four candles together and place them in his right hand; he's a grocer, he'll feel quite at home with them."

[...]

All this was done; and from then on, at each performance of *Freischütz*, just as Zamiel cries out: "I am here!," there is a flash of lightning, a tree comes crashing

136 The Occult Arts of Music

down, and our grocer, who was once so hostile to Weber's music, appears in the red glow of the Bengal lights, enthusiastically brandishing his lighted torch.[8]

Zamiel is, for all intents and purposes, the Devil. The hero, Max, is a terrible shot, which is very unfortunate for him, because hitting a bull's-eye is the only way he can ever hope to win the hand of the beautiful Agathe, who is the prized trophy of a shooting competition organized in her honor. Realizing he will never be able to win Agathe without supernatural intervention, Max enlists the help of Kaspar, who is in league with Zamiel. In the dead of night Max and Kaspar make their way to the Wolf's Glen to forge seven magic bullets that will not fail to find their mark.

Weber uses the symbolism of different musical keys to suggest the demonic, equating the forces of good with C major and the forces of evil with F-sharp minor. Not only did Christian Schubart define F-sharp minor as "gloomy" but the relationship between C major and F-sharp minor is also that of a tritone, because the tonics of each key are separated by an augmented forth, the so-called "Diabolus in musica." Amid the gloomy F-sharp minor surroundings of the Wolf's Glen, Kaspar duly invokes the Devil and holds the magic bullets up to the light of the moon, and with each ballistic blessing increasingly supernatural events occur. Everything starts quietly, however, with owls hooting, an effect Weber created with tritonic flutes. A storm wind gathers and black boars run across the scene, followed by four fiery wheels, a procession of ghostly huntsmen across the sky and finally a terrific storm. The music Weber provides for these episodes is so graphic and overwhelming that it caused a positive sensation at its premiere, fully the nineteenth-century equivalent of Hammer's original impact in the late 1950s. And just as was the case with Hammer's competitors, opera composers now wanted to jump on the bandwagon of Weber's success.

Hot on the heels of *Der Freischütz* came an opera based on the story written by Lord Byron's private physician, Dr. John Polidori, during the haunted Swiss house party of 1816 that also gave birth to Mary Shelley's *Frankenstein*. Polidori's story, economically titled "The Vampyre," is the first modern vampire tale, and was largely based on the despotic personality of his poetical employer. In the opera, the action takes place in Scotland, thanks to the popularity at the time of Sir Walter Scott's novels, which did for the Highlands what Bram Stoker later did for Transylvania. Consequently, it is perhaps rather amusing to contemporary eyes to see etchings of the production that show Lord Ruthven, as the vampire is known, dressed not in a cloak but rather a kilt. Ruthven must drink the blood of three virgins by midnight to avoid being dragged down to hell. If he succeeds, he will be granted another year of undead existence.

## Seven. Phantoms at the Opera

The most occult aspect of the work occurs right at the beginning with a chorus of witches and ghosts summon their Vampire Master with an invocation that bears some relation to Shakespeare's witches in *Macbeth* with their famous "Double, double, toil and trouble" recipe:

> Schlange, Natter hör ich zischen,
> Irrlicht flackert hör' dazwischen
> Molche, Kröten, schwarze Katzen,
> Kobold, Hexen, Teufelsfratzen
> Kommt und schlingt den muntern Reihn!
> Eul' und Uhu, irh sollt schrein.
>
> (Snake and viper I hear hissing,
> Will-o'-the-wisp flickers and among them,
> Newts, toads, black cats,
> Goblins, witches, devils grimaces.
> Come and close the merry circle!
> Owl and eagle-owl, you should shriek.)

As one might expect, everything ends in a terrific thunderstorm and Ruthven, who fails to do what the Vampire Master commanded at the beginning, is dragged down to hell, rather as Mozart's Don Giovanni similarly meets his doom. The music, however, is much more demonic than Mozart's admittedly frightening finale. It was composed by Heinrich Marschner (1795–1861) and in many ways it sounds like the music of one of his greatest admirers, Richard Wagner. In fact, Wagner so admired *Der Vampyr,* as Marschner's version was called, that he even wrote extra words and music for it, which were first performed by Wagner's brother, Albert, when Wagner was conducting the opera in Würzburg in 1833, only five years after the work's premiere in Leipzig.

In 1992 *Der Vampyr* was dusted off by the BBC and turned into a soap opera, updating the action to the present day and making an effectively ironic satire of what we used to call yuppie corporate greed. Vampires are, after all, a very good symbol of capitalism, as Karl Marx knew quite well. As for the opening chorus of witches and demons, the reworked libretti by Charles Hart turned the proceedings into a slick Black Mass with Satan himself being hailed in the back room of a trendy London art gallery.

Wagner was also a huge admirer of Weber, admitting in his memoirs that "*Freischütz,* though mainly because of its spooky plot, affected my imagination with characteristic intensity. The excitement of horror and fear of ghosts constitute a singular factor in the development of my emotional life."[9] Indeed, the subject of the supernatural runs throughout Wagner's oeuvre, but before we look into that, it is important to mention another composer who equally inspired him. This was Giacomo Meyerbeer, who, despite his

Salle Le Peletier during a performance of "Robert le diable," Paris, 1832.

Italian name, was actually a German composer originally called Jakob Liebmann Beer. So ubiquitous did his *Robert le diable* become that it was even mentioned in Alexandre Dumas' novel, *The Count of Monte Cristo*, where chapter 52 is subtitled "Robert le diable" because it takes place during a performance of this work at the Paris Opéra, for which it had originally been composed. Dumas doesn't say much about the opera itself, but the mere title of the piece is enough to add a certain glamour and mystery to the persona of the mysterious Count:

> "Do you observe," said the Countess G— to Albert, who had returned to her side, "that man does nothing like other people; he listens most devoutly to the third act of *Robert le diable,* and when the fourth begins makes a precipitate retreat."[10]

For good measure, Dumas also refers to *Der Vampyr* in this chapter, or at least to the character of Lord Ruthven, "the Vampire of the Salle Argentino."[11]

The most occult scene of *Robert* occurs in the finale to Act III, which is set in the ruins of the Convent of Saint Rosalie. As the curtain rises, we dimly perceive the dark and shadowy cloisters of the place. To the left stand the moldering tombstones of long-dead nuns, and in the center the marble statue of the abbey's patron saint surveys the scene, holding a magic cypress branch in its hands. It is this branch that Robert seeks, for it will give him resistless power. At the diabolical suggestion of Bertram, a fiend disguised as a human being (who also happens to be Robert's father), Robert has been persuaded

## Seven. Phantoms at the Opera

to enter the convent at midnight, secure the branch and use it to win the hand of the fair Isabella, Queen of Sicily. It should not be too much of a surprise to learn that Bertram wants the cypress branch for himself, and is merely using Robert to achieve his own diabolical ends.

Bertram conjures the specters of dead nuns whose sins, during life, deprived the convent of its sanctity. They take on the alluring form of beautiful maidens, and by the light of the full moon, we watch the ghostly waftings of their funeral shrouds. Film director Roy Ward Baker captured this general mood perfectly in the exquisitely shot prologue to Hammer's *The Vampire Lovers* (1970), in which a similarly enshrouded specter wafts though a misty graveyard. Strangely, the original set for Meyerbeer's convent, by Pierre Luc-Charles Cicéri, is Romanesque rather than Gothic in style, which is perhaps a little disappointing, highly effective though it is, but just like the enshrouded vampire in *The Vampire Lovers*, Meyerbeer's shrouded specters are revealed to be actually rather alluring. Edgar Degas evocatively captured this compelling scene in a painting that now hangs in the Victoria and Albert Museum in London.

Robert enters and the nuns set about seducing him with three dances. The first one attempts to get him drunk, the second tempts him to gamble and the final one is frankly erotic. The abbess manages to extract a kiss from Robert but this sends a shiver down his spine. He swiftly snatches the branch and runs off. Bertram, meanwhile, is very pleased with how things have turned out and watches as demons emerge from hell to drag the unfortunate nuns back to their rightful place, their shrouds lying motionless on the moonlight flagstones of the convent.

The first performance of *Robert* was not without its unintentional sensations. At the beginning of the famous third act a dozen lighted lamps fell on the stage in front of Mlle Dorus, the soprano; the singer who created the role of Robert, Adolphe Nouritt, became so excited in the last act that he fell into a trapdoor and nearly killed himself; and during the resurrection of the nuns a curtain of clouds almost fell on Mlle. Taglioni, who, as the abbess, was about to rise from her tomb.

No one could ignore Meyerbeer, who was, while he lived, the God of the Paris Opéra. He was immensely influential but also equally kind and generous. When the young Wagner came to Paris to seek his fortune, Meyerbeer recognized his talent and graciously extended the hand of friendship. Characteristically, Wagner bit that hand clean off as soon as Meyerbeer had served his purpose. "It is not that I hate him," Wagner wrote in a letter to Liszt in 1851, "but that I find him infinitely repugnant."[12] Being Jewish, rich, successful and talented was too much of a celebrity constellation for Wagner to handle, and it is largely due to Wagner's subsequent smear campaign that Meyerbeer's posthumous reputation has suffered so much, but this did not stop Wagner from imitating Meyerbeer's style in *Rienzi,* his first major success.

Meyerbeer no doubt fully realized that Wagner, whatever else he might be, was a musical genius, and he encouraged Wagner with the composition and promotion of his second great success, *Der fliegende Höllander (The Flying Dutchman),* though Paris did not see the premiere of that work. The Flying Dutchman himself is also a distinctly supernatural figure: a cursed immortal, who seeks redemption through the love of a good woman. The opera follows a similar plot to that of the Werner Herzog 1979 remake of F. W. Murnau's *Nosferatu,* which is why Herzog chose to accompany that film with Wagnerian music. (In fact, he used the prelude to *Das Rheingold* rather than *Der fliegende Höllander,* but the inference is clear: Herzog wanted to place his film within the context of a specifically Wagnerian Romantic tradition, with its shared theme of redemption through love.) Klaus Kinski's lonely Count Dracula is redeemed by Isabelle Adjani's Lucy, who sacrifices herself to save her community from the plague of vampirism. She gives herself to the vampire, who in turn is overcome by the sunlight of dawn. A similar thing happens at the end of *The Flying Dutchman* when Senta hurls herself into the waves of the ocean and we see her spirit rising to heaven with that of her lover as the curtain falls. The music for the Dutchman himself contains some of the darkest and most brooding passages Wagner ever wrote and would have ideally suited Christopher Lee had he been able to follow the operatic career he so desperately desired. As Lee said of his own portrayal of Dracula, he wanted to convey the loneliness of that character's undead state: "his extraordinary stillness, punctuated by bouts of manic energy with feats of strength belying his appearance; his power complex; the quality of being done for but undead."[13] Most, if not all, of these characteristics apply to the Dutchman, who is basically a vampire without teeth.

Even at the other end of his career, the second act of Wagner's *Parsifal,* his final music drama, owes much to the structure of *Robert le diable's* third act. (In place of Bertram's seductive nuns, simply substitute the evil magician, Klingsor, and his seductive flower maidens.) *Parsifal* also has vampire imagery in common with Marschner's *Der Vampyr.* As we have seen, it is not hard to discern a racial subtext to all this that fits in well with Wagner's appallingly antisemitic essays written at the same time that he worked on the score, which contains the most ravishing music ever composed by anyone. Robert W. Gutman carefully quoted Shakespeare at the outset of his famous biography of Wagner with a quotation from *Macbeth:* "Such welcome and unwelcome things at once," as Macbeth puts it. "'Tis hard to reconcile."[14] Not that Bram Stoker, in his much less offensive way, was immune to casual antisemitism himself. In *Dracula* he refers to "a Hebrew of rather the Adelphi theatre type,

# Seven. Phantoms at the Opera 141

with a nose like a sheep, and a fez,"[15] but this is a long way from wanting to burn a theatre full of Jews in a single evening.

In *Parsifal*, Amfortas, due to his dalliance with Kundry, now suffers from a kind of spiritual syphilis. "The ebb of my own sinful blood in a mad tumult must surge back into me, to gush in wild terror into a world of sinful passion," is how he explains his situation in Wagner's flamboyantly macabre text. Compare that sense of impurity with Mina's reaction to the crucifix Van Helsing places against her forehead in Stoker's *Dracula*. Mina has also been polluted by mingling her blood with Dracula's, and the result is similarly catastrophic:

> She put before her face her poor crushed hands, which bore on their whiteness the red mark of the Count's terrible grip, and from behind them came a low desolate wail which made the terrible scream seem only the quick expression of an endless grief....
>
> "Unclean, unclean! I must touch him [Harker, her husband] or kiss him no more. Oh, that it should be that it is I who am now his worst enemy."[16]

Mina and Amfortas are both guilty of having illicit sex with the wrong person — the racially degenerate type. The upstanding heroes of Stoker's novel (if that's the right way to put it), along with the Grail knights of Wagner's opera, are, by contrast, sexually pure and desperate to remain that way.

Other vampire types prowl the surreal dream-text of *Parsifal*. The father of Amfortas, Titurel by name, is in a condition similar to that of Stoker's undead vampire. Titurel is kept alive by fresh infusions of divine blood from the Holy Grail, but the woeful state of the Grail community means that this reservoir is drying up. In the end, even his undead state proves terminal in the impressive funeral march of Act III. *Parsifal* also has examples of zombies in its cast list, for Klingsor's magic garden is guarded by slain Grail knights whom Klingsor has reanimated following a method that is presumably similar to that of John Carson in Hammer's *Plague of the Zombies*. In fact, the entire cast list of *Parsifal* would not be out of place in a Hammer or Universal Studios horror film. As Thomas Mann pointed out in his essay, "Sorrows and Grandeur of Richard Wagner,"

> The cast list of *Parsifal* — what a bizarre collection, at bottom! What an assemblage of extreme and repellent oddities! A sorcerer emasculated by his own hand; a desperate woman of split personality, half corrupter, half penitent Mary Magdalene, with cataleptic transitions between these two states of being; a love-sick high priest ... together they remind one of that motley bunch of freaks packed into Achim von Arnim's famous coach — the ambivalent gypsy witch, the dead layabout, the golem in female shape and the field marshal Cornelius Nepos, who is really a mandrake root grown beneath a gibbet.[17]

Klingsor's flower maidens, who soften up the hero, Parsifal, before Kundry

# 142 The Occult Arts of Music

gets to work on him, are also vampires in their own way—certainly seductive *femmes fatales.* And observe how Parsifal describes his encounter with Kundry, imagining as he does so the experience of all her other conquests:

> die Lippe, ja so zuckte sie ihm,
>> so neigt sich der Nacken,
>> so hob sich kühn das Haupt;
>> so flatterten lachend die Locken,
>> so schlang um den Hals sich der Arm -
>> so schmeichelte weich die Wange;
> mit aller Schmerzen Qual im Bunde,
>> das Heil der Seele
>> entküsste ihm der Mund![18]

(The lips—yes- they quivered for him, thus she bent her neck—thus boldly rose her head; thus laughingly fluttered her hair—thus her arms were twined around his neck—thus tenderly stroked her cheek; with all the powers of pain united, his soul's salvation these lips once kissed away!)

Compare that with Jonathan Harker's equally kinky seduction by the vampire brides of *Dracula*:

The fair girl went on her knees, and bent over me, fairly gloating. There was a deliberate voluptuousness which was both thrilling and repulsive, and as she arched her neck she actually licked her lips like an animal, till I could see in the moonlight the moisture shining on the scarlet lips and on the red tongue as it lapped the white sharp teeth.[19]

There is another connection between Wagner and Stoker: the curious coincidence that the Victorian actor-manager Sir Henry Irving, who was Stoker's rapacious employer, made something of a speciality of the role of the Flying Dutchman in a non-operatic version of the story at the Lyceum Theatre. In his early plans for *Dracula,* Stoker intended for Jonathan Harker to attend a performance of Wagner's *Der fliegende Höllander* at Munich's Hoftheater before embarking on his journey to Transylvania. The fact that Stoker drew a parallel between Dracula and the Flying Dutchman — especially Wagner's version of the story suggests that a vampiric affinity between Dracula, Irving and Wagner existed in Stoker's imagination. Indeed, Irving himself intended to out-Wagner Wagner with regard to the scenic effects on display at the Lyceum Theatre, having heard about Wagner's successes in Germany. In 1900, Stoker and his wife even attended a performance of *Der fliegende Höllander* at Wagner's Festspielhaus in Bayreuth. (A footnote remains: If one consults the program for the Royal Opera House, Covent Garden, issued in May 1903, one can read that the sets for Wagner's *Lohengrin* were designed

# Seven. Phantoms at the Opera 143

by one Joseph Harker — the same Harker who was part of Irving's staff at the Lyceum.)

During rehearsals for the premiere of *Parsifal* at Bayreuth it was discovered that there wasn't enough music to cover the time it took to change scenes between the exterior of the Grail Castle and the interior where the Grail is unveiled. Wagner intended the whole process to take place without a curtain drop in a somewhat proto-cinematic manner, and relied on the use of a cyclorama to give the impression of Gurnemanz and Parsifal walking to a new location. The man hired to write the extra music was Engelbert Humperdinck (1854–1921), one of the many musical assistants Wagner employed at the time. Humperdinck, however, had operatic projects of his own, and his *Hänsel und Gretel* (1893) features the infamous witch who lives in the gingerbread house. The witch is written for mezzo-soprano, but is sometimes sung by tenor, which gives this female role a suitably grotesque quality and emphasizes just how much the vocal writing for Humperdinck's witch was influenced by the music Wagner composed for the malicious dwarf Mime in *Siegfried*. Indeed, the whole thing is obviously influenced by Wagner, but the famous Witches' Ride ("Hexenritt"), delightful though it is, is rather more stately than Wagner's Ride of the Valkyries ("Walkürenritt").

Pyotr Tchaikovsky (1840–1893) notably disliked Wagner's music, even though it influenced him to some extent. As an admirer of Mozart, it is perhaps not surprising that Gothicisms should not have attracted him as much as his contemporaries. As we shall see later, fairy tales were more his style when it came to ballet, but Tchaikovsky's most occult opera is his setting of Puskin's story *The Queen of Spades* (1890), which gave him the opportunity to combine the eighteenth-century rococo elegance of Mozart with more Wagnerian undercurrents of psychological and occult terror. The Mozartian elements came to the fore in the *divertissement* in Act II, in which Tchaikovsky used a melody from Mozart's Piano Concerto in C major (K503) as the basis for a pastoral entertainment called *The Faithful Shepherdess*. This has little to do with the story, however, which concerns Hermann, an impoverished officer who wants to learn the secret of how to win at cards. A mysterious Countess, who is said to have been a lover of the even more mysterious Count Cagliostro, apparently knows the secret, and Hermann is determined to wrest it from her. The big scene between them takes place in the Countess' bedroom in Act II, scene 2, where Hermann hides, having managed to persuade the Countess' companion, Lisa, to give him the key to a secret door giving access to the room. There he waits for the Countess' servants to leave the old woman for the night. Tchaikovsky's music here is full of apprehension and tension, played out over an insistent ostinato in the strings, which suggests not only Hermann's obsession and the overall tension of the scene but also something

144      **The Occult Arts of Music**

of the occult secret the Countess knows but refuses to impart to Hermann. Or does she? Hermann so terrifies her that she dies of a heart attack, but later her ghost appears with the winning formula. This, however, could well be a hallucination on the part of the crazed Hermann, for it turns out she gave him the wrong cards—not "Three, Seven, Ace" but "Three, Seven, Queen." Hermann, having staked all on the wrong cards, shoots himself.

Thorold Dickinson's atmospheric 1949 film version of the same story, starring Anton Walbrook, cast Edith Evans in the role of the Countess and had music by Georges Auric, but for the crucial bed chamber scene, Auric did nothing. Instead, Dickinson relied on the sound effect of a sinister ticking clock to provide the occult mood. It is not only a symbolic heart beat but also fulfills the function of the kind of music used in operatic incantations. The clock stops dramatically when the Countess heart gives out, and the effect is so powerful music would only spoil the scene.

Operas continued to reflect occult and magical ideas in the twentieth century, though, as we shall see, this found more fertile ground (musically speaking) in the sphere of popular music. Busoni's *Doktor Faustus* (1925) emphasizes the occult much more than previous operatic adaptations of this story. Busoni wrote his own libretto but died before completing the music. The opera opens with the visit of three students from Kraków in Faust's study. They present him with a copy of the grimoire *Clavis Astartis Magica* (*The Key to the Magic of Astarte*), and in the next scene Faust performs the magical ceremony that will raise the Devil. As actors in occult horror films would do later (in fact, only one year later, in 1926, the same thing happened in F. W. Murnau's film of *Faust*), Faust draws a magic circle on the floor and summons the Devil. Five flames materialize, which are the Devil's servants, but these fail to impress the good doctor. With the arrival of a sixth flame, however, which announces itself as being "as swift as the thoughts of men," Faust recognizes it as the spirit of the diabolic power he seeks and succumbs to the Devil's offer of power in return for his soul. Faust duly signs the contract with his own blood.

At the end of the piece, Faust, full of remorse for his sins, attempts to perform one good deed by resurrecting a dead child. He once more draws a magic circle, takes the child inside it with him and transfers his own life-force into the corpse before dying himself.

As we have already seen, Busoni had a personal interest in the occult, and the mystical, otherworldly atmosphere of the opening prelude to *Doktor Faust* is in part based on his earlier orchestral work, *Nocturne symphonique*, characteristic elements of which return throughout the work and were associated with the various occult ceremonies.

Cyril Scott's opera *The Alchemist* premiered in the same year as *Doktor*

## Seven. Phantoms at the Opera      145

*Faust,* although it was composed during the last year of the First World War. *The Alchemist* is Scott's most overtly occult work, in which an adept magician raises an elemental spirit with a voracious appetite for magical tasks. The adept finds himself hard pressed to come up with new miracles to perform (each of which gave Scott an opportunity for increasingly spectacular musical effects—not to mention giving the stage designer a full evening's work). In the end, the Sage comes to the rescue and provides the final moral—the pursuit of material possessions can only bring unhappiness as such a desire is insatiable. *The Alchemist* was the only one of Scott's four operas to be published, though, as their titles suggest, two of the others, *Saint of the Mountain* (1924–1925) and *Shrine* (1925–1926), also inhabit a mystical terrain. Koot Hoomi apparently played a part in the rehearsals, as Scott's memoirs record:

> As the final rehearsal there was nearly a serious row, though I was not involved in it, and Mrs Chaplin [a medium with whom Scott was friendly at the time] had to send a mental S.O.S. to Master K. H. to come in one his subtle bodies and diffuse peace. However, on the evening of the actual performance the audience was friendly and gave the work a good reception, but the singers declined to appear with me to acknowledge the applause.[20]

Meanwhile, in Russia, Sergei Prokofiev (1891–1953) was hard at work on his magnum opus, *The Fiery Angel.* This was based on Valery Bryusov's novel of the same name, although Bryusov also included a lengthy subtitle, which succinctly sums up the action:

> The Fiery Angel; or, a True Story in which is related of the Devil, more than once appearing in the Image of a Radiant Spirit to a Maiden and seducing her to Various Sinful Deeds, of Unholy Practices of Magic, Astrology, Alchymy, and Necromancy, of the Trial of the Maiden under the Presidency of His Eminence the Archbishop of Trier, as well as of Encounters and Discourses with the Knight and thrice Doctor Agrippa of Nettesheim, and with Doctor Faustus, composed by an Eyewitness.[21]

The maiden is the sexually repressed Renata, who thinks she has been visited by an angel called Madiel, and believes him to be one and the same as the handsome Count Heinrich. Heinrich thus has an opportunity to seduce her but then leaves her in the lurch. With the help of a knight called Ruprecht, Renata starts her quest to locate the real Fiery Angel, and this involves them both in an occult odyssey, which results in Renata being burned at the stake as a witch by the Inquisition. The question remains: What kind of angel is the Fiery Angel—demonic or divine? Or is it anything more than Renata's unconscious libido projecting itself and creating poltergeist-like effects around her?

*The Fiery Angel* is perhaps the most occult opera of all time. Demons are

146 The Occult Arts of Music

everywhere, knocking on walls; there are also singing skeletons and possessed nuns, who in the opera's most infamous scene writhe around on stage as the Inquisitor attempts to exorcise them. The walls of the convent begin to shake, and thudding noises erupt all over the place, but Renata remains faithful to her angel, even though she knows that such a faith is likely to result in her own immolation at the hands of the Church. The cacophonous and relentlessly motoric music that accompanies all this, in which tritone relationships fully play their part, more than complements the demonic chaos on stage. As Simon Morrison puts it:

> The dementia reaches a climax at rehearsal number 545, when the chorus of nuns disintegrates into six parts, each assigned a rhythmic variant of Renata's leitmotif. The top two voices perform four pitches of the leitmotif ... in tandem, the lower two voices perform them down a tritone ... in tandem, and the middle two voice parts complete the consequent tritone-related harmonies.[22]

Prokofiev first stumbled upon Bryusov's novel in a bookstore in New York City in 1919 and immediately began work on the libretto himself, but he never lived to see the work performed, the whole subject matter of the piece being out of joint with the times—particularly in Soviet Russia, where Prokofiev's more extreme musical style was also out of favor and where the composer's life was in positive danger from Stalin. Prokofiev employs polytonality, combining music in C-sharp minor, for example, with music in F-sharp minor. He also uses ostinati to help suggest the general atmosphere of obsession and possession. Morrison describes the overall effect as an "oppressive onslaught of dissonance."[23]

Much more restrained was the two-act opera *The Medium* (1946) by Gian-Carlo Menotti (1911–2007), which concerns a fake medium who begins to believe her own lies—or are they lies? Ambiguity lies at the heart of the best ghost stories and this one ends in a tragic death as well. Madame Flora, the medium, has a daughter called Monica. During seances, Monica stands behind a curtain and provides the voices of the "spirits." Also involved in their fraudulent racket is a mute boy called Toby, who enjoys playing his tambourine and is in love with Monica. But something strange happens on the evening in question. During another routine séance, Madame Flora becomes convinced that phantom hands are pressing against her throat. Is she going mad? Or is it a real spiritual manifestation? At first, she blames Toby. Then she hears a voice and flies into a rage. Eventually, her anxieties lead to the bottle, which is in part responsible for the tragic dénouement. To those familiar with Hammer horror films, Menotti's opera will so far have reminded them of the opening scenes in *Hands of the Ripper* (dir. Peter Sasdy, 1971), in which much the same thing happens. In that film, Beryl Reid also plays a

## Seven. Phantoms at the Opera    147

medium, and Jack the Ripper's daughter Anna, played by Angharad Rees, whom Reid's character has taken into her dubious establishment, performs the ghostly impersonations. As in the opera, *Hands of the Ripper* begins with a séance involving grieving parents, and fake voices simultaneously comfort and disturb both sets of unfortunate clients. In addition, Reid's fraudster is eventually stabbed and pinioned against a door with a fire iron by the Rees' Ripper-possessed "innocent," whose latent evil has been awakened by the trigger of a glittering light followed by a kiss. In the opera, Madame Flora unwittingly shoots the innocent Toby, who has hidden in the trunk where he keeps his tambourine. Having accidentally woken Madame Flora while retrieving his tambourine, he hides in the trunk, but Madame Flora, thinking the sound was caused by a ghost, fires her revolver into it.

Menotti's music is nowhere near as disturbing as the action it accompanies, being far more conservative than anything to be found in Prokofiev's *Fiery Angel* — or Christopher Gunning's score for *Hands of the Ripper*, for that matter. Gunning's music for Anna's various frightening trance sequences turned out to be one of Hammer's most compelling musical cues. By surrounding a simple though unnerving 3- or 4-note harp ostinati with glockenspiels and vibraphones over sustained note clusters in strings, Gunning created the perfect musical impression of spiritual possession. Eric Porter's Freudian psychoanalyst, Dr. Pritchard, refuses to believe Anna is possessed, but has been persuaded to take her to Madame Bullard (Margaret Rawlings at her most imperious). She is a genuine medium and can feel the "horribly violent" spirit of Anna's father that is possessing her. Coupled with Gunning's music, this particular scene is a key moment in occult horror, and it ends with Madame Bullard's murder: having unwittingly primed Anna's state with a flashing light from her lorgnette, the medium kisses her client on the cheek, with devastating results. Gunning's music, which contrasts violence, possession and innocence (the latter quality expressed in a touchingly lyrical melody), plays a vital role in *Hands of the Ripper,* which it would not be unfair to claim as a far more compelling exploration of its subject matter than Menotti's opera.

In quite a different league, however, is Benjamin Britten's adaptation of Henry James' ghost story, *The Turn of the Screw,* which premiered in Venice in 1954. Britten (1913–1976) used this story about two children who may or may not have been corrupted by the former servants Miss Jessel and Peter Quint, and who may or may not be haunted by their ghosts, as a vehicle to discuss the forces of good and evil in general and the corruption of innocence in particular. The latter is a subject that resonates throughout much of the homosexual Britten's output and may well have had its origin in an incident during his own schooldays. Britten himself also claimed to have "premonitions" and "curious happenings"[24] and so he could be said to have been particularly well qualified to tackle such a subject. Myfanwy Piper's libretto took a distinctly cinematic form, and Britten's music a highly symbolic one. The opera is divided into fifteen scenes and a prologue, which affords the opportunity to intersperse each scene with orchestral interludes, with the prologue stating a theme, and the remaining fifteen interludes taking the form of variations on that theme. The theme itself is a twelve-note row, but it is not treated according to Schoenberg's serial principles. The first seven scenes are in so-called "white note" keys—in other words, keys that correspond to the white notes of the piano keyboard (e.g., C, D, E, F, G, A, B). The first "black note" key to be introduced is A-flat in a scene wherein the ghosts are first heard, and four of the eight scenes in part two are in these "black note" keys that are identified with the ghosts, suggesting (using conventional black-and-white symbolism) that they are emissaries of evil. Britten and Piper also interpolated a line from Yeats' poem "The Second Coming" ("the ceremony of innocence is drowned") to underline what is going on.

The film version of this story, called *The Innocents,* and directed some years later by Jack Clayton in 1961, starred Deborah Kerr as the governess. The ghosts, of course, may be figments of her own overheated imagination, for like Renata in *The Fiery Angel,* she is nothing if not repressed herself. Georges Auric (1899–1983), well versed in such supernatural movies from his time working on *Dead of Night* (various directors, 1945) and Dickinson's *The Queen of Spades,* brought an interesting mix of music, electronics and amplified sound effects to bear on this highly atmospheric dramatization. The climax of the film begins in the stuffy, humid and claustrophobic environment of a greenhouse. The governess is trying to force a confession from Miles, the boy in her charge, that it has been the ghost of Peter Quint (Peter Wyngarde) who has been haunting him. Miles (played with brilliant ambiguity by Martin Stevens) replies, "You don't fool me. I know why you keep on and on. It's because you're afraid. You're afraid you might be mad," and at this moment, the ghost of Quint appears behind the condensation of the greenhouse glass. Electronic effects accompany the apparition, suggesting the eerie "otherness" of this manifestation. "So you keep on and on," Miles complains, "trying to make me admit something that isn't true"—or is it? Are the ghosts real, or merely part of the Miss Giddens' imagination? Miles concludes by telling her exactly what he thinks of her—"A damned hussy. A damned dirty-minded hag"—but then he laughs and it seems just possible that the governess has been right all along. As someone on an internet posting of this clip commented, Miles could well be a "reverse pedophile." He hurls the tortoise he has been playing with through the glass and runs out into the garden. Auric's agitated music accompanies his flight, which results in him tripping and falling to the ground. The music then stops abruptly and a vaguely agitated bird calls out as the sound of a night breeze takes over. (The masterly use of sound effects here anticipated the rise of "sound design" in later movies, which sometimes replaces the emotional function of an underscore with imaginatively manipulated sound effects.) As Miss Giddens again presses Miles to confess that he has been corrupted by Quint, Miles shouts that she is "insane," and at this point Quint's ghost appears from above the ornamental circle of hedges in which Miles fell. It seems that the governess can see him but Miles apparently cannot. Quint raises a ghastly hand and electronic effects, like a roaring wind, imply the full demonic nature of the manifestation. All seems lost on Miles, however, who collapses dead in Miss Giddens' arms. As she grieves over the body and places a distinctly erotic kiss on the dead boy's lips, the bird call is once more heard singing in the dark, providing an acoustic ambiguity that has no need of musical support.

Although Clayton takes a much more subtle approach to the story than Hammer Films might have done, the cameraman was Freddie Francis, who would go on to direct many films for Hammer and Amicus, and the lyrics of the haunting "Willow Waly" song, which the children sing throughout the film, were written by Paul Dehn, the partner of Hammer's resident composer, James Bernard.

Another notable soundtrack for a British-made ghost story followed in 1963, with the truly disturbing combination of sound design and Humphrey Searle's mixture of Romantic and modern in *The Haunting.* This was directed by Robert Wise, better known for *The Sound of Music,* and Wise certainly knew about the music of sound. Muffled chanting, devilish laughter, a child's whimpering, footsteps, thumps and thuds and moaning wind all provide one of the most extreme uses of sound effects in any occult film, and they are emotionally heightened by Searle's modernist musical effects. A champion of serialism in his symphonic work, Searle uses various styles to accompany the action, ranging from the desolate Romanticism of the main theme and the traditionally "scary" trills and string tremolos and the vibraphone effects we often encounter in James Bernard horror film scores, to the shuddering of a cymbalom and fairly extreme avant-garde note clusters. The most unnerving moments, however, like those in *The Innocents,* are those that rely on sound effects rather than music, such as a distinctly unsettling scene in which a massive wooden door is pushed against by the "thing" beyond it — the door seems to breathe in and out creakily, not to mention creepily. If cinema is the offspring of opera, it truly came of age in films like *The Innocents* and *The Haunting,* which explored the dramatic potential of sound in ways of which Wagner could never have dreamed.

# Chapter Eight
## *Dancing with Death*

Gothic operas such as Meyerbeer's *Robert le diable* (1831) may have their ballet scenes but there are entire ballets devoted to narratives with an occult theme. The nuns of *Robert le diable* were unfaithful to their vows when still alive, but in *Giselle* (1841), the ballet by Adolphe Adam (1803–1856), we encounter the spirits of young girls who were jilted on their wedding nights. They are, essentially, the ballet equivalent of Charles Dickens' Miss Haversham in *Great Expectations.* Miss Haversham never danced, but she famously refused to remove her white (though increasingly decrepit) wedding gown, and the Wilis, as the specters in *Giselle* are known, similarly appear in bridal white — the epitome of the popular idea of what ballerinas should look like. Their whiteness is only enhanced by the light of the moon, which floods the sylvan scenery of Act II much as it had the ruins of the abbey in *Robert le diable*. *Giselle* is one of the most famous works in the history of ballet, and this is one of ballet's most supernatural scenes. Appropriately, the decor for the first production in 1841 was designed by Pierre-Luc-Charles Cicéri, who had worked such visual wonders for *Robert.* Indeed, Cicéri was a theatrical nineteenth-century equivalent of Hammer Films' set designer Bernard Robinson, providing the vital but often taken-for-granted atmosphere against which Petipa's choreography and Adam's music worked their magic.

The story of *Giselle* is simply told. Giselle, an equally simple peasant girl, falls in love with a disguised nobleman, who is merely out for some fun before marrying his fiancée. When Giselle finds out he has been deceiving her, she dies from a heart attack. A gamekeeper called Hillarion is also in love with Giselle and he warned her not to trust the nobleman, but, of course, she paid no attention to him. Stories such as this are, like *Titanic* films, really a pretext for the big scene, and the big scene in *Giselle* is the "white" second act, when the supernatural takes over from the rustic plot. The Wilis appear in all their ethereal weightlessness, but though the Wilis may look charming, they are in fact motivated entirely by their desire for vengeance on the opposite sex. They

## Eight. Dancing with Death          151

hurl Hillarion over a cliff and similarly condemn the nobleman to death. Only Giselle's abiding love saves him, and as a consequence, like a staked vampire, she is able to escape the clutches of the Wilis and return to her grave in everlasting peace.

The libretto for *Giselle* was in part concocted by Théophile Gautier (1811–1872), who also had a hand in the *La Péri* of Johann Friedrich Burgmüller. He based the action on a tale in Heinrich Heine's collection, *Geschichte der neuren schönen Literatur in Deutschland* (1833), and folk tales have often provided the inspiration for other ballets. Comparable to *Giselle*'s "white act," though composed much later, is Tchaikovsky's *Swan Lake* (1876), which may in part have been based on Russian folk tales, though the exact nature of the plot's origin is still in dispute. The supernatural element predominates in this tale of a swan queen who is under the domination of an evil magician, Rothbart, and in this respect the plot has certain things in common with Wagner's *Parsifal,* in which, as we have seen, Kundry is similarly under the spell of Klingsor. But *Swan Lake*'s occult credentials go further than the magic and enchantment of its plot. Its supernatural connotations were immediately exploited by Universal Studios for the Bela Lugosi *Dracula* film of 1931 (dir. Tod Browning). The famous oboe melody from the ballet, associated with the swans themselves, accompanies the main title of that film, and apart from brief extracts of Wagner's *Die Meistersinger* and Schubert's "Unfinished Symphony," this is the only music in the entire movie, which otherwise relies for its sonic shocks on sound effects alone (wolves howling, armadillos scuttling, coffin lids creaking, and, perhaps most potent of all, *silence*), for in those early days of sound cinema, audiences were still used to the wall-to-wall musical accompaniments of the so-called silent era; to be denied music in a dark cinema was a distinctly unnerving experience. The same *Swan Lake* excerpt became something of a signifier for Universal horror movies, for it was reprised in *The Mummy* (itself a kind of ancient Egyptian remake of *Dracula).*

Tchaikovsky's other ballets also contain occult elements. In *The Sleeping Beauty* (1890) the wicked fairy Carabose appears in a chariot drawn by six rats, and rats (or rather mice) also feature in his last ballet, *The Nutcracker* (1892). Tchaikovsky's answer to *The Magic Flute, The Nutcracker* is based on E.T.A. Hoffmann's tale in which the mouse king takes on an army of animated nutcracker soldiers. The somewhat sinister Herr Drosselmeyer ("Clockmaker and Arcanist"), the mastermind behind the story's fantasy events, is a kind of magician, and he has music of a somewhat grotesque nature, reflecting the bizarre person described in Hoffmann's story:

> Godpapa Drosselmeier was anything but a nice-looking man. He was small and lean, with a great many wrinkles on his face, a big patch of black plaster where

152                     The Occult Arts of Music

his right eye ought to have been, and not a hair on his head; which was why he
wore a fine white wig, made of glass, and a very beautiful work of art.[1]

Tchaikovsky composed some truly unusual music for the first entrance of
Drosselmeyer, which, as the composer's biographer, David Brown, puts it,
"is inspired — bizarre yet not really frightening, its grotesquerie springing
not only from its slightly eccentric melodic features but from its inventive
harmonic manoeuvring ... and especially from its implacable evasion of the
tonic chord till near the end."[2]

Hoffmann also inspired that other staple of ballet repertoire, *Coppélia*
(1870), the composer of which, Léo Delibes (1836–1891), Tchaikovsky rated
very highly, commenting that the former's *Les Sylphides* ballet was a thousand
times better than Wagner's *Ring* cycle. Delibes' *Coppélia* is a comic ballet,
though the original tale from which it was derived is a much more disturbing
one in which the hero, Nathaniel (Franz in the ballet), is driven mad and
eventually plunges to his death, tormented by his relationship with a sinister
lawyer named Coppelius, whom the hero equates with the legendary Sand-
man, who steals children's eyes. The story of Coppelius' automaton, with
which Nathaniel falls in love, is made quaint and charming in the ballet, but
Hoffmann's intentions were more disturbing. The eyes of the doll fall out,
causing Nathaniel to go mad. And if we wish to take a Freudian line of interpretation, loss of the eyes can be equated with a castration complex. Unfortunately, none of this left a trace in the ballet.

The appearance of Sergei Diaghilev's Ballets Russes in the early years of
the twentieth century was the balletic equivalent of Hammer's full-color horror films in the late 1950s. Horror, in an admittedly very stylized presentation,
was unleashed through the equally colorful sets and costumes of Diaghilev's
sensational productions. Leon Bakst, the designer of one of company's early
success, *Schéhérazade* (1910), swagged his set with huge, billowing curtains
and strewed cushions over a carpeted floor to create a fantasy of the East.
Against this riot of soft furnishings, the costumes clashed with gaudy opulence
in blues and crimsons, greens and pinks. The action had nothing much to do
with Rimsky-Korsakov's original program for the symphonic suite on which
it is based, but that wasn't the point. The point, in very cinematic terms, was
to create a sensation, and a sensation it most definitely achieved. The cast list
of odalisques, half-naked black slaves, diaphanously clad ladies of the harem,
a violent chief eunuch and a snake pit into which negroes are hurled all suggest the kind of things we find in Hammer's film adaptation of *She* (dir. Robert
Day, 1965) with Ursula Andress. Indeed, the mix of sex and violence proved
just as popular in the ballet. The finale of the ballet was a mass slaughter —
the vengeance of the Sultan on his faithless wives, who have been indulging
themselves with the negro slaves. Rimsky-Korsakov's music for this scene is

# Eight. Dancing with Death

simply called "Festival in Baghdad" but the ballet turned it into an admittedly highly aesthetic (though still distinctly bloodthirsty) kind of Iraq war and orgy, followed by a mass execution. Romola Nijinsky's description of the decor fully captures the Hammer-like, even rather campy excess of the affair:

> The scenery had no flats or practicable projections. It was all painted on the vivid walls and ceiling of the harem in motives of green and violet blue, rising from a shrill pink carpet. A voluptuous sensation was suggested by the mixing of these sensuous colours. The effect on the public was arousing of an immediate excitement. The front of the stage was draped in a gigantic curtain, its folds of varying greens, on which designs of blue and circular patterns of pink were sprayed. Colour had never before been so riotously used. In the blue background were three immense doors of silver, bronze, blue, gold. Huge Arabian lamps swayed from the ceiling squares, and heaps of enormous cushions sprawled all over the stage.[3]

Diaghilev's *Cléopâtre* of the previous year had prepared audiences to some extent for this precursor to an Eastmancolor sensation in Hammerscope. That ballet, again based on a story by Gautier, starred the Ursula Andress of ballet, Ida Rubinstein, as the Egyptian queen. The most famous ballet star of all time, Vaslav Nijinsky, danced the role of her slave, and Mikhail Fokine that of a young nobleman who agrees to a bargain: in return for a night of love with the queen, he must submit to drinking poison. The silent movies starring Theda Bara very much followed this cue, as did much of later Hollywood and Hammer-esque Egyptiana. Rubinstein's Cléopâtre anticipated the cycle of mummy movies that followed by making her entrance from a mummy-case, from which she was removed and then elaborately unwrapped. Also, the way in which the ballet's music was concocted was similar to the way in which the musical accompaniment of silent movies was often assembled from different pieces. In all, extracts from the works of six composers formed the score for this extravagant entertainment. Like a set designer for D. W. Griffith, Bakst provided massive pink-tinted statues of gods on either side of a view of the Nile. Columns, costumes and color created a whole new fashion among the public. "*Cléopâtre* brought the fullest houses," remembered Alexandre Benois, another of Diaghilev's designers, who also contributed to the event.[4] As Sir James Carerras once said, "You're the public. If you want Strauss waltzes, I'll make them." But as Christopher Lee observed, everyone was waltzing with death instead. "Hammer Horror had its dance card full."[5]

Horror elements continued in other Diaghilev productions. *Thamar* (1912) is another Hammer-esque conflation of sex and death. It was based on a tone poem of that name by the nineteenth-century Russian nationalist composer, Mili Balakirev (1837–1910), and featured a Bakst set, which, in its sheer vorticist verve, anticipated the astonishingly towering sets of Charles D. Hall for the laboratory scenes in James Whale's *Bride of Frankenstein* in 1935. Bakst's set featured the interior of a stone tower (all reds and purples) but painted in such a way that the audience was given the impression of staring right up to the top of the structure. An opulent bed of cushions, as in *Schéhérazade*, clustered around one corner, and against all this, blue and purple costumes moved almost psychedelically. The action revolves around a regal femme fatale (the Thamar of the title — as danced by Tamara Karsavina) who lures young men to her riverside abode and then, Cleopatra-like, hurls them from a window at the top of the tower after a night of passion.

Diaghilev was also fond of black magicians— not personally, but he knew what good box office they were. His version of Mocata (the devil-worshipper of *The Devil Rides Out*) is Katschei, the immortal sorcerer in Stravinsky's *The Firebird* (1910). Whereas Mocata attempts the transference of souls in Hammer's adaptation of Dennis Wheatley's occult classic, Katschei keeps his own soul in an egg and has imprisoned a princess in his magic garden, just as Mocata ensnared the unfortunate Tanith. Katschei also controls a kind of zombie army to protect his enchanted garden from intruders (rather like Klingsor in *Parsifal*). Needless to say, the hero of this work destroys Katschei by breaking the egg and releases the princess from her enchantment. All ends as happily, as does *The Devil Rides Out*.

Diaghilev and Fokine's answer to *Giselle* was *Les Sylphides* (1909), which took piano music by Chopin and orchestrated it for a drama set in another moonlit Gothic ruin (this time a monastery, atmospherically conjured up by Benois). Diaphanous white-clad ballerinas dutifully appeared amid this Romantic setting, alongside Nijinsky, Pavlova and Karsarvina, who all starred in the tale of a poet who dreams of sylphides, who are benign versions of *Giselle*'s Wilis. Quite harmless, they are the gentle spirits of departed lovers. The poet dances with these figments of his imagination, but eventually the moonbeams fade and the ballet ends with the poet still asleep but with one of the spirit lovers resting her head against his shoulder. It was in this ballet that audiences were first really amazed by Nijinsky's seemingly weightless leaps, as his wife recorded in her biography of him: "He floated, literally floated, and for a second stopped in the air. His unbelievable capacity of almost flying stupefied the audience and his *entre-chat dix* was another miracle. No one ever could achieve more than six *entre-chats*, or exceptionally eight."[6]

Later, in 1936, the choreographer Frederick Ashton created a similar kind of ballet called *Apparitions*, which adapted music by Liszt and was again set a Gothic environment — a gloomy chamber in a old mansion where a young poet sees a ghostly figure in each of the three long Gothic windows of the room. One of them is a soldier, another is a monk and the third is a beau-

## Eight. Dancing with Death

tiful woman. The poet immediately falls in love with the latter, but all too soon the apparitions vanish. In the next scene, the poet finds himself in a ballroom in the company of the ghostly soldier and the beautiful woman. To his annoyance, the poet watches her dance with the Hussar. Next he hears the tolling of bells and finds himself in a churchyard. The chimes of the bells are personified by more ballerinas and herald a funeral procession led by the ghostly monk. The corpse is, of course, the beautiful woman. The scene then changes to an illuminated cave. The same apparitions are present but are now dressed in scarlet and participate in a blasphemous orgy with devils and witches. The poet then wakes from his drug-induced dream and, in despair at being unable to find his ideal, he stabs himself. Another funeral procession now appears, including the beautiful woman. The mourners lift the body of the poet and bear it away.

Cecil Beaton's designs for *Apparitions* combined traditional Romantic Gothic with elements of German expressionist film, flying in the face of reality and the genuine horrors that were soon to engulf Europe during the Second World War. Indeed, the settings of both *Les Sylphides* and *Apparitions* are more in the spirit of Ann Radcliffe's picturesque late eighteenth-century Gothic novels than the more lurid aspects of the genre begun by Matthew Lewis' *The Monk,* and Benois' Romantic-Gothic ruins for *Les Sylphides* are almost a complete realization of Radcliffe's description in *The Romance of the Forest* (1791) of a similar ruin:

> He approached, and perceived the Gothic remains of an abbey: it stood on a kind of rude lawn, overshadowed by high and spreading trees, which seemed coeval with the building, and diffused a romantic gloom around. The greater part of the pile appeared to be sinking into ruins, and that, which had withstood the ravages of time, shewed the remaining features of the fabric more awful in decay. The lofty battlements, thickly enwreathed with ivy, were half demolished, and become the residence of birds of prey.[7]

These opening lines from the second chapter of Radcliffe's novel became the prototype of all the horror sets of future films, from Charles D. Hall's mouldering ruined castle in Tod Browning's 1931 *Dracula* to Bernard Robinson's ruined Castle Borski in *The Gorgon* (dir. Terence Fisher, 1964) — and beyond.

Gothic horror films have on occasion featured impressive dance sequences of their own. Don Sharp's *The Kiss of the Vampire* included a whole ballroom of dancing vampires, which went on to inspire Roman Polanski's atmospheric vampire comedy, *The Fearless Vampire Killers* (a.k.a. *Dance of the Vampires,* 1967), in which a rather more stately, eighteenth-century-style ball takes place. Jack MacGowran's Professor Abronsius and Polanski's Alfred,

Poster for *The Fearless Vampire Killers* (dir. Roman Polanski, 1967).

his assistant, join in, but unfortunately are exposed as interlopers when their reflections appear in the ballroom's immense mirrors, in which, of course, none of the vampires are reflected. James Bernard composed his own waltzes for *The Kiss of the Vampire*, but Harry Robinson relied on Johann Strauss' "Voices of Spring" waltz and the mazurka from Delibes' *Coppélia* in the dance scenes at the beginning of *The Vampire Lovers* (dir. Roy Ward Baker, 1970). Roger Corman's adaptation of Poe's *The Masque of the Red Death* (1964) also has its own ball scene, which reaches a macabre conclusion as the Red Death choreographs a Dance of Death while passing among the unfortunate guests of Vincent Price's wicked Prince Prospero.

The choreographic elements in Poe's story had previously been exploited by the British composer Joseph Holbrooke (known by some as "The Cockney Wagner"), whose ballet, *The Masque of the Red Death*, appeared in 1925 and gave ample opportunities for macabre maneuvers on stage. He divided the action into two scenes. The first is set outside Prince Prospero's palace; the second, based inside in the gigantic ballroom, comprises three numbers. Holbrooke also specified a lighting scheme that reflected the different colored rooms in Poe's tale: "The light changes throughout the scene — blue to purple,

## Eight. Dancing with Death

157

to green, orange white, violet and lastly a deep blood red. A tall ebony-black clock of sinister and lugubrious aspect stands C. between the windows." This clock, whose ticking Vincent Price in the Corman film describes as "the footsteps of an assassin," ultimately chimes out the midnight hour at the end of Holbrooke's ballet. This chiming effect was even more striking in André Caplet's mini-harp concerto, *Conte fantastique (Masque of the Red Death)* (1924), which he scored for harp and string quartet. Though not technically a ballet, the piece exploits waltz form throughout and calls for the harpist to rap the soundbox of his instrument when the Red Death first appears: Death knocking at the door, indeed.

Alan Birkinshaw's remake of Roger Corman's *Masque of the Red Death* for Harry Allan Towers in 1989 has a more up-to-date costume party dance scene with 1980s-style pop music in dubious taste. It all purportedly takes place inside Neuschwanstein, the fantasy castle of Richard Wagner's famous patron, King Ludwig II of Bavaria. Indeed, Prince Prospero is called Ludwig in this version, played by Herbert Lom, who must have wondered what on earth he was doing there. Birkinshaw actually took the trouble of going to Bavaria to film the exterior of this amazing inspiration of Disney's Cinderella castle, but failed to make much of its architectural opportunities, which would certainly make a splendid backdrop for any ballet.

Such Gothic ball scenes have a particular parallel in perhaps the twentieth century's most Gothic ballet, *The Haunted Ballroom* (1934), with music by Geoffrey Toye (1889–1942). The concert waltz from this work became extremely popular out of its original context, but the ballet as a whole (with choreography by Dame Ninette de Valois) tells the story of ghostly goings-on in the home of the Master of Tregennis. A house-party is under way, thrown by the Master's son, and all the guests are very impressed by the ghostly atmosphere of the old house. One room, however, is kept locked up (and where have we heard of that kind of thing before?). It is rumored to be haunted and naturally the houseguests want to experience this haunted ballroom for themselves. Thick cobwebs festoon the chandeliers and cover the frames of the old family portraits. The guests begin to dance about, despite the warnings of their host, and are only stopped by the Master of Tregennis himself, who insists they leave. Later that night, the walls of the ballroom become magically transparent and icy starlight gleams through them. A ghostly conductor appears and begins to conduct an invisible orchestra. Then ghostly dancers appear and indulge in a choreographic orgy. The Master of Tregennis is caught up with the spectral crew, who are in fact the ancestral portraits come to life. After dancing with one particularly beautiful woman, the Master, like the sacrificial virgin in Stravinsky's earlier *Rite of Spring* (1913), dances himself to death.

158 The Occult Arts of Music

Ninette de Valois achieved another huge macabre success with the chess-based ballet, *Checkmate,* with music and scenario by Sir Arthur Bliss (1891–1975), in 1937. This was Bliss' first ballet and was largely a response to the political situation of the time. Showcasing designs by Edward McKnight Kauffer, it dramatizes the moves of a chess game, with the ruthless Black Queen (the forces of fascism?) defeating the exhausted old Red King (unwitting, exhausted Europe?). As Bliss' own scenario puts it, "The Black Queen appears behind him with spear uplifted. She plunges it into his back and he falls lifeless. It is Checkmate." Whether the queen is Hitler or Mussolini, or both, is left to the imagination of the audience. The whole thing is in fact played out on a much more allegorical level. The prologue, rather like a Renaissance opera, pits Love and Death against each other. As in Ingmar Bergman's 1957 film, *The Seventh Seal,* in which Bengt Ekerot's Death plays chess with Max von Sydow's knight, Love and Death also play a game of chess but with human pieces. Bliss' experience as a film composer enormously enhanced the dramatic power of this ballet. Indeed, he included music he had written for the film adaptation of H. G. Wells' *Things to Come* (dir. William Cameron Menzies, 1936): for the "Entry of the Red Castles" in the ballet, he adapted the march he had written for the extensive montage sequence in that film showing the building of the subterranean Everytown.

A few years later in Hollywood, Disney began experimenting with the possibilities of animation ballet in *Fantasia* (1940). There are many occult elements at work here (most famously Mickey Mouse in *The Sorcerer's Apprentice*), but there are also many "magical" effects—dancing mushrooms, fauns and satyrs, and, perhaps the most occult element of all, the penultimate segment based on Mussorgsky's symphonic poem, *Night on the Bare Mountain.* This features a terrifying evocation of the demon Chernabog, who summons the dead from their graves, who then dance menically through the air until the sound of the Angelus bell destroys the spell and the dawn ushers in the final segment of the film, based on Schubert's *Ave Maria.* Intriguingly, some of the designs for the devils are reminiscent of those painted on the curtain drop of Bakst's original design for Stravinsky's *Petroushka* (1911), the whole ably demonstrating the kinship between ballet and animation in general.

But live action can also successfully aspire to the fantasy effects achieved so eloquently by animation. In 1951 Michael Powell and Emeric Pressburger followed up the immense success of their ballet-film *The Red Shoes* with an extravagant adaptation of Offenbach's opera, *The Tales of Hoffmann.* Though an opera, Powell and Pressburger employed the balletic talents of some leading dancers of the day to mime roles that were sung by others. The dancers included Robert Helpman, Frederick Ashton, Moira Shearer, Ludmilla Tchérina and, most evocatively of all, Léonide Massine, the star of the Ballets

## Eight. Dancing with Death     159

Russes who replaced Vaslav Nijinsky after Diaghilev fell out with his former lover when Nijinsky married Romola. In the "Tale of Giuletta," with its famous barcarolle and sinister Venetian setting, demonic red is the dominant color, and the story is introduced with one of the most dream-like sequences of all time, in which Tchérina and Helpman float down highly stylized Venetian canals in a giant gondola. This is Venetian Gothic at its most theatrical and it is the closest British cinema got to the extravagant style of Fellini until the advent of Ken Russell in the 1960s. The story is Faustian: The courtesan, Guiletta, has been promised a miraculous diamond if she steals Hoffmann's reflection from the mirror. She succeeds but the story ends with her drinking poison by mistake (it was prepared for someone else), and she falls dead in Hoffmann's arms. The story and production indeed summons a similar mood to Edgar Allan Poe's "The Assignation"— a suicide pact story, also set in Venice.

Leonard Salzedo (1921–2000), who scored Hammer's *The Revenge of Frankenstein* (dir. Terence Fisher, 1958), also contributed to the genre of the occult ballet in *The Witch Boy* in 1956. It originally received over 1,000 performances, and tells a story set in the American Midwest in which a girl witnesses the birth of the eponymous Witch Boy from under the cloak of the Conjor-Man. They fall in love and return to the girl's village, the inhabitants of which ostracize them, sensing that there's something strange and supernatural about the boy. Goaded by the local preacher, the villagers kill both the girl and Witch Boy but in the end the mysterious Conjor-Man reappears to witness the rebirth of his creation. Little heard these days, Salzedo's connection with Hammer should have revived interest in this powerfully strange ballet and stirred interest in the other sixteen he composed.

More recently, there have been both Frankenstein and Dracula ballets. David Nixon choreographed and designed the costumes of a Dracula dance drama for Britain's Northern Ballet Company in 2005 using music by Alfred Schnittke, Rachmaninoff and Arvo Pärt. Columbia City Ballet also adapted Stoker's novel for their Dracula ballet in 2011, which included quasi–belly dancing Orientalist female vampires dancing to the exuberant rock/jazz score of Thomas E. Semanski — and there was nothing stylized about the staking of vampires in that production. In fact, Dracula ballets are spreading across the United States like a virus. Companies in Texas, Sacramento and Carolina — to name but a few — all have Dracula ballets, but this is a trend that began with Aaron Copland's ballet *Grogh* in 1922 (revised 1935). This very odd (and, for Copland, rather uncharacteristic) work began as a response to F. W. Murnau's famous 1921 silent version of Dracula, *Nosferatu*. The story of the ballet, such as it is, was concocted for Copland by writer-director Harold Clurman, but it doesn't have anything to do with Stoker's novel or even with vampires. The general atmosphere, however, is assumed to have been derived from the expressionist mood of Murnau's adaptation. It begins with a cortege of Grogh's slaves. Grogh then performs magic on a corpse, which is reanimated. Then another corpse is reanimated — an opium-eater. The third corpse to be revived is a streetwalker whom Grogh unsuccessfully tries to embrace. Grogh then begins to hallucinate and kills the streetwalker. Everything grows dark and finally Grogh disappears as mysteriously as he appeared. One could well argue that the grotesque mood of the piece derives as much from Robert Wiene's *The Cabinet of Dr. Caligari* (1919) as from *Nosferatu*, and it also has some things in common with Stravinsky's *Petroushka*, which, with its story of an animated puppet and its unhappy love for a female doll, is also rather a macabre work. Grogh himself does, however, seem reminiscent of Max Schreck's seminal cabbage-eared vampire in Murnau's film and Copland's jazz-influenced score is certainly very grotesque, exploiting polytonality (i.e., two different keys playing simultaneously), advanced dissonance, and vibrant rhythms.

Finally, dance, the occult, Gothic horror and Hollywood made their most commercially successful partnership with Michael Jackson's *Thriller* music video, directed by John Landis in 1983, with its shimmying ranks of slickly choreographed zombies. Fresh from another film featuring partying ghouls (*The Monster Club,* directed by Roy Ward Baker in 1981), Vincent Price also lent his voice to the proceedings and even appeared at the end as a grimacing zombie himself. Death, it would appear, is quite a dirty dancer.

# Chapter Nine
## *Fairy Music*

Fairies are often said to be excellent musicians. As we have already seen, music has been regarded as the most metaphysical of the arts. E. T. A. Hoffmann went so far as to say that "music discloses to man an unknown realm, a world that has nothing in common with the external sensual world that surrounds him, a world in which he leaves behind him all definite feelings to surrender himself to an inexpressible longing."[1] Similarly, folklore suggests that fairy music can enchant those who hear it and make them forget everything about their human life. There are many folk tales that express the fairies' love of music. Thomas Keightley's celebrated compendium of fairy lore, *The Fairy Mythology* (1878), mentions how the effect of fairy music "seemed rather to be a thing divine than mortal,"[2] but it can also have somewhat less metaphysical consequences. Scandinavian fiddle players are wary of playing the "Elf-king's tune" because "as soon as it begins both old and young, and even inanimate objects, are impelled to dance, and the player cannot stop unless he can play the air backwards, or that some one comes behind him and cuts the strings of his fiddle."[3] Grieg's "Hall of the Mountain King" serves a similar function in its original context of Ibsen's *Peer Gynt*, but Grieg (1843–1907) hated composing it and, ironically, never rated it very highly. "I have also written something for the scene in the hall of the mountain king," he confessed in August 1874, "something that I literally can't stand to listen to because it absolutely reeks of cow pies, exaggerated Norwegian provincialism, and trollish self-sufficiency!"[4] No one who has heard it can forget it, but Norwegian troll music in general can also have an amnesiac effect. Keightley recounts the story of "The Girl at the Troll-Dance" who "spent, she thought, a few hours among the joyous hill-people."

> But when she came to the village she no longer found it the place she had left. All was changed; and when she entered the house in which she lived with her family, she learned that her father and mother had long been dead, and the house had come into the hand of strangers. She now perceived that for every hour that she

**162**                    **The Occult Arts of Music**

had among the Trolls, a year had elapsed in the external world. The effect on her mind was such that she lost her reason, which she never after recovered.[5]

So-called "Necks" are Danish river sprites who, again according to Keightley, sit on the water and play gold harps, "the harmony of which operates on all nature."[6] The "Strömkarl," who dwell rather more dramatically in waterfalls, are even more impressive musical geniuses, but if a human being wishes to learn the Strömkarl's musical arts, he must sacrifice a black lamb to him on a Thursday evening. Once taught, the aspirant will then be able to use this particular kind of fairy music to make trees dance and waterfalls stop.[7]

Related to these Scandinavian sprites are the legends of the Loreley. These beings inspired the famous poem by Heinrich Heine (1797–1856), which in turn formed the inspiration for numerous songs, one of the most dramatic of which is by Liszt. Heine's Loreley combs her golden hair,

> Und singt ein Lied dabei,
> Das hat eine wundersame,
> Gewaltge Melodei.
>
> (And sings a song the while.
> The song had a wondrous
> And powerful melody.)

Sailors who hear the music of the Loreley are in danger, however, as the seductive singing of the Loreley lures them to disaster on the rocks.

> Ich glaube, die Wellen vershlingen
> Am Ende Schiffer und Kahn,
> Und das hat mit irhem Singen
> Die Loreley getan.
>
> (I believe that in the end the waves
> Engulfed the boatman and his craft;
> And that was done
> By the Loreley and her singing.)

Wagner's Rheintöchter in the *Ring* cycle are also water sprites, and their singing indeed seduces the ugly dwarf Alberich, with catastrophic consequences. After the destruction of the world in *Götterdämmerung*, they return to drag him down beneath the overflowing waters of the Rhine and reclaim the ring of power he forged from the Rheingold at the beginning of the story. These daughters of the Rhine are also related to another water-sprite called Melusine, and not just mythologically speaking; there is also a musical connection because Wagner's leitmotif for the river Rhine in which they swim was indebted to the arpeggiated opening theme of Mendelssohn's 1833 *Ouver-*

## Nine. Fairy Music 163

*ture zum Märchen von der Schönen Melusine.* Mendelssohn (1809–1847) regarded this overture as the best thing he had composed, and the notoriously anti semitic Wagner obviously agreed, having no qualms about borrowing the Jewish Mendelssohn's watery motif for the *Ring* cycle.

Undine is another water sprite, and E. T. A. Hoffmann based his 1817 opera of that name on the story about her by Friedrich de la Motte Fouqué, which had appeared six years earlier. Carl Maria von Weber was very impressed by this opera, and in his essay on it, he claimed for it an honored place as one of the first truly German operas, by which he meant "an art work complete in itself, in which the partial contributions of the related and collaborating arts blend together, disappear, and, in disappearing, somehow form a new world."[8] Weber was here predicting the Wagnerian Gesamtkunstwerk, another parallel being the reference in Hoffmann's libretto to the concept of "Liebestod," which, as we have seen, would find its most famous expression in Wagner's *Tristan und Isolde.* For Weber, Hoffmann's music for this fairytale fully captured the magical quality of fairy music in folklore — "the great, mysterious secret of music, a secret to be felt but not to be expressed."[9]

Like the water sprite Rusalka, in the 1901 opera of that name by Dvořák (1841–1904), Undine falls in love with a human, but human and fairy worlds rarely mix without unfortunate consequences. An atmospheric operatic exploration of this particular problem is found in *The Immortal Hour* (1914), the opera by Rutland Boughton (1878–1960), which was based on a play by Fiona MacLeod, the *nom de plume* and alter-ego of William Sharp (1855–1905). Etain is a fairy who has drifted into the world of men, where Eohaidh, a human king, discovers her in a wood. (The role of Etain was created by Gwen Ffrangcon-Davies, who at the opposite end of her long theatrical career would appear in Hammer's supernatural thrillers *The Devil Rides Out* and *The Witches* [dir. Cyril Frankel, 1966].) Eohaidh marries Etain, but she is continually haunted by memories of her fairy past, particularly when she hears the opera's most famous melody, the "Faery Song":

> How beautiful they are, the lordly ones
> Who dwell in the hills, in the hollow hills.
> They have faces like flowers, and their breath is a wind
> That blows over summer meadows, filled with dewy clover.
> Their limbs are more white than the March wind.
> They laugh and are glad and are terrible.
> When their lances shake and glitter every green reed quivers.

Boughton based the melody for this song on a pentatonic scale (indeed, pentatonic elements inform the score as a whole), and this helps to create the

164 The Occult Arts of Music

required sense of strangeness, due to its contrast with the diatonic universe we all still take for granted as the musical norm. Boughton also accompanied the song with a harp, which is highly appropriate considering how often fairies have been associated with that instrument in folklore.

The harp is, indeed, a "magical" instrument in part due to such an association, but also because of its great antiquity. From ancient times, the harp has been credited with magical power. We learn in the myth of Amphion how Mercury gave Amphion a lyre with which Amphion was able to move stones and thus build the walls of the city of Thebes without having to struggle with the stones himself. The harp has consequently been frequently used by composers as a signifier of regression, transition and the supernatural. When Dvořák's Rusalka sings her melancholy lament to the moon, a harp again obliges with a regressively magical introduction to this most heart-achingly beautiful of questions: "Oh moon before you glide past me, tell me/Tell me, oh where does my loved one live?" Tchaikovsky included an extended harp cadenza in the introduction to his "Waltz of the Flowers" in *The Nutcracker* to suggest the magical atmosphere of dancing flowers. Even in the children's television series, *The Magic Roundabout* (dir. Serge Danot, and first screened in the 1960s), transitions from one part of the magic garden, in which the action is set, to another were always accompanied by a shimmering harp glissando.

Wagner similarly used harps to help suggest magical effects (i.e., the rainbow bridge that gives access to Valhalla at the end of *Das Rheingold*), to suggest regression into the timeless world of the Norns in *Götterdämmerung* or to indicate changes of scene (as, for example, in the transitional music that links the end of Siegfried's Funeral March in *Götterdämmerung* to Gutrune's monologue in the final scene of Act III). When Liszt orchestrated his *Mephisto Waltz No. 1* in 1861, it was almost a foregone conclusion that he would include a harp at the end of the piece, when the spell of Mephisto's fiddle is broken by the dawn. In Strindberg's fairy play *Swanwhite*, there is a magic harp that plays itself, which gave Sibelius (1865–1957) a good opportunity for exploiting the ethereal quality of the instrument when he wrote incidental music for the play in 1908.

The association of fairy mythology with harps was particularly the case in Wales. Keightley includes the story of "Rhys at the Fairy-Dance" in his *Fairy Mythology*, in which Rhys and Llewellyn, two servants, "heard the sound of many harps, and saw within a circle, about twenty feet across, great numbers of little people, of the size of children of three or four years old, dancing round and round."[10] This account has much in common with the rather more disturbing account of an incident related in a letter quoted by Keightley from "a pious young gentleman" on March 24, 1772, in which the correspondent

## Nine. Fairy Music

discusses how he and his sister, with two other girls, "playing at noon of a summer's day in a field,"

> saw a company of dancers, about seventy yards from them. Owing to the rapidity of their whirling motions, they could not count them, but guessed them at fifteen or sixteen. They were in red, like soldiers, with red handkerchiefs spotted with yellow, on their heads. As they were gazing and wondering at them, one of the dancers came running towards them. The children, in a fright, made for an adjacent stile. The girls got over, but the boy was near being caught, and on looking back when over, he saw a red man stretching his arms after him over the stile, which it would seem he had not the power to cross. When they came home to the house, which was close at hand, they gave the alarm, and people went out to search the fields, but could see nothing. The little man was very grim-looking, with a copper-coloured face. His running-pace was rather slow, but he took great strides for one of his size.[11]

This letter formed part of the Rev. Edward Jones' *A Relation of Apparitions of Spirits in the County of Monmouth and the Principality of Wales* (1780). Alan Garner, who also quotes this letter in his own anthology, *A Book of Goblins*, comments that Jones "appears to have been a gullible man, and he preserved some queer gossip,"[12] but the letter does have a ring of truth about it. The small people who chased the children are reminiscent of the fairy folk in Keightley's retelling of "The Two Fiddlers." One Christmas, the two fiddlers of the title decided to try their luck in Inverness, found lodgings there and were visited by a "venerable-looking grey-haired old man, who not only found no fault with [them], but actually offered to double their terms if they would go with him."

> They agreed, and he led them out of the town, and brought them to a very strange-looking dwelling which seemed to them to be very like a Shian. The money, however, and the entreaties of their guide induced them to enter it, and their musical talents were instantly put into requisition, and the dancing was such as in their lives they had never witnessed.
>
> When morning came they took their leave highly gratified with the liberal treatment they had received. It surprised them greatly to find that it was out of a hill and not a house that they issued, and when they came to the town, they could not recognise any place or person, every thing seemed so altered. While they and the townspeople were in mutual amazement, there came up a very old man, who on hearing their story, said: "You are then the two men who lodged with my great-grandfather."[13]

Once again, the fairies seduce men out of their own human world and transport them to a timeless "other" dimension. A similar thing happens in a story related by Robert Kirk in *The Secret Commonwealth of Elves, Fauns and Fairies* (1691) concerning one John Jenkinson:

## 166 The Occult Arts of Music

He sat down one morning to listen to a bird singing in a tree by a fairy hill. When the bird had finished its song, John got up, and he was very puzzled to find that the tree, which had been a sapling at the beginning of the song, was now a hollow stump. He turned back to his house, but his footsteps grew slower and slower, his shadow bent and trembling, and when he reached his doorstep, John Jenkinson crumbled into a thimbleful of black dust.[14]

In Celtic tradition, fairies were believed to have originally been angels, seduced into revolting against God by Satan and consequently cast down to earth. Indeed, Nick Willing's 1997 film, *Photographing Fairies,* to which we will be returning, also refers to this belief. Irish tradition concurs, though credits the fairies with having been "less guilty than the rest"—hence their earthly habitation.[15] Shetland Islanders believed that fairy rings were the result of fairies dancing to the music of which they are so very fond:

A Shetlander lying awake in bed before day one morning, heard the noise of a party of Trows [Trolls] passing by his door. They were preceded by a piper, who was playing away lustily. The man happened to have a good ear for music, so he picked up the tune he heard played, and used often after to repeat it for his friends under the name of a Fairy-tune.[16]

Kirk included a Welsh version of this story in his *Secret Commonwealth,* which tells of a shepherd who heard fairy music at twilight on Halloween:

The music gradually moulded itself in something like a tune, though it was a tune I had never heard before. And then there appeared at the mouth of the cave a figure well known to me by remembrance. It was dimly visible; but it was Iolo ap Hugh—I could see that at once.[17]

Iolo ap Hugh was a fiddler who had previously attempted to solve the riddle of the cave's mysterious music, but who was never seen again. The shepherd describes his reappearance in sinister terms: "He was capering madly to the music of his own fiddle, with a lantern dangling at his breast."

Suddenly, the moon cleared through the mist, and I saw poor Iolo for a single moment—oh, but it was clearly! His face was pale as marble, and his eyes stared deathfully. His head dangled loose and unjointed on his shoulders. His arms seemed to keep his fiddle stick in motion without his will.[18]

Like Keightley's Shetlander, Kirk's shepherd notated the (in fact unremark-able) music he heard and it is reproduced in Kirk's text.

Though well established in mythology, and of considerable interest to Renaissance writers such as Shakespeare and Edmund Spencer, fairies did not make a strong impression on Western art until the nineteenth century, when Romanticism's interest in mythology in general and the idea of "inspiration" in particular gained a hold on the aesthetic of the times. Purcell had composed music for a masque based on Shakespeare's *A Midsummer Night's Dream* (1692), but in the nineteenth century, fairies were treated as metaphors for that aspect of the psyche that gave access to other worlds, to altered states of consciousness and consequently to the fount and origin of human creativity. They represented that childlike instinct so lauded by Romantic theoreticians, rather than the logical concerns of the earlier age of reason. Consequently, Mozart wrote no fairy operas.

The first landmark of nineteenth-century fairy music was Hoffmann's *Undine*. In his essay on "The Poet and the Composer," Hoffmann expressed his ideas about what Romantic opera should be:

> A genuinely romantic opera is written only by a gifted and inspired poet, for only such a one can bring to life the wondrous phenomena of the spirit world; on his wings we are lifted over the chasm which otherwise divides us from it, and, grown accustomed to the strange country, we believe in the marvels which, as inevitable effects of the action of higher natures on our being, take place visibly and bring about all the strong, powerfully affecting situations which fill us, now with awe and horror, now with the highest bliss.[19]

Undine, like Rusalka, is a personification of nature's elemental power. She has many advantages over human beings, but is denied the most important thing of all — an immortal soul. "We should be far better off than you other human beings," she says to Huldbrand, the knight whom she eventually marries in Motte Fouqué's original story,

> —for human beings we consider ourselves, having the semblance and the body of humanity — but for one great disadvantage. We and those who resemble us in the other elements, we vanish and are gone, breath and body, so that no trace of us remains behind, and when you others on some future day shall wake to a purer life, we shall be what sand and smoke and winds and waves are made of. For no souls have we; It is the element that loves us, often, so long as we live, obeys us, when we die, turns us to dust; and we rejoice, without a peevish sigh, as do nightingales and little golden fishes and the other pretty children of nature. Yet all creatures desire to rise to higher things. So my father, who is a mighty prince of the waters in the Mediterranean Sea, desired that his daughter should in measure possess a soul, and in consequence should share many of the sufferings of those in whom souls are born. But one of us can only win a soul by the most intimate union in love with one of your race.[20]

Undine's longing for a soul can be interpreted as the longing of matter to understand itself — the basis, as we have seen, of Philip Pullman's *His Dark Materials* trilogy. The plight of Undine is, in a way, shared by the audience of Romantic operas, for, in Hoffmann's words, "in an opera the action of higher natures on our being must take place visibly, thus opening up before our eyes a romantic existence in which language, too, is raised to a higher power, or rather, is borrowed from that faraway country—from music, that is, from song—where action and situation themselves, vibrating in powerful harmonies, take hold of us and transport us the more forcefully."[21] Undine needs a soul to become "whole" and to be able to understand herself; humanity needs art to put it into contact with the world from which Undine comes— the world of instinct and intuition.

Undine, a child of the ocean kingdom, has been brought up by a fisherman and his wife, their own daughter having been lost at sea. Undine grows up and marries the knight Huldbrand, but the fisherman's real daughter, Bertalda, captures Huldbrand's heart. The heart broken Undine is drawn back to the ocean kingdom and the water spirits decide that Huldbrand must die. Undine appears at the marriage of the knight and Bertalda, and the former love Huldbrand felt for her rekindles in his heart:

> She kissed him with a heavenly kiss, but she released him not, she pressed him ever closer and closer to her, and wept as if she would weep away her soul. The tears flooded the eyes of the knight, and in a sweet agony of woe they so whelmed his bosom that at length they bore his breath away, and he sank back a corpse out of those lovely arms on to the cushions of the bed of rest.
>
> "I have wept him to death!" she said to a servant who met her in the antechamber, and through the midst of the terror-stricken retainers she glided slowly out into the fountain.[22]

Undine's soulless nature was captured once again in 1909 by Ravel in the first piece of his suite, *Gaspard de la Nuit,* where she appears in a more menacing manner in one of the most demanding pieces of piano music ever written. Ravel also uses the remote, "otherworldly" key of C-sharp major for this movement. A rapid tremolo effect in the right hand accompanies a languid melody in the left, eloquently paralleling Aloysius Bertrand's accompanying poem: "Ecoute!—Ecoute!—C'est moi, c'est Ondine qui frôle de ces gouttes d'eau les losanges sonores de ta fenêtre illuminée par les mornes rayons de la lune!" ("Listen! Listen! It's me, it's Ondine who brushes the diamond panes of your window by the dull light of the moon.")

Hoffmann's *Undine* was greatly admired by Carl Maria von Weber, "since," as he put it, "everything, as it stands there, is necessary exactly as it is and not otherwise."[23] His own response to the fairy world was based on a play by Christoph Martin Wieland (1733–1813), and it was composed for English audiences right at the end of Weber's life in 1826. The poster advertising the first production at London's Covent Garden lists the various scenes as "Oberon's Bower with a Distant View of England, and the adjacent Country on the Banks of the Tigris *By Sunset,*" the "INTERIOR of NAMOUNA's COTTAGE, VESTIBULE and TERRACE in the HAREM of the CALIPH overlooking the Tigris, GRAND BANQUETTING CHAMBER of HAROUN,

## Nine. Fairy Music

GARDENS of the PALACE, **PORT OF ASCALON,** RAVINE amongst the ROCKS of a DESOLATE ISLAND, The Haunt of Spirits of the Storm," "**Perforated Cavern on the Beach,** With the OCEAN — in a STORM — a CALM — by SUNSET," and so forth. As the list of scenery suggests, this concoction has little in common with Shakespeare's *A Midsummer Night's Dream,* which Wieland had earlier translated. Weber's librettist, James Robinson Planché, further adapted Wieland's play, which served Weber ill, but the disadvantages of the text notwithstanding, Weber composed some of the most ravishing fairy music ever written up to that time. As John Warrack points out, "Part of his genius as a composer was to make the timbre of instruments essential to the musical invention, rather than a colouring of it."[24] The overture, for example, begins with the evocative sound of horns, which, due to its association with the traditional hunting horn call and its connotation of distance (one call answering another), immediately transports us into that equally distant land of dreams and faeries. Weber's use of woodwinds and strings also led the way for Mendelssohn and Berlioz in their own fairy pieces.

Mendelssohn composed his overture to *A Midsummer Night's Dream* in 1826 and this set the standard for all the fairy music that followed. The opening four bars are a musical equivalent of "Once Upon a Time," with their harmonic "strangeness" (resulting from the juxtaposition of an implied E major chord which a B major chord, which then moves to A minor before returning to E major) creating a sense of magical remoteness. When intoned by ethereal wind instruments, as they are, the transition to the land of faery is complete. Mendelssohn used standard sonata form for the overture, and skillfully arranged its various sections to present the principle characters in the drama. The first subject of the succeeding exposition represents the fairies. *Leggiero,* high-pitched strings suggest their ability to fly, as well as their rapid movement, and many of the harmonies echo the traditional intervals of the horn call (third, fifth, sixth and vice versa). By referencing these sonorities, Mendelssohn exploits their deep-rooted connotations of distance and longing — distance due to the aforementioned reasons touched on with regard to Weber's *Oberon,* and longing due to the nostalgia they evoke for a past time. (Beethoven had similarly used the horn call in his "Les Adieux" sonata [1809 – 1810], in which he included the word "Le-be-wohl" ["Farewell"] under the opening three measures of the first movement. Horst Janowski also used horn calls in his 1965 instrumental hit, *A Walk in the Black Forest,* which helps explain its considerable popularity at the time.) Music associated with the Lovers, the "Rude Mechanicals" and the braying of Bottom as a donkey also forms part of Mendelssohn's mix, but the most significant element from our point of view is the opening of the overture.

Fairies also played a role in the early years of Wagner's career. In 1833, when he was only twenty, he composed his first opera, based on Carlo Gozzi play titled *La donna serpente* (*The Snake Woman*). The characteristic elements familiar from the legend of Undine are here. Ada, half fairy and half mortal, marries Arindal, King of Tramond. Anticipating Lohengrin's insistence that Elsa should never ask his name, Ada places the same condition on Arindal, but like Elsa, Arindal cannot restrain his curiosity, and Ada consequently disappears. The only way that Arindal can be reunited with her is to pass a series of tests. Arindal fails these, however, and Ada is turned to stone for a hundred years. The myth of Orpheus and Euridice also forms part of the story, as Arindal is able to bring Ada back to life by venturing into the underworld and reviving her with the power of music. Arindal and Ada are thereafter able to live happily ever after in the fairy kingdom. Unfortunately, the same cannot be said of Wagner's original manuscript, as it was later given to Adolf Hitler and was presumably destroyed in the Führer's Berlin bunker during the Second World War. Combining influences from Weber, Marschner and the *bel canto* style of Bellini, Wagner's filigree score for this work contrasts markedly with his later music, though, having said that, there are many indications of what would later flower in *Lohengrin*, and the opening bars of the overture even point the way to the luminous textures of *Parsifal*.

Rapidity and lightness of touch are another significant element in the musical depiction of fairies, not that Wagner's music for *Die Feen* really suggests the ethereal nature of his fairies, his concern being to be rather more philosophically weighty than fantastically weightless, but Mendelssohn again put rapidity and a *leggiero* quality to good use in the scherzo ("Allegro molto vivace") of his incidental music to *A Midsummer Night's Dream*, which he wrote some sixteen years after the overture. And in the celebrated Nocturne, horns are again exploited for their qualities of longing and distance, which in this context suggest the psychological distance of unconsciousness and sleep.

Berlioz was very relieved that Mendelssohn did not act on an observation Berlioz himself made when both men shared a riding excursion in the Roman Campagna. Berlioz pointed out that no composer had yet made a musical response to Mercutio's speech about Queen Mab, the queen of sleep, in Shakespeare's *Romeo and Juliet*. "For several years afterwards I dreaded hearing that he had used the subject," Berlioz confessed. "Had he done so it would have been impossible, or at any rate very unwise to make the double attempt."[25] The "Queen Mab" Scherzo, which opens the fourth part of Berlioz's *Roméo et Juliette* symphony (1839), takes Mendelssohn's fairy style to even more ethereal heights. The rapidity is there (a *prestissimo* scherzo in 3/8), but the orchestration is more clearly defined. Strings and woodwinds create the required filigree texture, often alternating with each other, with

## Nine. Fairy Music

171

plenty of *staccato* and *pizzicato* to suggest the gravity-defying nature of fairy-folk. Berlioz also exploits *acciaccatura* to suggest playfulness, along with string and harp harmonics to connote the supernatural element. Toward the end, antique cymbals in B and F add a further gossamer layer of charm, magic and weightlessness.

This exquisite masterpiece of orchestration was nonetheless equated with a noise reminiscent of "a badly oiled syringe"[26] by one of Berlioz's unsympathetic critics, which may have been due to a poor performance. Berlioz was well aware of the movement's technical difficulty. He himself described the effect he wanted to achieve in his memoirs:

"Queen Mab in her microscopic chariot, drawn at full gallop by her team of little atomies and driven by the murmuring gnat that buzzes and hovers on summer eves, danced her mad revels."[27]

As if this miraculous scherzo were not enough, Berlioz anticipated it in a recitative and scherzetto earlier in the symphony in which the choir and tenor alternate as they sing:

> Mab, la messagère
> Fluette et lègere!
> Elle a pour char une coque de noix
> Que l'ecureuil a façonnée
> On filé ses harnois.

(Mab, the light and agile messenger! Her chariot is a nutshell made by a squirrel, a spider's fingers wove her harness.)

Berlioz realized that there was no point in trying to "improve" on Shakespeare by setting his words to music, and so commissioned Emile Deschamps to provide paraphrases of the original text, more suitable for musical treatment.

*Lélio,* Berlioz's curious sequel to the *Symphonie fantastique,* contains a fantasy based on Shakespeare's *The Tempest,* a play with its own references to fairy music, controlled by the occult magician, Prospero. As his slave Caliban puts it:

> Be not afeard: the isle is full of noises,
> Sounds, and sweet airs, that give delight, and hurt not.
> Sometimes a thousand twangling instruments
> Will hum about mine ears; and sometimes voices,
> That, if I then had wak'd after long sleep,
> Will make me sleep again: and then, in dreaming,
> The clouds methought would open and show riches
> Ready to drop upon me; that, when I wak'd,
> I cried to dream again.[28]

172                    The Occult Arts of Music

Music plays a much larger role in this play than in any other by Shakespeare. Ariel invokes his magic by means of song. Ferdinand, who has been shipwrecked on Prospero's island, realizes that "This music crept by me upon the waters,/Allaying both their fury, and my passion,/With its sweet air."[29] There are masques, songs and stage directions that abound with musical instructions: "*Solemn and strange music; and PROSPERO above, invisible. Enter below several strange Shapes, bringing in a banquet*"[30] Alonso wonders, "What harmony is this? my good friends, hark!" to which Sebastian replies, "Marvellous sweet music!"—and visions of ethereal shapes are accompanied by "soft music" later in the scene.

The text of *The Tempest* is significantly shorter than other Shakespeare plays because of the important role music played in the original production, and it was the play's musical nature that obviously attracted Berlioz. His *Fantasie dramatique sur la Tempête* was completed in 1830 and suggests Ariel's voice at the beginning by employing the high-pitched, ethereal timbres of solo violins, clarinets, flutes, piccolos and, most unusually in an orchestral work of this period, figurations played by four hands on the piano. Berlioz, who could not play the piano, wrote very little for that instrument, and perhaps felt it to be a strange, "impossible" sound, suitable to summon fairy magic. Unfortunately, a real-life tempest accompanied the premiere. As Berlioz recalled in his memoirs, "A mighty cloudburst turned the streets into veritable rivers and lakes; all traffic, wheeled or on foot, became virtually impossible. During the whole of the first half of the evening, just as my own little Tempest was supposed to be raging, the Opéra was almost deserted."[31]

Almost a century later, in 1925–1926, Sibelius composed a complete suite of incidental music for *The Tempest*, a project that not only provided him with an opportunity to set all the various song texts but also gave him full rein to explore textures that suggest both Ariel's fairy nature and various natural phenomena, as seen in the stormy overture, the choral "Chorus of the Winds" with its harp accompaniment, and the music for the rainbow in Act IV.

Fairies gradually went out of fashion as the nineteenth century progressed, though, as we have seen, Tchaikovsky included them in his *Sleeping Beauty* ballet at the end of his life, and also created one of the most evocative musical characterizations of faery nature in *The Nutcracker*'s "Dance of the Sugar Plum Fairy" by scoring it for the then novel timbre of the celesta. Fairies regained a considerable amount of their lost territory in Maurice Maeterlinck's fairy play, *The Blue Bird* (1890), which was particularly popular in Edwardian England. Maeterlinck's story of two children in search of the Blue Bird of Happiness takes the characters to many supernatural locations populated with various kinds of fairy beings. When the play was mounted at the

## Nine. Fairy Music                                                173

Haymarket Theatre, London, in 1909, Norman O'Neill (1875–1934) was commissioned to write incidental music for the production. In those days before CDs and cast recordings, a suite of piano pieces from the orchestral score was published by Elkin, the publisher of O'Neill's student friend Cyril Scott (who, along with H. Balfour Gardiner, Percy Grainger and Roger Quilter, had formed part of the so-called "Frankfurt Group," all of them having studied there in their youth). The rest of O'Neill's score is sadly lost, but the remaining four dances give an impression of the delicate and nostalgic quality of the whole. The first dance, a waltz, describes the "Mist Maids" who live in the land of memory, wherein the two children discover the shades of their grandparents. The second dance is another slow waltz for Fire and Water, who inevitably compete with each other. Fire retreats to the fireplace and water sinks exhausted into the ground. The "Dance of the Stars," an *Allegretto grazioso* in 2/4, occurs in the Palace of Night, where, according to Maeterlinck's stage directions, "stars in the shape of beautiful girls, veiled in many-coloured radiancy, escape from their prison, disperse over the hall, and form graceful groups on the steps and round the columns. THE PERFUMES OF THE NIGHT, who are almost invisible, the WILL-O'-THE-WISPS, the Fireflies and the transparent DEW join them, while the SONG OF THE NIGHTINGALES streams from the cavern and floods the Palace of NIGHT."[32] The last dance, the "Dance of the Hours," is an *Andante* waltz, and it originally accompanied an early scene in the play when, by means of a magical diamond, the face of a clock is magically brought to life and smiles while the door of the pendulum case opens and the Hours pour out and dance to the music, "holding one another by the hand and laughing merrily."[33]

One might have thought that with the outbreak of the First World War, fairies and stories of the supernatural would have disappeared, but that wasn't the case at all. Arthur Machen's story "The Bowmen" (1914) famously gave birth to the legend of the Angels of Mons, who supposedly led British troops to heroic deeds on the battlefield; no doubt the very human need for a supernatural explanation of wartime chaos helped fuel this delusion. Similarly, Boughton's *The Immortal Hour* enjoyed unprecedented success in the 1920s. As Gwen Ffrangcon-Davies recalled, "It was a cult. People ... were so glad to see something of beauty and hope and removal from the grossly material world, into the world of 'the land of heart's desire,' 'the land of the ever-young,' the beauty: and the beauty of the music and the strangeness of the atmosphere after all the filth and the dreadfulness of those four years of misery and agony of the trenches in the war.... I've never been anywhere in the world but somebody hasn't come up and said, 'I saw *The Immortal Hour*. I shall never forget it.' It did have a magical effect on people."[34]

In 1928 there were more fairies in Stravinsky's reworking of music by

174                       The Occult Arts of Music

Tchaikovsky in his ballet *Le Baiser de la fée* (*The Fairy's Kiss*). In it, Stravinsky interpreted Hans Christian Andersen's tale of *The Snow Maiden* as an allegory of Tchaikovsky's own genius, as he explained in the conversation books compiled by Robert Craft: "The fairy's kiss on the heel of the child is also the muse marking Tchaikovsky at his birth — though the muse did not claim Tchaikovsky at his wedding, as she did the young man in the ballet, but at the height of his powers."[35]

Stravinsky regarded Tchaikovsky's strengths as being elegance and "a certain sense of humour,"[36] and these were the qualities he wanted to emphasize in the score, but he later realized that "even this Tchaikovsky was derided as a sentimental absurdity." Stravinsky aimed to cleanse the music of all that by means of his own orchestrations, and later observed that on hearing a concert of "the saccharine source material for that work, I almost succumbed to diabetes."[37]

Fairies, it now seemed, could only be taken seriously when they were stripped of those fantastic qualities that had made them so appealing in earlier times. They retreated from high art but found a welcome resting place in popular culture. Erich Wolfgang Korngold (1897–1957) arranged Mendelssohn's music for the Warner Brothers' production of *A Midsummer Night's Dream* (dir. William Dieterle and Max Reinhardt, 1935), in which the perhaps unlikely figure of Mickey Rooney played Puck. With its visual references to German Romantic artists such as Arnold Böcklin (1827–1901) and Hans Thoma (1839–1924), it was in many ways a last gasp of the venerable Romantic tradition that was being perverted before being stamped out by the Nazis. The film's spiraling choirs of diaphanous fairies and grotesque fairy musicians were really refugees, just as Korngold himself became shortly after having completed his work on this film. Walt Disney Studios also offered sanctuary to fairies who could no longer survive in the ironic climate of postwar Europe. From *Peter Pan* (dir. Clyde Geronimi and Wilfrid Jackson, 1953)to *Sleeping Beauty* (dir. Clyde Geronimi, 1959), the fairies that had populated nineteenth-century opera and ballet found a new home in the cinema, and the music to which they appeared was also derived from earlier models. Disney's Tinkerbell, for example, is accompanied in Oliver Wallace's score not only by her trail of stars but also by the indispensable fairy sounds of the flute, celesta, glockenspiel and (less often) harp. She also indulges in a short waltz with her own reflection on top of a hand mirror as Peter Pan searches for his shadow in the children's bedroom. The three good fairies of *Sleeping Beauty*, who take on rather housewifely personae, also require celestas and tuned percussion when using their magic wands. George Bruns' adaptation of Tchaikovsky's ballet also adds another layer of continuity with the past.

Howard Greenfield and Jack Keller's iconic theme music for the TV com-

## Nine. Fairy Music

edy series *Bewitched* (1964–1972) also exploits these essential timbres, for though not technically a fairy, Samantha the witch (played by Elizabeth Montgomery) shares many of the attributes of the three good fairies in Disney's *Sleeping Beauty.* Along with harps, celestas and the glockenspiel, the oscillating "magic" of the vibraphone also accompanies Samantha's various magical transformations in the opening animated sequence. Her classic nose-wiggling alternative to a magic wand was always accompanied by a xylophone.

Even as late as 1997, Simon Boswell's music for Nick Willing's *Photographing Fairies* exploits the traditional association of faery folk with harps, though flutes and rapid strings also play their part in his music. The film concerns the use of an hallucinogenic flower that causes whoever eats it to see fairy visions. Toby Stephens plays the skeptical, grief-stricken photographer, Charles Castle, who begins by debunking the infamous Cottingley fairy photographs, which at one time convinced Sir Arthur Conan Doyle, but the film ends with Castle so convinced of the reality of the fairies he has experienced and photographed that he willingly goes to his execution for murder in the firm conviction that he will be reunited with his lost wife in paradise. When we are first shown the Cottingley photographs during a meeting of the Theosophical Society (filmed, incidentally, in the suitably Gothic surroundings of Horace Walpole's Strawberry Hill), Simon Boswell's score begins their association with the harp, and thereafter the harp accompanies all the other "sightings." Boswell also references the first four notes of one of the most famous waltzes in Tchaikovsky's *Swan Lake* as the film's overall theme. *Swan Lake* is not, admittedly, a fairy ballet, but its story of enchantment and its generic connection with Tchaikovsky's two other fairy ballets make this an appropriate musical reference here.

In some ways *Photographing Fairies* could be compared with Michelangelo Antonioni's *Blow Up* (1966), as both films feature enlarging of photos to gain evidence of a mystery, and both films are also primarily concerned with the nature of illusion and reality. In *Photographing Fairies,* Charles Castle expands the shot of a child's eye, the surface of which reveals a reflection of the fairy she has purportedly been photographed watching. Is the fairy therefore "real"? The film allows for ambiguity on that question.

So fairies survived until the end of the twentieth century and, thanks to Philip Pullman's *His Dark Materials* trilogy, into the twenty-first as well.

# Chapter Ten

## *Satan Rocks: Popular Music and the Occult*

Robert Irwin's 1999 novel, *Satan Wants Me,* is set in London during the summer of 1967. It takes the form of a magical diary kept by the book's hero, Peter, who is a PhD student at the London School of Economics. While researching a thesis on "Inter-group dynamics and peer-group reinforcement on a North-London coven of sorcerers," he becomes involved with an occult organization called the Black Book Lodge. This is run by a certain Dr Felton, a pompous follower of Aleister Crowley, who pedantically corrects the diary he insists his young adept keep. Peter eventually discovers that the Lodge believes him to be the reincarnation of Crowley and wants him to get together with Dr. Felton's daughter, Maud, to create a magical child, along the lines described in Crowley's novel, *Moonchild.* The overall tone of the book is much more ironic than such a precis might suggest, however, and it is really only a pretext for Irwin's exploration of the role that permissiveness, popular culture and occultism played in the spirit of the times. The novel closes with a disillusioned epilogue that catches up with Peter in 1997, his student idealism long since a thing of the past, the Summer of Love a distant memory and Maud now dead. Peter realizes he is not the reincarnation of Crowley, but at least the delusion of his student years brought him together with Maud and made life more interesting, more optimistic, and more colorful. Since those heady days, he says,

> Everybody sold out. I lived through the years of the Great Betrayal and Sell-Out of the hippy dream. We were going to change things. We were going to set free the hearts and minds of our generation — and not just our generation....
>
> But we lost. The old bankers, generals, policemen and professors prevailed. And I am they. They, the men in suits, who every morning walk across Waterloo Bridge, heading for the City are no better than war criminals.[1]

Throughout the novel, Irwin also drenches the reader in the popular

## Ten. Satan Rocks     177

music of the period, which ranges from Alan Price's "Simon Smith and His Amazing Dancing Bear" and Jeff Beck's "Silver Lining" to the Rolling Stones' "Have You Seen Your Mother, Baby?," Jefferson Airplane's "White Rabbit," The Beatles' "Strawberry Fields," Pink Floyd's "Piper at the Gates of Dawn" and Procol Harum's "Whiter Shade of Pale." (The name "Procol Harum," incidentally, was adopted quite arbitrarily by the band after a friend's cat. Only later did they realize that if spelled "Procul Harem" it could, though in a grammatically incorrect sense, be interpreted as Latin for "beyond these things"—or, in the common parlance of the time, "far out," which would have given the group an unintended "occult" and groovy aura, fully in tune with the zeitgeist.)

*Satan Wants Me* is, in fact, a rather more convincing and realistic account of the life style Hammer bravely tried to evoke (three or four years too late) in Alan Gibson's *Dracula* A.D. *1972*, with its group of swinging middle-class hippies hanging out at the Cavern Club (Peter hangs out at Middle Earth) while listening to drug-drenched progressive rock. ("They were all zonked out when they recorded this," says Christopher Neame's devil-worshipper Johnny Alucard in the film. "Aren't they always?" languidly replies Marsha Hunt's Gaynor.) Peter, in *Satan Wants Me,* similarly confesses to "scoring four ampoules of methedrine, a couple of ampoules of amyl nitrate, half a dozen cubes of LSD, a tiny sachet of heroin and a couple of grams of dope."[2] Also like Peter, the teenagers of *Dracula* A.D. *1972* get involved with the occult — in their case, unwittingly assisting at Dracula's resurrection. There's even a party scene at the beginning of the movie with Stoneground's approximation of the sort of music to which Peter likes to groove. And in the movie, the bookshelves in the study of Peter Cushing's ultra-respectable academic vampire hunter, Lorrimer Van Helsing, are filled with the kind of books Peter would no doubt have borrowed from the library (though some of them weren't actually published in 1967). They include the Richard Wilhelm translation of *The I Ching,* a new edition and translation of *The Secret Grimoire of Turiel,* Colin Wilson's *The Occult* and Bernard Bromage's *The Occult Arts of Ancient Egypt.* As Stephanie Beacham's purple-trousered Jessica Van Helsing puts it, "You can buy that sort of stuff in any shady shop in Soho. They think it's all kinky." Precisely.

Dennis Wheatley himself also makes an appearance in Irwin's novel, though only via a letter he sends to the protagonist, couched in the manner of his famous disclaimer in *The Devil Rides Out,* in which he warns the reader of the "very real and concrete nature" of Satanism's dangers. ("What a wonderful come-on," is Peter's perceptive reaction to all that.)

Like many budding occultists, Peter is attracted to the black magic in Wheatley's sensationally lurid books, and he is quick to take in Hammer's film adaptation of *The Devil Rides Out* (though, in fact, this wasn't released until 1968). "I grooved on the film," Peter records, "especially Charles Gray being sleek and unctuous as the Satanist Mocata."[3] The Hammer film, despite its conservative and rather old-fashioned approach to the subject, was, with the possible exception of the occult scenes in *The Kiss of the Vampire*, the first British film to deal explicitly with Satanism, and thus owes its existence to the liberal mood generated in 1967. Roman Polanski's *Rosemary's Baby*, which was also released in 1968, reflected that mood even more, but distanced itself from the way horror films usually used music by having remarkably little of it. Christopher Komeda's main title theme is an ironic pastiche of a nursery rhyme, with its "la, la, la" lyrics providing an unnerving anticipation of what will happen at the end of the film when Rosemary is confronted with the devil-child she has spawned and rocks in its cradle. There is also an important cue for the scene in which the demon baby is conceived. Rosemary, suitably drugged, hallucinates in an appropriately 1960s manner, imagining she's nude on a yacht. Later, guilt-ridden Catholic that she is, she sees the Sistine Chapel ceiling, with God creating Adam. Soon, however, it is the Devil who helps create Rosemary's baby. She agrees to have her legs bound, to allow him easy access, so to speak, and all through this monstrous "dream sequence," which she eventually realizes is no dream at all, Komeda presents a two-note theme, which again echoes the opening notes of the *Dies Irae* chant. The film certainly needs music here, but otherwise Polanski keeps it very much in abeyance. While the film was being made, however, pop music was very much center-stage, and the previous year, when Ira Levin's novel was first published, it formed the soundtrack to the summer of love.

In June 1967, the Monterey International Pop Music Festival in California attracted some 90,000 people over its three-day span. Organized partly by John Phillips of Mamas and the Papas, it inaugurated the so-called Summer of Love, which continued with a gathering of 100,000 people at the Haight-Ashbury suburb of San Francisco. Phillips' song "San Francisco" was a rallying call (his detractors would call it a kind of Pied Piper seduction) to join in all the fun. However, Phillips also had connections with Charles Manson, who, in 1969, infamously organized the murder of Sharon Tate, Roman Polanski's wife. Phillips later claimed that he had narrowly avoided being another of Manson's victims, but Polanski convinced himself that Phillips had organized the whole thing in revenge for his own affair with Phillips' wife, Michelle. Polanski, as if enacting a scene from one of his own movies, held a kitchen knife to Phillips' neck in an attempt to force a confession from him. Such goings-on, combined with the shock impact of *Rosemary's Baby* and Phillips' drug addiction, fueled the retrospective conspiracy theory among the paranoid that Monterey had been some kind of Satanic convention.

## Ten. Satan Rocks

The Woodstock Music and Art Fair followed in August 1967, continuing the celebration of the alternative "hippie" lifestyle, which brought together pop and rock music, anti-commercialism, drugs, sexual liberation, political liberalism and all-around "creativity." As part of this psychedelic, drug-induced state of mind, an occult revival also burst out across the Western world, albeit mainly among young people, which drew much of its inspiration from an earlier occult revival that had its roots in the turn of the nineteenth century with organizations such as the Order of the Golden Dawn and the works of Aleister Crowley. As is well known now (but not, perhaps, when the album was first released), Crowley's face peers out of the background of Peter Blake and Jann Haworth's pop art cover for The Beatles' *Sgt. Pepper's Lonely Hearts Club Band*, which was released on June 1, 1967. Crowley had died twenty years earlier in 1947, though on December 1 rather than June 1, which is disappointing for conspiracy theorists who like to suggest that Sgt. Pepper was a cipher for Crowley, and who cite the opening line of the lyric about it having been twenty years to the day since Sergeant Pepper first taught them to play as evidence of this sinister alias.

Crowley features as one of the people The Beatles said "we like and admire,"[4] and he shares the psychedelic limelight with Karlheinz Stockhausen, Sigmund Freud, Carl Jung, Edgar Allan Poe, Oscar Wilde, and Aldous Huxley, all of whom formed a cohesive collection of pioneers into the unconscious and alternative states of mind, often combined with an interest in the occult. Apparently, John Lennon also wanted Hitler, Gandhi and Christ as part of the blend, in an effort, no doubt, to outrage as many people as possible. Poe and Oscar Wilde are obvious literary candidates for The Beatles' personal hall of fame, particularly Poe, with his death-obsessed mysticism and that line in "The Raven" that speaks of pouring over "many a quaint and curious volume of forgotten lore." Poe even proposed an explanation of the universe in his often impenetrable essay "Eureka" of 1848. Wilde also professed an interest in the occult, which *The Picture of Dorian Gray* reflects; his wife, Constance, even joined the Order of the Golden Dawn. But Crowley outstripped these literary luminaries with his notoriety and serious commitment to the study and practice of occultism.

Jung (1875–1961) likewise devoted much of his energy to occult investigation. His first publication was his MD dissertation concerning the psychiatric analysis of a medium. His complete works contain eight essays on the subject, including "On the Psychology and Pathology of So-Called Occult Phenomena," "On Spiritualistic Phenomena," "The Psychological Foundations of Belief in Spirits," "The Soul and Death" and "On Spooks: Heresy or Truth?" According to Jung's biographer, Richard Noll, Jung went much further than that in private and based his entire system on a foundation of late

180                    The Occult Arts of Music

nineteenth-century occultism and neo-paganism, ultimately coming to regard
himself as the Aryan Christ and consequently falsifying the results of his scientific research to fit this mystical self-image.[5] Freud distanced himself from
all that, but his theories were of obvious interest to the sexual aims of hippie
counter-culture. Stockhausen (1928–2007), the high priest of the musical
avant-garde, was also deeply interested in esoteric wisdom, believing himself
to be from another planet and his music to be therefore extra-terrestrial as
well.

As for Aldous Huxley, it was he, of course, who wrote about the mind-
expanding potential of Mescalin in *The Doors of Perception* (1954), the title
of which is derived from William Blake but which also inspired the name of
that archetypal 1960s rock group, The Doors, who were very much "Riders
on the Storm" of the 1960s. Jim Morrison, its lead singer, was certainly interested in the occult. The cover of the *Doors 13* album even shows a photo of
Morrison with a bust of Crowley. He married Patricia Kennealy-Morrison in
a Celtic pagan ceremony, and film interviews reveal that he really believed he
had been possessed by the spirits of two American Indians and had seen Satan
or a satyr. Drug use no doubt played a part in these visions, as did the occult
atmosphere of the time, but some people think more supernatural forces were
at work.

The *Sgt. Pepper* cover, then, does seem to reflect the general interest in
esoteric and psychological concerns of the music business in the 1960s, which
have subsequently fueled a host of Internet sites run by evangelical Christians,
Satanists and other obsessives, all keen in their various ways to prove that
Satan was genuinely being invoked by pop and rock music. The fact that the
Woodstock Festival was dubbed "An Aquarian Festival," giving rise to the
birth of the phrase "The Age of Aquarius," has been interpreted by them in
a negative light, as an indication that the age of Pisces was now over (Pisces,
due to the fish imagery of Jesus Christ, the fisher of men, represented the age
of Christianity). The drug-induced muddy chaos of Woodstock has also been
interpreted by such theorists as an inherently Satanic affair, the kind of event,
indeed, that Anthony Burgess depicted in his novel *Earthly Powers* (1980), in
which a crazed guru, Godfrey Manning, encourages a multitude of followers
to commit suicide in his name. Burgess based Manning on Jim Jones, who
presided over the Peoples' Temple Agricultural Project in Guyana. In 1978,
over 900 people died there of self-inflicted cyanide poisoning on Jones' orders,
but nothing of the sort happened at Woodstock. Tragically, two people did
die — one from an overdose, another from being run over by a tractor — but
Satan was not involved.

John Lennon and Paul McCartney have also been portrayed as practicing
Satanists. A photo of Ringo Starr and George Harrison, for example, shows

## Ten. Satan Rocks

The Beatles pose for at the premiere of *Yellow Submarine* (dir. George Dunning, 1968).

them holding up a picture of the Yellow Submarine, which features in the film of that name. Lennon and McCartney are in the foreground, Lennon gesturing what conspiracy theorists would claim to be a "Satanic" sign, but which is traditionally associated with warding *off* the evil eye, not attracting the Devil. (It is now, however, a badge of honor among fans of heavy metal music.) McCartney, meanwhile, signals an "OK" gesture, which some like to see as a secret signal of 666, the number of the Beast (Crowley's favorite self-appellation). However, Satanism in the 1960s was also a fashion item and did not necessarily signify anything more than just another way to *épater le bourgeoisie*. Having said that, Crowley did exert an influence on the ideas of The Beatles and many of the bands who followed in their wake. Lennon famously claimed that the whole idea of The Beatles was to "do what you want."[6] This was one of the central tenents of Crowley's Law of Thelema ("Do what thou wilt shall be the whole of the law"), but it is important to realize that Crowley's ideas were themselves deeply indebted to François Rabelais (1494–1553), who provided the blueprint for Crowleyan philosophy in his *Gargantua and Pantagruel*. In Rabelais' Abbey of Theleme (with an "e" rather than Crowley's "a"), the Thelemite monks anticipate the ideals of Crowley by three centuries:

> All their life was spent not in laws, statutes, or rules, but according to their own free will and pleasure. They rose out of their own beds when they thought good; they did eat, drink, labour, sleep, when they had a mind to it, and were disposed for it. None did awake them, none did offer to constrain them to eat, drink, nor do any other thing; for so had Gargantua established it. In all their rule and strictest tie of their order, there was but this one clause to be observed:
> DO WHAT THOU WILT[7]

Crowley's catchphrase, therefore, was nothing particularly new. And "doing your own thing" doesn't necessarily have to be Satanic, as right-wing apologists try to suggest. Crowley, after all, was not advocating irresponsible hedonism. As Simon Iff, his fictional detective, put it, "It is our right and duty ... to expand upon our own true centre, to pursue the exact orbit of our destiny."[8] This is what Crowley meant by "Do what thou wilt." In other words, "explore and be yourself." This message was doubtless delivered long before its time, for Edwardian society was very much against doing one's own thing, but this idea found fertile ground in the 1960s as part of a mix of ideas favoring individualism, sexual freedom and anti-establishment liberalism.

In an attempt to prove Lennon's apparently Satanic beliefs, the evangelical right also like to quote his provocative statement that "Christianity will go. It will vanish and shrink. I needn't argue about that. I'm right and I will be proved right.... We're more popular than Jesus."[9] This predictably outraged the Catholic Church, but the accusation of Satanism hardly squares with the lyrics of The Beatles' "All You Need Is Love" (1967). Attacking Christianity does not automatically make you a Satanist, but doubtless Crowley was an influence here, just as Friedrich Nietzsche possibly was as well. Like Lennon, Nietzsche also felt he had replaced Christianity with his own philosophy, and Lennon's comments here are really no more than a simplified version of what Nietzsche spent most of his writing career elucidating, which is summed up in *Ecce Homo* (1888):

> No one has yet felt *Christian* morality *beneath* him: that requires a height, a far-sightedness, a hitherto altogether unheard-of psychological profundity and abysmalness. Christian morality has hitherto been the Circe of all thinkers—they stood in its service.— Who before me has entered the caverns out of which the poisonous blight of this kind of ideal —*world-calumny!*— wells up? Who has even ventured to suspect *that* these caverns exist?[10]

Nietzsche, who regarded himself as the most musical of all philosophers, claimed that "blindness in the face of Christianity is the *crime par excellence*—

*the crime* against life."[11] For him, Christianity was the ultimate manifestation of negation and resentment *against* life. Christianity, in Nietzsche's eyes, rejected existence in the here and now in favor of the delayed gratification of a fantasy called "heaven." Lennon's song "Imagine" (1971) is, therefore, very much a Nietzschean text, advocating a world beyond religion and repressive morality, where life can be lived to the full, and happiness and fulfillment can be shared by everyone. In many ways this is also in full agreement with Crowley's agenda.

What is of far more interest than whether pop and rock musicians were or were not practicing Satanists is the question of how far occultism as an idea and a style influenced music at this time, and there is no question that it did. Led Zeppelin's guitarist, Jimmy Page, was a student of Crowley's works, and his success as a musician gave him the means to purchase not only a vast collection of Crowley first editions and ephemera but also Crowley's infamous Boleskine House on the shores of Loch Ness, where, unreliable rumor has it, he continued Crowley's magical work. It may have been a somewhat unnerving place to live, for it was there that Crowley worked on the ritual of Abra-Melin the Mage, which, if one is to believe Colin Wilson, one of Crowley's biographers, raised "shadowy shapes." Visitors were apparently seized with panic and fled. Crowley's coachman became an alcoholic and his housekeeper disappeared. A workman went mad and even tried to murder the magician.[12] Distracted from this time-consuming and complex occult operation by a former Golden Dawn magus, Samuel Liddell MacGregor Mathers, Crowley went off to Paris but failed to complete the ritual, leaving spirits to do their worst and ultimately to plague Crowley with bad luck during the rest of his life.

Whatever Jimmy Page got up to at Boleskine House, there is no doubt that he had "So mote be it. Do what thou wilt" inscribed on the vinyl of Led Zeppelin's third album, *Led Zeppelin III* (1970) — yet another reference to Crowley's Rabelaisian Law of Thelema. It is also alleged that when the vinyl disc of "Stairway to Heaven" (1971), Zeppelin's most celebrated hit, is played backward, it is possible to hear Satanic messages. Page additionally composed the soundtrack score (later discarded) for Kenneth Anger's occult film, *Lucifer Rising*, in 1972, the same year that the more sensationally occult *Dracula A.D. 1972* was released. Page's score was replaced with one by the convicted murderer and cohort of Charles Manson, Bobby Beausoleil, which was proudly advertised as the only soundtrack album "recorded entirely in prison." Both Page and Beausoleil also appeared in the film. Page had the smaller role, carrying a reproduction of the Stele of Ankh-ef-en-Khonsu (a.k.a. the Stele of Revealing), which inspired Crowley to create his new religion back in 1904.[13] Page holds the Stele while gazing up at a photo of Crowley's face, which is wreathed in a circular frame of laurel leaves. Marianne Faithfull, yet another

Poster for *Lucifer Rising* (dir. Kenneth Anger, 1972).

musical luminary of the period, also appeared as Lilith, resplendent in a magnificent Egyptian costume based on hieratic representations of Isis. Filmed on location in Egypt, she gestures to Donald Cammell's Osiris before we cut to shots of Anger himself in a coat of many colors; Anger eventually strips off, takes a bath and wakes up in a sarcophagus. Various other mystical happenings occur, the non-action alternating between Egypt and Stonehenge.

## Ten. Satan Rocks                                                                185

The weather gets mixed up too (lightning juxtaposed against the desert heat, etc.), before a pink UFO hovers over the ruins of ancient Egypt, presumably announcing the arrival of the new humanity and the age of Horus. Hammer's *Dracula A.D. 1972* and *The Devil Rides Out* used similar imagery to rather more compelling narrative effect, but the reputation and provenance of Anger's film was always more important than the film itself.

Chris Jagger, younger brother of Mick, also appeared in *Lucifer Rising* but had his part drastically cut. He nonetheless still features as the "Man in the Yellow Tunic." Chris went on to act in six more films (including a part in the Joan Collins vehicle, *The Stud* [dir. Quentin Master, 1978], and also made eight record albums of his own, but he was always overshadowed by his much more famous brother, the lead singer of the Rolling Stones. The Stones, actively promoted as the rough-and-ready alternative to the originally squeaky clean Fab Four, were similarly interested in Crowley, and much has been made of the killing of Meredith Hunter at the Altamont Music Festival in 1969 during a Stones performance. It is often claimed that the murder of Hunter took place during a rendition of the song "Sympathy for the Devil," and countless turgid conspiracy theories, linking the event with the CIA, British military intelligence and international occult networks, have thrived on the tragic events of that day. In fact, the killing, which was committed by a member of the local Hell's Angels, who had been hired to police security, took place during a different number that was performed some time after "Sympathy for the Devil" (which, it is true, had been interrupted by scuffles). If one bothers to read the lyrics of "Sympathy for the Devil," however, it is fairly obvious that the title is ironic: The Devil has been around for a long time — since the time of Christ, in fact. He was there at the time of Rasputin and during the two world wars. He was present at the killing of President Kennedy, which wasn't entirely his fault. It was everyone. He is in each one of us. No one is entirely good. Cops are partly criminals, and saints are partly sinners. The song is hardly a paean to his Satanic Majesty, but rather a recognition of a sad fact of life, and in its own way rather Nietzschean in the sense that the Devil is, like the title of Nietzsche's third book, *Human, All Too Human*. Indeed, in one line the Devil says he needs restraint. However, none of that stopped the Stones from calling the album from which the song came *Their Satanic Majesties Request* (1967).

"Sympathy for the Devil" strangely prophesied Meredith Hunter's murder, but simultaneously invested the tragedy with more Satanic significance than it truly had. The reality was much more prosaic. Drug-fueled as the audience was, anything could have happened. What did happen was that Hunter pulled a gun and seemed to be aiming it at Jagger. He was swiftly stabbed by a Hell's Angel and died soon after. Chaos, rather than conspiracy, would seem to have prevailed, but with Hunter's death, the optimism and liberation of the 1960s died as well. The Summer of Love was over, but the influence of occultism on popular music was far from dead.

Looking back over the schedules of British TV during the early 1970s, it is intriguing to realize how many shows for both adults and children alike were inspired by the interest in occultism that the period inspired. Two good examples of such mainstream programs were *Zodiac* (1974) and *Ace of Wands* (1970–1972), both produced by ITV's Thames Television.

In the former, Anouska Hempel starred as an astrologer who assisted Anton Rodgers in solving crimes. *Ace of Wands* took a similar approach, though it was made specifically for children. Each episode began with overt occult imagery that today might be considered inappropriate by many perhaps overly protective parents. A magic circle enclosing a pentagram and five-pointed Seal of Solomon is formed and then replaced by a pair of eyes (belonging to Michael Mackenzie, who performed the leading role). These are then adorned with various hippie/mystical symbols, which would not have been out of place on the painted faces of fans at Woodstock or Monterey: snakes, a starry sky, and two more seals of Solomon, one on each cheek of the implied face. Then, Mackenzie's face is revealed in full (rather like the heads of the various Dr. Whos in their respective time tunnel title sequences) and the actor's hand makes a magical pass over the screen, revealing the torso of Mackenzie in a hieratic pose. Accompanying all this was the iconic theme song composed by Andy Brown, who soon after joined Status Quo. The song, which was released as a single at the time, is another kind of occult incantation, appropriate for a show in which a magician with psychic powers solves crimes and mysteries. With its nonsense rhyming lyrics, it evokes the psychedelic occult revival of the 1960s but from within the overall context of the musical incantation of old. The repetition of the tune and its repeating acoustic guitar riff generates in this "occult" context a more specifically incantatory connotation, and the appearance of a wordless female vocal with the instrumental break at one point adds another signification of vaguely creepy mysticism here.

A similar approach was taken by Dudley Simpson in his rather frightening title music for Thames Television's science fiction series for children, *The Tomorrow People* (1973–1979). Though not strictly speaking an occult series, it nonetheless included aspects of the occult, such as telepathy, telekinesis and other psychic powers. Another product very much of its time, Simpson's mix of electric and acoustic instruments featured guitar riff that echoed the effect of Andy Brown's *Ace of Wands*, and the show's premise of a superior form of humanity gave birth to the phrase "homo superior," which also found its way into David Bowie's song "Oh! You Pretty Things." That song, from

## Ten. Satan Rocks     187

Bowie's 1971 *Hunky Dory* album, predated the first transmission of *The Tomorrow People* because he had been shown a draft script by the series' creator, Roger Price, who, at the time, was producing another show Bowie was involved with. Bowie appropriated the phrase and released his album before *The Tomorrow People* aired. Like "Quicksand" on the same album, "Oh! You Pretty Things" was also influenced by Crowley and Nietzsche, anticipating, as it does, the emergence of some kind of *Übermensch* — a man who, in Nietzsche's terms, has overcome his limitations, or, in Crowley's, a human who has become a man-god, that ultimate aim of occultists through the ages. One might also detect the influence of Sir Edward Bulwer-Lytton (later Lord Lytton, 1803–1873), considering Bowie's reference to "a coming race" (the title of Bulwer-Lytton's only science fiction novel of 1871). Also, John Wyndham's *The Midwich Cuckoos* (1957) might have inspired the song's reference to strangers who have come to stay, and who are now going to replace homo sapiens, which have outgrown their usefulness.

*Zodiac* and *Ace of Wands* were both examples of "soft" occult entertainment, but heavy metal bands had other ideas. In 1970, a Birmingham-based group called Earth released a track called "Black Sabbath" and, on the strength of its success, renamed themselves after the song. Satanism now became fashionable, but not much more than that.

"The Wizard" followed, which was about exorcism rather than devil worship, but there were evidently no wizards around as Black Sabbath's lead singer, Ozzy Osborne, eventually damaged his brain with drugs and alcohol. However, the band certainly performed Satanic rituals on stage. The song "Mr. Crowley" asks what went on in The Great Beast's head? A very good question indeed, and one that suggests Ozzy Osborne is a student of Crowley himself, but like Iron Maiden (with their "Number of the Beast") and Marilyn Manson's reference to the Abbey of Thelema and 666 in "Misery Machine" (1994), how much these gestures reflect a commitment to occult philosophy, or even a serious interest in figures such as Crowley, is debatable.

David Bowie's interest in Crowley is well informed. "Quicksand" from the *Hunky Dory* album (1971) is a rather more reflective response to the history of twentieth-century occultism and to Crowley's ideas in general. This song includes a reference to the Golden Dawn, and also to Crowley's support of Hitler and Crowley's habit of biting his scarlet women on the lips — the so-called "serpent's kiss," which Bowie refers to as kissing the fang of a viper. Whatever meaning life may or may not have, death will enlighten us. Alive, we are merely mortals, but perhaps mortals with the potential to become gods. Such a song reflects an intellectual engagement with Crowley's ideas, though the ultimate "message" suggests a rather more Schopenhaurian nihilism. Don't fool yourself with beliefs seems to sum up what Bowie is saying here.

# The Occult Arts of Music

Rock music now uses Crowley's image as a convenient shorthand for teenage rebellion without really bothering to think about what Crowley was saying. The 1980s goth band Stiff Kittens, for example, released "Happy Now" in 1986 with its reiterated claim that they have made an art of desecrating the sanctuaries (presumably of the orthodox), and how this breaks their hearts. "Contempt" is of the same vintage, and both singles were adorned with photographs of (or graphics based on) Crowley, whose aura elevated both songs to a rather higher plane than they might otherwise have attained. Taking their cue from James Bernard's orgy music in *The Devil Rides Out,* much heavy metal and goth music depends on hypnotic and usually very rapid percussion, repeated sequences and a general mood of relentlessness; however, Bernard's score helped raise the Goat of Mendes in the film, which is more than can be said of the Stiff Kittens, despite their Christian detractors.

The catchphrases and visual clichés of Satanism are now so closely associated with heavy metal that bands of this persuasion can hardly afford to do without them if they are to be accepted into the head-banging brotherhood. So, in Megadeath's "The Conjuring" (1986) the band boasts of being the Devil's advocate — a salesman for Satan, on the lookout for souls to drag to hell. Metallica's "Jump in the Fire" (1984) urges its audience to do just that, and in "The Prince" (1989) they confess to a disdain for heaven, preferring instead to sell their souls to the devil, which is hardly a very original proposal, and one that Marlowe's Faust took up with rather more interesting results. Iron Maiden's "Number of the Beast" (1982) is an obvious candidate for nervous Christian hysteria, even though the band's bass guitarist, Steve Harris, claimed it was inspired by a nightmare he had after watching *Damien: Omen II.*[14] Iron Maiden's lead singer, Bruce Dickinson, however, has a more scholarly interest in Crowley, and wrote the screenplay of *Chemical Wedding* (dir. Julian Doyle, 2008), in which Simon Callow plays Crowley, reincarnated in the body of a Cambridge academic. (The opening scene has the magnificent John Shrapnel as the original Crowley, and one rather wishes that Dickinson's aim of filming a historical drama had not been thwarted by lack of funds: hence the rewrite in a cheaper, contemporary setting, and the plot device of reincarnation by means of a virtual reality machine.) Dickinson also wrote the main title song and performed a small cameo role in the film.[15]

Finally (though by no means exhaustively), that other British heavy metal band, Warfare, combined elements of Hammer horror films (both soundtrack dialogue and James Bernard's music) with their own material in the 1991 album appropriately titled *Hammer Horror.* In "Prince of Darkness" a reference is made to *Dracula* A.D. *1972* and *The Satanic Rites of Dracula* by sampling Christopher Lee's lines as Dracula. From the former comes Dracula's imperious response to Johnny Alucard's demand that he be given the power of immortality: "You demand! I have returned to destroy the house of Van Helsing forever, the older through the young. You and your line have been chosen." From the latter comes "I have chosen four messengers of death, four horsemen of my created apocalypse, four carriers of the plague who will infect their miserable brethren. You, Van Helsing, are now one of the four." Given the distinctly occult context of these late-vintage Hammer Draculas, Warfare's reference to them not only qualifies the album as an example of occult-inspired heavy metal but also creates an intriguing conflation of styles.

# *Epilogue*

Though there may, in fact, be nothing to believe in, the act of belief itself is what generates culture, even if that is only self-belief. To create anything at all is a leap of faith — a challenge to disaster, an invocation to whatever gods one chooses that the project will come to fruition and one's aims will not be swallowed up by the blank sheet of paper before the work is complete. None of the ideas explored in this book are any stranger than those of orthodox religion, the beliefs of which, though normalized through social convention and the power of a particular dominant ideology, are nonetheless truly strange. As Christopher Lee's Lord Summerisle in Robin Hardy's *The Wicker Man* observes, belief in pagan parthenogenesis is no different from the idea of an immaculate conception.

"Sir, have these children never heard of Jesus Christ?" asks Edward Woodward's Christian copper, Sgt. Howie.

"Himself the son of a virgin, impregnated, I believe, by a ghost," Summerisle replies, much to Howie's indignation.

The masterpieces based on what champions of reason would regard as nonsense are, of course, manifold. Bach's *St. Matthew Passion* and Scriabin's *Prometheus* are both responses to an irrational belief system and simultaneously supremely human. This, I think, is what evangelists of reason like Richard Dawkins overlook in their passionate rejection of the irrational component of the human psyche. In their understandable desire to make logic and rational inquiry paramount in human affairs, they forget that a great deal of the world's art comes from a very different place, and that the world would be not only poorer but also unendurable without it. Just as humanity is equally responsible for the Sistine Chapel and Auschwitz, so too are reason and irrationality equal and opposite sides of human experience, and they cannot be severed from each other without a profound sense of loss and dislocation. Would not humanity get along with itself better by accepting and assimilating its contradictions, painful though they may be, rather than raging with Caliban at its own reflection or pretending that it was something it never has been and never will be?

And anyway, who is to say what truth is? The answer to that question is, unfortunately, the fundamentalists among us, but in the realm of metaphysical speculation there are only questions. And atheism is quite as much of a belief system as that of a convinced Christian or a follower of Madame Blavatsky. There is no way to prove the nonexistence of God and vice versa. One might consequently advocate the advantages of not believing in anything, which, in other words, is to keep an open mind. Having said that, there is no doubt that belief generates meaning, and meaning generates purpose, just as ideas generate convictions for which people unfortunately have been willing to die (and kill). George Bernard Shaw's Don Juan in *Man and Superman* was convinced that "you can make any of these cowards brave by simply putting an idea into his head."[1] But ideas and convictions also create art.

Absurd though some of occultism's ideas may be, a completely rational world would be an intolerably boring place. The occult revival of the 1960s may have been fake, but the ideals of that time were better than the hard-nosed materialism to which Peter and his friends sold out at the end of Robert Irwin's *Satan Wants Me*. It was a similar imbalance that the nineteenth-century occult revival attempted to redress. Perhaps we need the irrational in order to remain sane. This problem was articulated by W. H. Auden in his 1969 poem "Moon Landing," an indignant response to the Apollo space mission, which was a phallic triumph for male reason at the expense of "female" emotional intuition and imagination. What do we gain in emotional terms from knowing that the moon is a lump of sterile rock? Was it not more emotionally nourishing when it was a goddess? The tragedy is that we can no longer regard the moon in those terms. Reason has ripped up that beautifully irrational conception. It is the use of nature as a metaphorical articulation of human emotion that the worldview of the ultra-rationalist would have us turn our backs upon.

Edgar Allan Poe attempted a reconciliation of science and poetry in his ultimately pantheistic essay "Eureka," in which he approached cosmology from a purely intuitive perspective. His principal theme is this: "*In the Original Unity of the First Thing lies the Secondary Cause of all Things, with the Germ of their Inevitable Annihilation.*"[2] In other words, everything, in all its diversity, is part of the original simple *Oneness*: "*All* phænomena are referable to one, or to the other, or to both combined."[3] We are part of "a novel Universe swelling into existence, and then subsiding into nothingness, at every throb of the Heart Divine.... And now — this Heart Divine — what is it? *It is our own.*"[4] According to Poe, since we are each a part of the universe, our *intuitions* are all we need to understand it. "Poetry and Truth are one.... Man cannot long or widely err, if he suffer himself to be guided by his poetical, which I have maintained to be his truthful ... instinct."[5]

Such an emphasis on intuitive understanding has certain things in common with Richard Cavendish's definition of magic. Usually regarded as a primitive form of science, Cavendish argues that magic is actually more like poetry, and it is in this poetic quality that the real value of occultism lies— the power of analogy, metaphor and association: "The whole magical universe itself is built on the analogy of the human body.... Magic makes use of all kinds of associations and connections between things whose relationship to each other is a matter of similarities and parallels.... This is a natural parallel for the mind to draw."[6] Perhaps both scientific truth and great art spring from the same intuitive place. Great art has been inspired by some profoundly irrational ideas, just as Poe anticipated some of the major ideas of particle physics, such as the Big Bang theory—not to mention Einstein's theory of relativity—in his purely intuitive essay. No one denies the value and benefit of reason, but if we drain the irrational marshlands of poetry and intuition to make way for a dubious utopia of pure reason, we might lose more than we bargained for.

*Quod superius est sicut quod inferius et quod inferius est sicut quod superius ad perpetranda miracula rei unius.*[7]

# Chapter Notes

## PREFACE

1. Percy Bysshe Shelley, *The Complete Poetical Works of Percy Bysshe Shelley*, ed. Thomas Hutchinson (London: Oxford University Press, 1905), 531 ("Hymn to Intellectual Beauty," lns. 49–52).

2. Percy Bysshe Shelley, *Essays and Letters by Percy Bysshe Shelley*, ed. Ernest Rhys (London: Walter Scott, 1886), 27 ("A Defence of Poetry").

3. Mary Shelley, *Frankenstein* (London: J. M. Dent, 1941), 30.

4. Johann Wolfgang von Goethe, *Faust Part One*, trans. David Luke (Oxford: Oxford University Press, 1987), 17.

## CHAPTER ONE

1. Iamblichus, *Life of Pythagoras or Pythagoric Life*, trans. Thomas Taylor (London: J. M. Watkins, 1818), 63.

2. Eduard Hanslick, *The Beautiful in Music*, trans. Gustav Cohen (London: Novello, 1891), 21.

3. Ibid., 63.

4. R. Larry Todd, ed., *Mendelssohn Studies* (Cambridge: Cambridge University Press, 1992), 217 (letter from Felix Mendelssohn to Eduard Devrient, March 10, 1832).

5. Oliver Strunk, ed., *Source Readings in Music History*, vol. 1, *Antiquity and the Middle Ages* (London: Faber and Faber, 1981), 16 (Aristotle's "Politics").

6. Roy Howat, *Debussy in Proportion: A Musical Analysis* (Cambridge: Cambridge University Press, 1983), 171.

7. Arthur Honegger, *I Am a Composer* (London: Faber and Faber, 1966), 78.

8. Jacques Barzun, *Pleasures of Music* (London: Michael Joseph, 1954), 268 (Heine, "Letters on the French Stage," 1837).

9. Thomas Mann, *Doctor Faustus*, trans. H. T. Lowe-Porter (London: Secker & Warburg, 1949), 131.

10. Francis Barrett, *The Magus or Celestial Intelligencer* (London: Lackington, Allen, 1801), Book I, 99–100.

11. Plato, *The Essential Plato*, trans. Benjamin Jowett (London: Softback Preview, 1999), 409–19 (*The Republic*).

12. Ibid., 411.

13. Ibid., 632–33 (*Phaedo*).

14. Strunk, *Source Readings in Music History*, vol. 1, *Antiquity and the Middle Ages*, 84.

15. Ibid., 85.

16. Jens Peter Jacobsen, *Niels Lynne*, trans. Tiina Nunnally (Harmondsworth: Penguin, 2006), 16.

17. Marcus Hearn and Alan Barnes, *The Hammer Story* (London: Titan Books, 1997), 111.

18. Henry Cornelius Agrippa, *Three Books of Occult Philosophy or Magic*, Book II, trans. J. French (London: Gregory Moule, 1651), chapter 25. www.esotericarchives.com

19. Mircea Eliade, *From Primitives to Zen: A Thematic Sourcebook of the History of Religions* (London: Collins, 1979), 98.

20. Ibid., 96.

21. Joscelyn Godwin, ed., *Music, Mysticism and Magic* (London: Routledge & Kegan Paul, 1986), 261.

22. Jill Purce in conversation with the author for the BBC Radio 3 documentary, *Cosmic Harmonies*, produced by Andrew Kurowski, July 29, 2001.

23. Thomas Mann, *Pro and Contra Wagner*, trans. Allan Blunden (London: Faber and

**193**

Faber, 1985), 108 ("The Sorrows and Grandeur of Richard Wagner").

24. Richard Wagner, *My Life*, trans. Andrew Grey (Cambridge: Cambridge University Press, 1987), 36.

25. Plato, *The Essential Plato*, 288–89 (*The Republic*).

26. Marsilio Ficino, *Three Books on Life*, trans. Carol Kaske and John Clark (Binghamton, NY: Medieval & Renaissance Texts & Studies in conjunction with the Renaissance Society of America, 1989), 361.

27. Agrippa, *Three Books of Occult Philosophy or Magic*, Book II, chapter 26.

28. Jamie James, *The Music of the Spheres: Music, Science and the Natural Order of the Universe* (London: Abacus, 1993), 104.

29. William Shakespeare, *The Oxford Shakespeare*, ed. W. J. Craig (Oxford: Oxford University Press, 1905), 672 (*Troilus and Cressida*, Act I, scene 3, lns. 83–110).

30. Ibid., 214 (*The Merchant of Venice*, Act V, scene 1, lns. 83–88).

31. H. P. Lovecraft, *The Fiction* (New York: Barnes and Noble, 2008), 178 ("The Music of Erich Zann").

32. Ibid., 179.

33. James, *The Music of the Spheres*, 133.

34. Sir Thomas Browne, *Religio Medici* (Oxford, Oxford University Press, 1831), 135.

35. John Milton, *Paradise Lost* (London: Frederick Warne, 1896), 220 (Book V, lns. 618–27).

36. James D'Angelo in *Cosmic Harmonies*, BBC Radio 3 documentary, written and presented by David Huckvale (produced by Andrew Kurowski), July 29, 2001.

37. Stanley Sadie, ed., *The New Grove Dictionary of Music and Musicians*, vol. 8 (London: Macmillan, 1998), 584.

38. Hans Kayser, *The Textbook of Harmonics*, trans. Ariel and Joscelyn Godwin, http://www.sacredscience.com/archive/Kayser.htm.

## CHAPTER TWO

1. Philippa Faulks and Robert L.D. Cooper, *The Masonic Magician: The Life and Death of Count Cagliostro and His Egyptian Rite* (London: Watkins, 2008), 141.

2. Jean Terrasson, *The Life of Sethos: Taken from the Private Memoirs of the Ancient Egyptians*, vol. 1, trans. Thomas Lediard (London: J. Walthoe, 1732), i.

3. Faulks and Cooper, *The Masonic Magician*, 42.

4. Erik Hornung, *The Secret Lore of Egypt: Its Impact on the West*, trans. David Lorton (Ithaca, NY: Cornell University Press, 2002), 125.

5. M. F. M. van den Berk, *The Magic Flute: Die Zauberflöte: An Alchemical Allegory* (Leiden and Boston: Brill Academic Publications, 2004).

6. Colin Wilson, *The Occult* (London: Granada, 1973), 139.

7. Terrasson, *The Life of Sethos*, 18.

8. Ibid., 164.

9. Ibid., 155.

10. Wolfgang Amadeus Mozart, *The Magic Flute*, ed. Nicholas John (London: John Calder, 1980), 118–20 (Act II, scene 28).

11. Terrasson, *The Life of Sethos*, 158.

12. Mozart, *The Magic Flute* (English National Opera Guide 3) , 118–20 (Act II, scene 28).

13. Jacques Chailley, *The Magic Flute — Masonic Opera*, trans. Herbert Weinstock (New York: Alfred A. Knopf, 1971), 86.

14. Ibid., 89.

15. Ibid., 94–96.

16. Alexander Wheelock Tayer, *Tayer's Life of Beethoven*, ed. Elliot Forbes, trans. H. E. Krehbiel (Princeton, NJ: Princeton University Press, 1970), 802.

17. Maynard Solomon, *Late Beethoven* (Berkeley and Los Angeles: University of California Press, 2003), 146.

18. Tayer, *Tayer's Life of Beethoven*, 481.

19. Ibid., 482.

20. Ibid., 481.

21. Ibid., 440.

22. Solomon, *Late Beethoven*, 150.

23. Brian S. Gaona, "Through the Lens of Freemasonry: The Influence of Ancient Esoteric Thought on Beethoven's Late Works," http://www.ideals.illinois.edu/bitstream/handle/2142/16092/1_Gaona_Brian.pdf.

24. William Kinderman, *The String Quartets of Beethoven* (Urbana: University of Illinois Press, 2006), 198 (entry no. 94d of Beethoven's Tagebuch).

25. Mann, *Doctor Faustus*, 55.

26. William Kinderman, *Beethoven* (Berkeley and Los Angeles: University of California Press, 1995), 276.

27. Mark Evan Bonds, ed., *Beethoven Forum*, vol. 8 (Lincoln & London: University of Nebraska Press, 2000), 108 (Maynard Solomon quoted).

28. Marion M. Scott, *Beethoven* (London: Dent, 1974), 272.

## Notes—Chapter Three

29. Ibid., 274.
30. Ibid., 273.
31. Juan Mascaró, trans., *The Bhagavad Gita* (Harmondsworth: Penguin, 1962), 80.
32. Scott, *Beethoven*, 273.
33. Anthony Burgess, *You've Had Your Time: Being the Second Part of the Confessions of Anthony Burgess* (London: Heinemann, 1990), 60.
34. Ibid., 245.
35. Ibid., 60.
36. Ibid., 61.
37. Mann, *Doctor Faustus*, 46–47.
38. Burgess, *You've Had Your Time*, 246.

### CHAPTER THREE

1. Johann Peter Eckermann and Frédéric Soret, *Conversation of Goethe with Eckermann and Soret*, trans. John Oxenford (London: G. Bell, 1883), 527.
2. Arthur Schopenhauer, *The World as Will and Representation*, vol. 1, trans. E. F. J. Payne (New York: Dover, 1969), 257.
3. Nicolay Rimsky-Korsakov, *My Musical Life*, ed. Carl van Vechten, trans. Judah A. Joffe (London: Eulenburg, 1974), 400.
4. Eckermann and Soret, *Conversation of Goethe with Eckermann and Soret*, 526.
5. Ibid., 111.
6. Eero Tarasti, *Myth and Music* (Helsinki, Finland: Suomen Musiikkitieteellinen Seura, 1978), 111.
7. Eckermann and Soret, *Conversation of Goethe with Eckermann and Soret*, 525.
8. Cyril Scott, *Music — Its Secret Influence Throughout the Ages* (Wellingborough, UK: Aquarian, 1976), 142.
9. Ibid.
10. Erik Levi, *Music in the Third Reich* (Basingstoke, UK: Macmillan, 1994), 121.
11. Tarasti, *Myth and Music*, 113.
12. Faubion Bowers, *The New Scriabin: Enigma and Answers* (Newton Abbot, UK: David & Charles, 1974), 180.
13. Ibid., 181.
14. Ibid., 121.
15. Richard Cavendish, *The Black Arts* (New York: Perigree, 1983), 5.
16. Bowers, *The New Scriabin*, 116.
17. Shelley, *The Complete Poetical Works*, 268 (*Prometheus Unbound*).
18. Tarasti, *Myth and Music*, 108.
19. Ibid., 110.
20. J. K. Huysmans, *Là-bas (Lower Depths)* (London: Dedalus, 1986), 40.

21. E. T. A. Hoffmann, *Tales of Hoffmann*, ed. Christopher Lazare (New York: A. A. Wyn, 1946), 104 ("Don Juan").
22. Tarasti, *Myth and Music*, 112.
23. Gaston Leroux, *The Phantom of the Opera* (London: Michael O'Mara, 1987), 198.
24. Anthony Burgess, *The Devil's Mode* (London: Vintage, 1990), 98 ("1889 and the Devil's Mode").
25. Ferdinand Gregorovius, *The Roman Journals, 1852–1874*, trans. G. W. Hamilton (London: G. Bell, 1911), 230.
26. George Du Maurier, *Novels of George Du Maurier: Trilby, The Martians, Peter Ibbetson* (London: Pilot Press/Peter Davies, 1947), 226.
27. Ibid., 448–49.
28. George Moore, *Evelyn Innes* (London: T. Fisher Unwin, 1898), 73.
29. John Sugden, *Paganini* (London: Omnibus, 1980), 134.
30. Ibid., 54.
31. Fred Mustard Stewart, *The Mephisto Waltz* (London: Michael Joseph, 1969), 24.
32. John Meade Falkner, *The Lost Stradivarius*, London: Hesperus, 2006, pp. 121–122.
33. Ibid., p. 126.
34. Ibid., pp. 22–23.
35. Ibid., pp. 72.
36. Ibid., p. 112.
37. Ibid., p. 100.
38. H. Douglas Thomson, ed., *The Mystery Book* (London: Odhams, 1934), 1006 (Sax Rohmer's "Tchériapin").
39. Ibid., 1002.
40. Ibid.
41. Ibid., 1006–7.
42. Ibid., 1019.
43. The story is recorded by Joseph Jérôme Lalande in *Voyage d'un Français en Italie* (1769).
44. Helena Petrovna Blavatsky, *Nightmare Tales*, www.theosociety.org/pasadena/nightmar/night-9.htm ("The Ensouled Violin").
45. Roger Nicols, ed., *Ravel Remembered* (London: Faber and Faber, 1987), 50.
46. Mann, *Doctor Faustus*, 486–87.
47. For more information regarding Paul Glass' score for *To the Devil a Daughter ...*, see David Huckvale, *Hammer Film Scores and the Musical Avant Garde* (Jefferson, NC: McFarland, 2008), chapter 10.

## CHAPTER FOUR

1. Schopenhauer, *The World as Will and Representation*, vol. 1, 261.
2. Ibid., 258.
3. Ibid., 411.
4. Arthur Schopenhauer, *Essays and Aphorisms*, trans. R. J. Hollingdale (Harmondsworth: Penguin, 1970), 48.
5. Wolfgang Osthoff, *Richard Wagner's Buddha Project "Die Sieger" ("The Victors")* (Zurich: Museum Rietberg, 1996), 13–14.
6. Alan Walker, *Hans von Bülow: A Life and Times* (Oxford: Oxford University Press, 2009), 112ff.
7. Richard Wagner, *Selected Letters of Richard Wagner*, ed. Barry Millington, trans. Stewart Spencer (London: Dent, 1987), 321–22 (letter to Hans von Bülow, October 26, 1854).
8. Richard Wagner, "Wagner programme notes (3) — Prelude to *Tristan und Isolde*," *Wagner: The Journal of the London Wagner Society* 11, no. 3 (August 1990), 112.
9. Ibid., 113.
10. Schopenhauer, *The World as Will and Representation*, vol. 1, 411–12.
11. Friedrich Nietzsche, *The Birth of Tragedy and the Wagner Case*, trans. Walter Kaufmann (New York: Random House, 1967), 176 ("The Wagner Case").
12. Robert W. Gutman, *Richard Wagner: The Man, His Mind, and His Music* (New York: Time-Life Records Special Edition, 1972), 431.
13. Richard Wagner, *Religion and Art*, trans. William Ashton Ellis (Lincoln and London: University of Nebraska Press, 1994), 238 ("Know Thyself").
14. Ibid., 274.
15. Gutman, *Richard Wagner*, 427.
16. See Paul Lawrence Rose, *Wagner — Race and Revolution* (London: Faber and Faber, 1992), and Marc A. Weiner, *Richard Wagner and the Anti-Semitic Imagination* (Lincoln and London: University of Nebraska Press, 1995).
17. Helena Petrovna Blavatsky, *The Secret Doctrine*, vol. 2 (Los Angeles: The Theosophy Co., 1982), (Facsimile Edition), 200.
18. Ibid., 195.
19. Wagner, *Religion and Art*, 238 ("Religion and Art").
20. Ibid., 241–42.
21. Ibid., 225.
22. Ibid., 233.
23. Max Heindel, *The Rosicrucian Cosmo-Conception* (Oceanside, CA: Rosicrucian Fellowship, 1911), 290.
24. Ibid., 304.
25. Ibid., 306.
26. Ibid., 314–15.
27. Max Heindel, *Mysteries of the Great Operas* (Oceanside, CA: Rosicrucian Fellowship, 1921), 130.
28. Ibid., 150.
29. Ibid., 153–54.
30. Ibid., 161.
31. Ibid., 163.
32. Ibid., 83.
33. Ibid., 118–19.
34. Ibid., 66.
35. Ibid., 151.
36. Richard Wagner, *Parsifal* (English National Opera Guide 34), ed. Nicholas John (London: John Calder, 1986), 90 (Gurnemanz's narration, Act I).
37. Wagner, *Selected Letters of Richard Wagner*, 457 (letter to Mathilde Wesendonck, May 30, 1859).
38. Ibid., 458–59 (letter to Mathilde Wesendonck, May 30, 1859).
39. Wolfram von Eschenbach, *Parzival*, trans. A. T. Hatto (Harmondsworth: Penguin, 1980), 239.
40. C. G. Jung, *Psychology and Alchemy*, trans. R. F. C. Hull (London: Routledge & Kegan Paul, 1980), 313ff.
41. Richard Wagner, *The Artwork of the Future*, trans. William Ashton Ellis (Lincoln and London: University of Nebraska Press, 1993), 346–47 ("A Communication to My Friends").
42. Richard Wagner, "Wagner's programme notes (3) — Prelude ('The Holy Grail')," *Wagner: The Journal of the London Wagner Society* 11, no. 3 (August 1990), 110.
43. Wagner, *Selected Letters of Richard Wagner*, 869 (letter to Carl Friedrich Glasenapp, June 25, 1977).
44. Schopenhauer, *The World as Will and Representation*, vol. 1, 382.
45. Wagner, *Religion and Art*, 213 ("Religion and Art").
46. James, *The Music of the Spheres*, 217.
47. Rudolf Steiner, *Goethe's World View*, trans. William Lindeman (New York: Mercury Press, 1985), 77.
48. James, *The Music of the Spheres*, 219.
49. Rudolf Steiner, *Four Mystery Dramas*, trans. Ruth and Hans Pusch (North Vancouver, BC: Steiner Book Centre, 1973), 74–75 (*The Soul's Probation*).

## Notes—Chapter Five

50. James, *The Music of the Spheres*, 219.

51. Honoré de Balzac, *Seraphita* (Champaign, IL: Standard Publications, 2007), 113.

52. Ibid., 127.

53. James, *The Music of the Spheres*, 224.

54. John Covach, "Schoenberg and the Occult: Some Reflections on the 'Musical Idea,'" www.ibiblio.org/johncovach/asoccult.htm.

55. Joan Peyser, *Boulez: Composer, Conductor, Enigma* (London: Cassell, 1977), 26.

56. James, *The Music of the Spheres*, 218.

57. Balzac, *Seraphita*, 85.

58. Feruccio Busoni, *Letters to His Wife*, trans. Rosamund Ley, http://www.rodoni.ch/busoni/bibliotechina/letteregerdaEN/gerdaEN1.html (letter of July 21–22, 1902).

59. Joseph Henry Auner, *A Schoenberg Reader: Documents of a Life* (New Haven: Yale University Press, 2003), 75 (Arnold Schoenberg's letter to Busconi, August 24, 1909)..

60. Ferruccio Busoni, *A Sketch of a New Esthetic of Music*, trans. Th. Baker (New York: Schirmer, 1911), 13.

61. Ibid., 36.

62. James, *The Music of the Spheres*, 223.

63. Michael Hall, *Leaving Home: A Conducted Tour of Twentieth-Century Music with Simon Rattle* (London: Faber and Faber, 1996), 64–65.

64. Arnold Schoenberg, *Theory of Harmony*, trans. Roy E. Carter (London: Faber and Faber, 1978), 431–32.

65. Rudolf Steiner, *The Way of Initiation; or, How to Attain Knowledge of the Higher Worlds* (London: Theosophical Publishing Society, 1912), 66.

66. C. W. Leadbeater and Annie Besant, *Thought-Forms*, www.gutenberg.org/files/16269/16269-h/16269-h.htm.

67. Emanuel Swedenborg, *Arcana Coelestia*, vol. 1, trans. John Clowes (West Chester, PA: Swedenborg Foundation, 2009), 154.

68. See Ingo Cornils, ed., *A Companion to the Works of Hermann Hesse* (Rochester, NY: Camden House, 2009), 139 ("*Klingsors letzer Sommer* and the Transformations of Crisis" by Ralph Freedman).

69. Modris Eksteins, *Rites of Spring: The Great War and the Birth of the Modern Age* (London: Papermac, 2000), 82.

70. Wassily Kandinsky, *Concerning the Spiritual in Art*, trans. Michael T. H. Sadler, www.gutenberg.org/cache/epub/5321/pg5321/html (introduction to part 1).

71. Ibid., from part 2.

72. Ibid., from part 5.

## Chapter Five

1. See John Harrison, *Synaesthesia: The Strangest Thing* (Oxford: Oxford University Press, 2001), 123.

2. Cyril Scott, *The Philosophy of Modernism — Its Connection with Music* (London: Waverley, 1910), 116.

3. Joscelyn Godwin, *Music and the Occult: French Musical Philosophies, 1750–1950* (Rochester, NY: University of Rochester Press, 1995), 13.

4. Ibid., 15.

5. Ibid., 159.

6. Ibid.

7. Ibid., 104.

8. Balzac, *Seraphita*, 76.

9. Ella Adelia Fletcher, *The Law of the Rhythmic Breath: Teaching the Generation, Conservation and Control of the Vital Force* (New York: R. F. Fenno, 1908), 284–85.

10. Ibid., 285.

11. E. T. A. Hoffmann, *E. T. A. Hoffmann's Musical Writings: Kreisleriana, the Poem and the Composer, Music Criticisms*, ed. David Chartlon, trans. Martyn Clarke (Cambridge: Cambridge University Press, 2003), 164 ("Johannes Kreisler's Certificate of Apprenticeship").

12. Ibid., 105.

13. J. K. Huysmans, *À Rebours (Against the Grain)* (London: Fortune Press, 1946), 111.

14. Simon Morrison, *Russian Opera and the Symbolist Movement* (Berkeley/Los Angeles/London: University of California Press, 2002), 199.

15. Richard Wagner, letter to Theodor Uhlig, September 20, 1850, http://www.-bayreuther-festspiele.de/documents/a_rough_theatre_of_planks_and_beams_built_according_to_this_plan_of_mine_338.html.

16. Hagen Biesantz and Arne Klingborg, *The Goetheanum: Rudolf Steiner's Architectural Impulse* (London: Rudolf Steiner Press, 1979), 46.

17. Bowers, *The New Scriabin*, 191.

18. Roy Prendergast, *Film Music: A Neglected Art* (New York: W. W. Norton, 1977), 196–98.

19. Aldous Huxley, *The Doors of Perception and Heaven and Hell* (Harmondsworth: Penguin, 1959), 25.

## Chapter Six

1. Bowers, *The New Scriabin*, 53.
2. Ibid., 181.
3. Ibid., 60.
4. Alexander Scriabin, *Complete Works for Piano* ("Préludes I") (Budapest: Könemann Music, 1997), concluding remarks.
5. Bowers, *The New Scriabin*, 108.
6. Faubion Bowers, *Scriabin: A Biography*, vol. 2 (Tokyo: Kodansha International, 1969), 134.
7. Ibid., 112.
8. Bowers, *The New Scriabin*, 111.
9. Ibid., 112.
10. Bowers, *Scriabin: A Biography*, 135.
11. Bowers, *The New Scriabin*, 122.
12. Helena Petrovna Blavatsky, *The Secret Doctrine*, vol. 3 (Cambridge: Cambridge University Press, 2011), 509.
13. Ibid., 483.
14. Bowers, *The New Scriabin*, 82.
15. Ibid., 108.
16. Ibid., 125–26.
17. Ibid., 193.
18. Shelley, *The Complete Poetical Works*, 208 (*Prometheus Unbound*, lns. 31–36).
19. Bowers, *Scriabin: A Biography*, 135.
20. The asteroid is called 6549Skryabin.
21. Shelley, *Essays and Letters*, 26–27.
22. Hugh Macdonald, *Skryabin* (Oxford: Oxford University Press, 1978), 44.
23. Alexander Pasternak, *A Vanished Present*, trans. Ann Pasternak-Slater (Oxford: Oxford University Press, 1984), 73.
24. Helena Petrovna Blavatsky, *Studies in Occultism* (The Dennis Wheatley Library of the Occult) (London: Sphere, 1974), 8 (Dennis Wheatley's introduction).
25. Bowers, *The New Scriabin*, 95.
26. Osbert Sitwell, *Great Morning* (London: Macmillan, 1948), 238.
27. Ibid.
28. Bowers, *The New Scriabin*, 95.
29. Raymond Head, "Astrology and Modernism in 'The Planets,'" http://raymondhead.com/planets, 3.
30. Fred Gettings, *Secret Symbolism in Occult Art* (New York: Harmony Books, 1987), 18–19.
31. Imogen Holst, *Gustav Holst* (London: Oxford University Press, 1938), 34–35.
32. Robert Hitchens, *The Garden of Allah*, http://www.gutenberg.org/files/3637/3637-h/3637-h.htm (chapter 4).
33. Ibid. (chapter 6).
34. Ibid. (chapter 8).
35. Ibid.
36. Ibid. (chapter 10).
37. Ibid. (chapter 30).
38. Holst, *Gustav Holst*, 31.
39. Ibid., 139–40.
40. Scott, *Music — Its Secret Influence Throughout the Ages*, 152–53.
41. Ibid., 203.
42. Ibid., 204.
43. Cyril Scott, *The Initiate: Some Impressions of a Great Soul* (London: Routledge & Kegan Paul, 1920), xi.
44. Stephen Banfield, *Gerald Finzi* (London: Faber and Faber, 1997), 28.
45. Stephen Lloyd, *H. Balfour Gardiner* (Cambridge: Cambridge University Press, 1984), 14.
46. Malcolm MacDonald, *John Foulds and His Music: An Introduction* (New York: Pro/Am Music Resources, 1989), 15.
47. Ibid., 22.
48. Ibid., 40.
49. Ibid.
50. Ibid., 46–47.
51. Ibid., 45.
52. Robert Delevoy, *Symbolists and Symbolism* (London: Macmillan, 1982), 90.
53. Robert Orledge, *Debussy and the Theatre* (Cambridge: Cambridge University Press, 1982), 265–66.
54. Ibid., 124.
55. Ibid., 128.
56. Ibid., 126.
57. Edward Lockspeiser, *Debussy: His Life and Mind*, vol. 2, *1902–1918* (London: Cassell, 1965), 273.
58. Orledge, *Debussy and the Theatre*, 127.
59. Ibid., 356.
60. Lockspeiser, *Debussy: His Life and Mind*, vol. 2, *1902–1918*, 277.

## Chapter Seven

1. Cavendish, *The Black Arts*, 253.
2. Dante Alighieri, *The Divine Comedy*, trans. Rev. Henry F. Cary (New York: Thomas Y. Crowell, 1897), 77 (*Inferno*, Canto IX , lns. 24–25).
3. Johann Wolfgang von Goethe, *Goethe's Faust*, trans. John Anster (London: Routledge, 1883), 96 ("The Second Part of Goethe's Faust").
4. See Christian Schubart, *Ideen zu einer Aesthetik der Tonkunst* (Vienna: Degen, 1806).

## Notes—Chapters Eight, Nine · 199

5. Ibid.

6. Christopher Hogwood, *Handel* (London: Thames and Hudson, 1984), 64.

7. Hector Berlioz, *The Memoirs of Hector Berlioz*, trans. and ed. David Cairns (London: Sphere, 1990), 50.

8. Hector Berlioz, *Evenings in the Orchestra*, trans. C. R. Fortescue (Harmondsworth: Penguin, 1963), 77–78.

9. Wagner, *My Life*, 13.

10. Alexandre Dumas, *The Count of Monte Cristo* (London: Routledge, n.d.), 388.

11. Ibid.

12. Wagner, *Selected Letters of Richard Wagner*, 222 (letter to Franz Liszt, April 18, 1851).

13. Christopher Lee, *Tall, Dark and Gruesome — An Autobiography* (London: Gollancz, 1997), 184.

14. Gutman, *Richard Wagner*, 427.

15. Bram Stoker, *The Annotated Dracula*, ed. Leonard Wolf (London: New English Library, 1976), 20–22.

16. Ibid., 251–52.

17. Mann, *Pro and Contra Wagner*, 129.

18. Wagner, *Parsifal* (English National Opera Guide No. 34), 114 (Act II).

19. Stoker, *The Annotated Dracula*, 39–40.

20. Cyril Scott, *Bone of Contention* (London: Aquarian, 1969), 188–89.

21. Simon Morrison, *Russian Opera and the Symbolist Movement* (Berkeley/Los Angeles/London: University of California Press, 2002), 244.

22. Ibid., 280.

23. Ibid., 282.

24. Michael Kennedy, *Britain (The Dent Master Musicians)* (London: Dent, 1993), 64.

### Chapter Eight

1. E. T. A. Hoffmann, *The Nutcracker and The Golden Pot* (New York: Dover, 1993), 72.

2. David Brown, *Tchaikovsky: The Years of Fame, 1878–1893* (London: Gollancz, 1992), 341.

3. Romola Nijinsky, *Nijinsky* (London: Sphere, 1970), 93–94.

4. Richard Buckle, *Diaghilev* (London: Weidenfeld, 1995), 150.

5. Lee, *Tall, Dark and Gruesome*, 187.

6. Nijinsky, *Nijinsky*, 77.

7. Ann Radcliffe, *The Romance of the Forest*, ed. Chloe Chard (Oxford: Oxford University Press, 1986), 15.

### Chapter Nine

1. Oliver Strunk, ed., *Source Readings in Music History*, vol. 5, *The Romantic Era* (London: Faber and Faber, 1981), 35–36.

2. Thomas Keightley, *The Fairy Mythology* (London: G. Bell, 1878), 49.

3. Ibid., 79.

4. Finn Benestad and Dag Schjelderup-Ebbe, *Edvard Grieg: The Man and the Artist*, trans. William H. Halverson and Leland B. Satern (Gloucester: Alan Sutton, 1988), 185.

5. Keightley, *The Fairy Mythology*, 125.

6. Ibid., 149.

7. Ibid., 152.

8. Strunk, *Source Readings in Music History*, vol. 5, *The Romantic Era*, 63.

9. Ibid., 64.

10. Keightley, *The Fairy Mythology*, 145–46.

11. Ibid., 414.

12. Alan Garner, *A Book of Goblins* (Harmondsworth: Penguin, 1972), 219.

13. Keightley, *The Fairy Mythology*, 387–88.

14. Garner, *A Book of Goblins*, 93.

15. Keightley, *The Fairy Mythology*, 363.

16. Ibid., 165.

17. Garner, *A Book of Goblins*, 94.

18. Ibid.

19. Strunk, *Source Readings in Music History*, vol. 5, *The Romantic Era*, 48.

20. Freidrich de la Motte Fouqué, *Undine: A Tale*, trans. Edmund Gosse (London: Sidgwick & Jackson, 1912), 105–6.

21. Strunk, *Source Readings in Music History*, vol. 5, *The Romantic Era*, 48–49.

22. Motte Fouqué, *Undine: A Tale*, 201–2.

23. Strunk, *Source Readings in Music History*, vol. 5, *The Romantic Era*, 66.

24. Jane Martineau, ed., *Victorian Fairy Painting* (London: Merrell Holberton, 1997), 34 ("Fairy Painting" by John Warrack).

25. Berlioz, *The Memoirs of Hector Berlioz*, 122.

26. Ibid., 197.

27. Ibid., 254.

28. William Shakespeare, *Shakespeare — Complete Works*, ed. W. J. Craig (Oxford: Oxford University Press, 1905), 14 (*The Tempest*, Act III, scene 3, lns. 147–55).

29. Ibid., 6 (*The Tempest*, Act I, scene 2, lns. 389–91).

30. Ibid. (*The Tempest*, Act II, scene 3).

31. Berlioz, *The Memoirs of Hector Berlioz*, 86.

32. Maurice Maeterlinck, *The Blue Bird: A Fairy Play in Six Acts*, trans. Alexander Teixeira de Mattos (London: Methuen, 1929), 108.

33. Ibid., 33.

34. Gwen Ffrangcon-Davies interviewed on film by Susan Gau in *A Life in the Theatre* (1983).

35. Igor Stravinsky and Robert Craft, *Expositions and Developments* (London: Faber and Faber, 1981), 83.

36. Ibid.

37. Igor Stravinsky and Robert Craft, *Dialogues* (London: Faber and Faber, 1982), 27.

## CHAPTER TEN

1. Robert Irwin, *Satan Wants Me* (Sawtry: Dedalus, 1999), 317.

2. Ibid., 221.

3. Ibid., 54.

4. *Hit Parade* magazine, October 1976, 14.

5. See Richard Noll, *The Aryan Christ: The Secret Life of Carl Gustav Jung* (London: Macmillan, 1997).

6. John Lennon and Yoko Ono, *The Playboy Interviews with John Lennon and Yoko Ono: The Complete Texts Plus Unpublished Conversations and Lennon's Song-by-Song Analysis of His Music* (New York: Putnam, 1981), 61.

7. François Rabelais, *The Works of Rabelais* (London: Chatto and Windus, 1875), 113.

8. Aleister Crowley, *The Simon Iff Stories & Other Works*, ed. William Breeze (Ware, UK: Wordsworth, 2012), 52 ("The Artistic Temperament").

9. *San Francisco Chronicle*, April 13, 1966, 26.

10. Friedrich Nietzsche, *Ecce Homo*, trans. R. J. Hollingdale (Harmondsworth: Penguin, 1979), 131.

11. Ibid.

12. Colin Wilson, *Aleister Crowley: The Nature of the Beast* (Wellingborough, UK: Aquarian Press, 1987), 53.

13. See David Huckvale, *Ancient Egypt in the Popular Imagination: Building a Fantasy in Film, Literature, Music and Art* (Jefferson, NC: McFarland, 2012), 99–100.

14. Mick Wall, *Iron Maiden: Run to the Hills — The Authorized Biography* (London: Sanctuary, 2004), 224.

15. See Huckvale, *Ancient Egypt in the Popular Imagination*, 87–88.

## EPILOGUE

1. George Bernard Shaw, *The Complete Plays of Bernard Shaw* (London: Odhams Press, 1950), 377 (*Man and Superman*).

2. Edgar Allan Poe, *The Science Fiction of Edgar Allan Poe*, ed. Harold Beaver (Harmondsworth: Penguin, 1976), 211.

3. Ibid., 233.

4. Ibid., 307.

5. Ibid., 300.

6. Cavendish, *The Black Arts*, 21.

7. "That which is above is like that which is below and that which is below is like that which is above, to achieve the wonders of the one thing." This is the famous inscription on the Emerald Table of Hermes Trimegistus. See Cavendish, *The Black Arts*, 12.

# Bibliography

Agrippa, Henry Cornelius. *Three Books of Occult Philosophy or Magic.* Book II. Translated by J. French. London: Gregory Moule, 1651.

Alighieri, Dante. *The Divine Comedy.* Translated by Rev. Henry F. Cary. New York: Thomas Y. Crowell, 1897.

Arnim, Bettina von, and Johann Wolfgang von Goethe. *Goethe's Correspondence with a Child.* Boston: Ticknor and Fields, 1861.

Balzac, Honoré de. *Seraphita.* Champaign, IL: Standard Publications, 2007.

Banfield, Stephen. *Gerald Finzi.* London: Faber and Faber, 1997.

Barrett, Francis. *The Magus or Celestial Intelligencer.* London: Lackington, Allen, 1801.

Barzun, Jacques. *Pleasures of Music.* London: Michael Joseph, 1954.

Benestad, Finn, and Dag Schjelderup-Ebbe. *Edvard Grieg: The Man and the Artist.* Translated by William H. Halverson and Leland B. Satern. Gloucester: Alan Sutton, 1988.

Berlioz, Hector. *Evenings in the Orchestra.* Translated by C. R. Fortescue. Harmondsworth: Penguin, 1963.

_____. *The Memoirs of Hector Berlioz.* Translated and edited by David Cairns. London: Sphere, 1990.

_____. *The Secret Doctrine.* Vol. 3. Cambridge: Cambridge University Press, 2011.

Biesantz, Hagen, and Arne Klingborg. *The Goetheanum: Rudolf Steiner's Architectural Impulse.* London: Rudolf Steiner Press, 1979.

Blavatsky, Helena Petrovna. *NightmareTales.* www.theosociety.org/pasadena/nightmar/night-9.htm ("The Ensouled Violin").

_____. *The Secret Doctrine.* Los Angeles: The Theosophy Co., 1982 (Facsimile Edition).

_____. *Studies in Occultism* (The Dennis Wheatley Library of the Occult). London: Sphere, 1974.

Bonds, Mark Evan, ed. *Beethoven Forum.* Vol. 8. Lincoln and London: University of Nebraska Press, 2000.

Bowers, Faubion. *The New Scriabin: Enigma and Answers.* Newton Abbot, UK: David & Charles, 1974.

_____. *Scriabin: A Biography.* Tokyo: Kodansha International, 1969.

Brown, David. *Tchaikovsky: The Years of Fame, 1878–1893.* London: Gollancz, 1992.

Browne, Sir Thomas. *Religio Medici.* Oxford, Oxford University Press, 1831.

Buckle, Richard. *Diaghilev.* London: Weidenfeld, 1995.

Burgess, Anthony. *The Devil's Mode.* London: Vintage, 1990.

_____. *You've Had Your Time: Being the Second Part of the Confessions of Anthony Burgess.* London: Heinemann, 1990.

Busoni, Feruccio. *Letters to his Wife.* Translated by Rosamund Ley. http://www.rodoni.ch/busoni/bibliotechina/lettere gerdaEN/gerdaEN1.html.

_____. *A Sketch of a New Esthetic of Music.* Translated by Th. Baker. New York: Schirmer, 1911.

Cavendish, Richard. *The Black Arts.* New York: Perigree, 1983.

Chailley, Jacques. *The Magic Flute — Masonic Opera.* Translated by Herbert Weinstock. New York: Alfred A. Knopf, 1971.

Cornils, Ingo, ed. *A Companion to the Works of Hermann Hesse.* Rochester, NY: Camden House, 2009.

# Bibliography

Covach, John. "Schoenberg and the Occult: Some Reflections on the 'Musical Idea.'" www.ibiblio.org/johncovach/asoccult.htm.

Crowley, Aleister. *The Simon Iff Stories & Other Works.* Edited by William Breeze. Ware, UK: Wordsworth, 2012.

Delevoy, Robert. *Symbolists and Symbolism.* London: Macmillan, 1982.

Dumas, Alexandre. *The Count of Monte Cristo.* London: Routledge, n.d.

Du Maurier, George. *Novels of George Du Maurier: Trilby, The Martians, Peter Ibbetson.* London: Pilot Press/Peter Davies, 1947.

Eckermann, Johann Peter, and Frédéric Soret. *Conversations of Goethe with Eckermann and Soret.* Translated by John Oxenford. London: G. Bell, 1883.

Eksteins, Modris. *Rites of Spring: The Great War and the Birth of the Modern Age.* London: Papermac, 2000.

Eliade, Mircea. *From Primitives to Zen: A Thematic Sourcebook of the History of Religions.* London: Collins, 1979.

Eschenbach, Wolfram von. *Parzival.* Translated by A. T. Hatto. Harmondsworth: Penguin, 1980.

Falkner, John Meade. *The Lost Stradivarius.* London: Hesperus, 2006.

Faulks, Philippa, and Robert L.D. Cooper. *The Masonic Magician: The Life and Death of Count Cagliostro and His Egyptian Rite.* London: Watkins, 2008.

Ficino, Marsilio. *Three Books on Life.* Translated by Carol Kaske and John Clark. Binghamton, NY: Medieval & Renaissance Texts & Studies in conjunction with the Renaissance Society of America, 1989.

Fletcher, Ella Adelia. *The Law of the Rhythmic Breath: Teaching the Generation, Conservation and Control of the Vital Force.* New York: R. F. Fenno, 1908.

Gaona, Brian S. "Through the Lens of Freemasonry: The Influence of Ancient Esoteric Thought on Beethoven's Late Works." http://www.ideals.illinois.edu/bitstream/handle/2142/16092/1_Gaona_Brian.pdf.

Garner, Alan. *A Book of Goblins.* Harmondsworth: Penguin, 1972.

Gettings, Fred. *Secret Symbolism in Occult Art.* New York: Harmony Books, 1987.

Godwin, Joscelyn. *Music and the Occult: French Musical Philosophies, 1750–1950.* Rochester, NY: University of Rochester Press, 1995.

_____, ed. *Music, Mysticism and Magic.* London: Routledge & Kegan Paul, 1986.

Goethe, Johann Wolfgang von. *Faust Part One.* Translated by David Luke. Oxford: Oxford University Press, 1987.

_____. *Goethe's Faust.* Translated by John Anster. London: Routledge, 1883.

Gregorovius, Ferdinand. *The Roman Journals, 1852–1874.* Translated by G. W. Hamilton. London: G. Bell, 1911.

Gutman, Robert W. *Richard Wagner: The Man, His Mind, and His Music.* New York: Time-Life Records Special Edition, 1972.

Hall, Michael. *Leaving Home: A Conducted Tour of Twentieth-Century Music with Simon Rattle.* London: Faber and Faber, 1996.

Hanslick, Eduard. *The Beautiful in Music.* Translated by Gustav Cohen. London: Novello, 1891.

Harrison, John. *Synaesthesia: The Strangest Thing.* Oxford: Oxford University Press, 2001.

Head, Raymond. "Astrology and Modernism in 'The Planets.'" http://raymondhead.com/planets.

Hearn, Marcus, and Alan Barnes. *The Hammer Story.* London: Titan Books, 1997.

Heindel, Max. *Mysteries of the Great Operas.* Oceanside, CA: Rosicrucian Fellowship, 1921.

_____. *The Rosicrucian Cosmo-Conception.* Oceanside, CA: Rosicrucian Fellowship, 1911.

Hitchens, Robert, *The Garden of Allah.* http://www.gutenberg.org/files/3637/3637-h/3637-h.htm.

*Hit Parade* magazine, October 1976.

Hoffmann. E. T. A. *E. T. A. Hoffmann's Musical Writings: Kreisleriana, the Poem and the Composer, Music Criticisms.* Edited by David Chartlon. Translated by Martyn Clarke. Cambridge: Cambridge University Press, 2003.

_____. *The Nutcracker and The Golden Pot.* New York: Dover, 1993.

_____. *Tales of Hoffmann.* Edited by Christopher Lazare. New York: A. A. Wyn, 1946.

Hogwood, Christopher. *Handel.* London: Thames and Hudson, 1984.

Holst, Imogen. *Gustav Holst.* London: Oxford University Press, 1938.

Honegger, Arthur. *I Am a Composer.* London: Faber and Faber, 1966.

Hornung, Erik. *The Secret Lore of Egypt: Its*

# Bibliography

*Impact on the West.* Translated by David Lorton. Ithaca, NY: Cornell University Press, 2002.

Howat, Roy. *Debussy in Proportion: A Musical Analysis.* Cambridge: Cambridge University Press, 1983.

Huckvale, David. *Ancient Egypt in the Popular Imagination: Building a Fantasy in Film, Literature, Music and Art.* Jefferson, NC: McFarland, 2012.

_____. *Hammer Film Scores and the Musical Avant Garde.* Jefferson, NC: McFarland, 2008.

Huysmans, J. K. *À Rebours (Against the Grain).* London: Fortune Press, 1946.

_____. *Là-bas (Lower Depths).* London: Dedalus, 1986.

Huxley, Aldous. *The Doors of Perception and Heaven and Hell.* Harmondsworth: Penguin, 1959.

Iamblichus. *Life of Pythagoras or Pythagoric Life.* Translated by Thomas Taylor. London: J. M. Watkins, 1818.

Irwin, Robert. *Satan Wants Me.* Sawtry: Dedalus, 1999.

Jacobsen, Jens Peter. *Niels Lynne.* Translated by Tiina Nunnally. Harmondsworth: Penguin, 2006.

James, Jamie. *The Music of the Spheres: Music, Science and the Natural Order of the Universe.* London: Abacus, 1993.

Jung, C. G. *Psychology and Alchemy.* Translated by R. F. C. Hull. London: Routledge & Kegan Paul, 1980.

Kandinsky, Wassily. *Concerning the Spiritual in Art.* Translated by Michael T. H. Sadler. www.gutenberg.org/cache/epub/5321/pg5321/html.

Kayser, Hans. *The Textbook of Harmonics.* Translated by Ariel and Joscelyn Godwin. www.sacredscience.com/archive/Kayser.htm.

Keightley, Thomas. *The Fairy Mythology.* London: G. Bell, 1878.

Kinderman, William. *Beethoven.* Berkeley and Los Angeles: University of California Press, 1995.

_____. *The String Quartets of Beethoven.* Urbana: University of Illinois Press, 2006.

Leadbeater, C. W., and Annie Besant. *Thought-Forms.* www.gutenberg.org/files/16269/16269-h/16269-h.htm.

Lee, Christopher. *Tall, Dark and Gruesome — An Autobiography.* London: Gollancz, 1997.

Lennon, John, and Yoko Ono. *The Playboy Interviews with John Lennon and Yoko Ono: The Complete Texts Plus Unpublished Conversations and Lennon's Song-by-Song Analysis of His Music.* New York: Putnam, 1981.

Leroux, Gaston. *The Phantom of the Opera.* London: Michael O'Mara, 1987.

Levi, Erik. *Music in the Third Reich.* Basingstoke, UK: Macmillan, 1994.

Lloyd, Stephen. *H. Balfour Gardiner.* Cambridge: Cambridge University Press, 1984.

Lockspeiser, Edward. *Debussy: His Life and Mind.* Vol. 2, *1902–1918.* London: Cassell, 1965.

Lovecraft, H. P. *The Fiction.* New York: Barnes and Noble, 2008.

Macdonald, Hugh. *Skryabin.* Oxford: Oxford University Press, 1978.

MacDonald, Malcolm. *John Foulds and His Music: An Introduction.* New York: Pro/Am Music Resources, 1989.

Maeterlinck, Maurice. *The Blue Bird: A Fairy Play in Six Acts.* Translated by Alexander Teixeira de Mattos. London: Methuen, 1929.

Mann, Thomas. *Doctor Faustus.* Translated by H. T. Lowe-Porter. London: Secker & Warburg, 1949.

_____. *Pro and Contra Wagner.* Translated by Allan Blunden. London: Faber and Faber, 1985.

Martineau, Jane, ed. *Victorian Fairy Painting.* London: Merrell Holberton, 1997.

Mascaró, Juan, trans. *The Bhagavad Gita.* Harmondsworth: Penguin, 1962.

Milton, John. *Paradise Lost.* London: Frederick Warne, 1896.

Moore, George. *Evelyn Innes.* London: T. Fisher Unwin, 1898.

Morrison, Simon. *Russian Opera and the Symbolist Movement.* Berkeley/Los Angeles/London: University of California Press, 2002.

Motte Fouqué, Friedrich de la. *Undine: A Tale.* Translated by Edmund Gosse. London: Sidgwick & Jackson, 1912.

Mozart, Wolfgang Amadeus. *The Magic Flute.* Edited by Nicholas John. London: John Calder, 1980.

Nicols, Roger, ed. *Ravel Remembered.* London: Faber and Faber, 1987.

Nietzsche, Friedrich. *The Birth of Tragedy and the Wagner Case.* Translated by Walter Kaufmann. New York: Random House, 1967.

# Bibliography

_____. *Ecce Homo.* Translated by R. J. Hollingdale. Harmondsworth: Penguin, 1979.

Nijinsky, Romola. *Nijinsky.* London: Sphere, 1970.

Noll, Richard. *The Aryan Christ: The Secret Life of Carl Gustav Jung.* London: Macmillan, 1997.

Orledge, Robert. *Debussy and the Theatre.* Cambridge: Cambridge University Press, 1982.

Osthoff, Wolfgang. *Richard Wagner's Buddha Project "Die Sieger" ("The Victors").* Zurich: Museum Rietberg, 1996.

Pasternak, Alexander. *A Vanished Present.* Translated by Ann Pasternak-Slater. Oxford: Oxford University Press, 1984.

Payser, Joan. *Boulez: Composer, Conductor, Enigma.* London: Cassell, 1977.

Plato. *The Essential Plato.* Translated by Benjamin Jowett. London: Softback Preview, 1999.

Poe, Edgar Allan. *The Science Fiction of Edgar Allan Poe.* Edited by Harold Beaver. Harmondsworth: Penguin, 1976.

Prendergast, Roy. *Film Music: A Neglected Art.* New York: W. W. Norton, 1977.

Rabelais, François. *The Works of Rabelais.* London: Chatto and Windus, 1875.

Radcliffe, Ann). *The Romance of the Forest.* Edited by Chloe Chard. Oxford: Oxford University Press, 1986.

Rimsky-Korsakov, Nicolay. *My Musical Life.* Edited by Carl van Vechten. Translated by Judah A. Joffe. London: Eulenburg, 1974.

Sadie, Stanley, ed. *The New Grove Dictionary of Music and Musicians.* Vol. 8. London: Macmillan, 1998.

*San Francisco Chronicle*, April 13, 1966.

Schoenberg, Arnold. *Arnold Schoenberg Letters.* Edited by Leonard Stein. Translated by Leo Black. Los Angeles: University of California Press, 1975.

_____. *Theory of Harmony.* Translated by Roy E. Carter. London: Faber and Faber, 1978.

Schopenhauer, Arthur. *Essays and Aphorisms.* Translated by R. J. Hollingdale. Harmondsworth: Penguin, 1970.

_____. *The World as Will and Representation.* Vol. 1. Translated by E. F. J. Payne. New York: Dover, 1969.

Schubart, Christian. *Ideen zu einer Aesthetik der Tonkunst.* Vienna: Degen, 1806.

Scott, Cyril. *Bone of Contention.* London: Aquarian, 1969.

_____. *The Initiate: Some Impressions of a Great Soul.* London: Routledge & Kegan Paul, 1920.

_____. *Music — Its Secret Influence Throughout the Ages.* Wellingborough, UK: Aquarian, 1976.

_____. *The Philosophy of Modernism — Its Connection with Music.* London: Waverley, 1910.

Scott, Marion M. *Beethoven.* London: Dent, 1974.

Scriabin, Alexander. *Complete Works for Piano* ("Préludes I"). Budapest: Könemann Music, 1997.

Shakespeare, William. *The Oxford Shakespeare.* Edited by W. J. Craig. Oxford: Oxford University Press, 1905.

Shaw, George Bernard. *The Complete Plays of Bernard Shaw.* London: Odhams Press, 1950.

Shelley, Mary. *Frankenstein.* London: J. M. Dent, 1941.

Shelley, Percy Bysshe. *The Complete Poetical Works of Percy Bysshe Shelley.* Edited by Thomas Hutchinson. London: Oxford University Press, 1905.

_____. *Essays and Letters by Percy Bysshe Shelley.* Edited by Ernest Rhys. London: Walter Scott, 1886.

Sitwell, Osbert. *Great Morning.* London: Macmillan, 1948.

Solomon, Maynard. *Late Beethoven.* Berkeley and Los Angeles: University of California Press, 2003.

Steiner, Rudolf. *Four Mystery Dramas.* Translated by Ruth and Hans Pusch. North Vancouver, BC: Steiner Book Centre, 1973.

_____. *Goethe's World View.* Translated by William Lindeman. New York: Mercury Press, 1985.

_____. *The Way of Initiation; or, How to Attain Knowledge of the Higher Worlds.* London: Theosophical Publishing Society, 1912.

Stewart, Fred Mustard. *The Mephisto Waltz.* London: Michael Joseph, 1969.

Stoker, Bram. *The Annotated Dracula.* Edited by Leonard Wolf. London: New English Library, 1976.

Stravinsky, Igor and Robert Craft. *Dialogues.* London: Faber and Faber, 1982.

_____. *Expositions and Developments.* London: Faber and Faber, 1981.

Strunk, Oliver, ed. *Source Readings in Music History.* Vol. 1, *Antiquity and the Middle Ages.* London: Faber and Faber, 1981.

# Bibliography

_____, ed. *Source Readings in Music History.* Vol. 5, *The Romantic Era.* London: Faber and Faber, 1981.

Sugden, John. *Paganini.* London: Omnibus, 1980.

Swedenborg, Emanuel. *Arcana Coelestia.* Vol. 1. Translated by John Clowes. West Chester, PA: Swedenborg Foundation, 2009.

Tarasti, Eero. *Myth and Music.* Helsinki, Finland: Suomen Musiikkitieteellinen Seura, 1978.

Tayer, Alexander Wheelock. *Tayer's Life of Beethoven.* Edited by Elliot Forbes. Translated by H. E. Krehbiel. Princeton, NJ: Princeton University Press, 1970.

Terrasson, Jean. *The Life of Sethos: Taken from the Private Memoirs of the Ancient Egyptians.* Vol. 1. Translated by Thomas Lediard. London: J. Walthoe, 1732.

Thomson, H. Douglas, ed. *The Mystery Book.* London: Odhams, 1934.

Todd, R. Larry, ed. *Mendelssohn Studies.* Cambridge: Cambridge University Press, 1992.

van den Berk, M. F. M. *The Magic Flute: Die Zauberflöte: An Alchemical Allegory.* Leiden and Boston: Brill Academic Publications, 2004.

Wagner, Richard. *The Artwork of the Future.* Translated by William Ashton Ellis. Lincoln and London: University of Nebraska Press, 1993.

_____. Letter to Theodor Uhlig, September 20, 1850. http://www.bayreuther-festspiele.de/documents/a_rough_theatre_of_planks_and_beams_built_according_to_this_plan_of_mine_338.html.

_____. *My Life.* Translated by Andrew Grey. Cambridge: Cambridge University Press, 1987.

_____. *Parsifal* (English National Opera Guide 34). Edited by Nicholas John. London: John Calder, 1986.

_____. *Religion and Art.* Translated by William Ashton Ellis. Lincoln and London: University of Nebraska Press, 1994.

_____. *Selected Letters of Richard Wagner.* Edited by Barry Millington. Translated by Stewart Spencer. London: Dent, 1987.

_____. "Wagner's programme notes (3)—Prelude ('The Holy Grail')." *Wagner: The Journal of the London Wagner Society* 11, no. 3 (August 1990).

_____. "Wagner programme notes (3)—Prelude to *Tristan und Isolde*." *Wagner: The Journal of the London Wagner Society* 11, no. 3 (August 1990).

Walker, Alan. *Hans von Bülow: A Life and Times.* Oxford: Oxford University Press, 2009.

Wall, Mick. *Iron Maiden: Run to the Hills—The Authorized Biography.* London: Sanctuary, 2004.

Wilson, Colin. *Aleister Crowley: The Nature of the Beast.* Wellingborough, UK: Aquarian Press, 1987.

_____. *The Occult.* London: Granada, 1973.

# *Index*

Numbers in **bold italics** indicate illustrations

*À Rebours* (J. K. Huysmans) 103
Abraham, F. Murray 11
*Ace of Wands* 186, 187
Achin von Arnim, Ludwig 141
*Adagio and Fugue in C-minor* (J. S. Bach) 51
Adam, Adolphe 150
Adjani, Isabelle 140
*The Affair of the Necklace* (dir. Charles Shyer) 33
Agrippa, Heinrich Cornelius 2, 11, 17, 145
Alberti, Ignaz **29**
*The Alchemist* (Cyril Scott) 122, 144–145
Alda, Alan **60**
*Alien* (dir. Ridley Scott) 16, 36
Allan, Maud 127
*Amadeus* 11
Andersen, Hans Christian 174
Andress, Ursula 152, 153
*The Angel of Splendor* (Jean Delville) 116
Anger, Kenneth 183–185, **184**
Antonioni, Michelangelo 175
*Aphorisms* (Shostakovitch) 55
*Apparitions* (Frederick Ashton) 154–155
*Aquarelles* (John Foulds) 134
*Arcana* (Edgar Varèse) 92–93
*Arcana Coelestia* (Swedenborg) 95, 101
Aristotle 7
Ashton, Frederick 154, 158
"The Assignation" (Poe) 159
Auden, W. H. 190
Augustine, St. 42
Auric, Georges 144, 148
Austen, Jane 1
*Ave Maria* (Schubert) 158
Averdonk, Severin Anton 39

Bach, Johann Sebastian 40, 43, 57, 62, 91, 106, 190
Bacon, Francis 15
*Bagatelles*, op. 119 (Beethoven) 39

Baigent, Michael 127
Bailly, Edmond 128
*Le Baiser de la fée* (Stravinsky) 174
Baker, Roy Ward 139, 156, 160
Bakst, Leon 152, 153–154, 158
Balakirev, Mili 153
*Un ballo in maschera* (Verdi) 133–134
Balsamo, Guiseppe *see* Cagliostro
Balzac, Honoré de 88–89, 90, 101
Banks, Don 48
Banks, Tony 16
Bantock, Sir Granville 124
Bara, Theda 153
Bardi, Giovanni de' 17
Bargagli, Girolamo 17
Barrett, Francis 7
Barry, John 106
Bates, Alan 13
Baudelaire, Charles 100, 101, 102
Baxter, Les 107
Beacham, Stephanie 177
The Beatles 54, 107, 126, 177, 177, 179, 181, **181**
Beaton, Cecil 155
Beaumont, Anthony 92
Beausoleil, Bobby 183
Beck, Jeff 176
Bedford, David 25
Beethoven, Ludwig, van 16, 35–41, 43, 57, 69, 102, 169
Bellini, Vincenzo 170
"The Bells" (Poe) 51
*The Bells* (Rachmaninoff) 51
*Beneath the Twelve-Mile Reef* (dir. Robert D. Webb) 121
*Beni Mora* (Holst) 119–120, 121, 122
Benois, Alexandre 153, 154, 155
Bergman, Ingmar 35, 158
Berk, M. F. M. van den 28
Berlioz, Hector 1, 53–55, 62, 135, 169, 170–172

207

## 208　　Index

Bernard, James 10, 11, 44, 46, 47, 49–50, 56, 67, 107, 131, 134, 149, 156, 187
Bertrand, Aloysius 168
Besant, Annie 95, 108, 111, 124
*Bewitched* (TV series) 175
*Bhagavad Gita* 37, 39
Binder, Maurice 106
Birkinshaw, Alan 157
Bisset, Jacqueline 44, 60
*The Black Arts* (Richard Cavendish) 131
*The Black Cat* (dir. Edgar G. Ulmer) 51
"The Black Mass: An Electric Storm in Hell" (White Noise) 65
Black Sabbath 187
"Black Sun" (*Space: 1999* episode, dir. Lee H. Katzin) 101
Blackwood, Algernon 117
Blake, Peter 179
Blake, William 180
Blavatsky, Helena Petrovna 65, 78–79, 81, 82, 98, 109, 110, 111, 112, 113, 116, 123, 125, 190
Bliss, Sir Arthur 158
*Blood from the Mummy's Tomb* (dir. Seth Holt) 36, 42
*Blow Up* (dir. Michelangelo Antonioni) 175
*The Blue Bird* (Maeterlinck) 172–173
*Blütenstaub* (Novalis) 96
Böcklin, Arnold 55, 174
Boethius 9–10, 11, 25
Bogarde, Dirk 54
Bois, Jules 128, 129
*Boléro* (Ravel) 66
*A Book of Goblins* (ed. Alan Gardner) 165
Born, Ignaz Edler von 29
*Born of Fire* (dir. Jamil Dehlavi) 19, 20
Boswell, Simon 175
Botticelli, Sandro 118
Boughton, Rutland 163–164, 173
Boulez, Pierre 90
Bowers, Faubion 48, 108, 108, 113, 114
Bowie, David 187–188
"The Bowmen" (Arthur Machen) 173
Boyer, Charles 121
Branagh, Kenneth 35
Brancusi, Constantin 112
Brianchaninov, Alexander 108
*The Bride of Frankenstein* (dir. James Whale) 154
Britten, Benjamin 125, 147–148
Brommage, Bernard 177
Brown, Andy 186
Brown, Dan 127
Brown, David 152
Browne, Sir Thomas 22
Browning, Tod 151, 155
Bruckner, Anton 49
Bruns, George 174
Bryusov, Valery 145–146
Bülow Hans von 72–73
Bulwer-Lytton, Sir Edward 187

Bunyan, John 125
Bürger, Gottfried August 36, 55
Burgess, Anthony 42, 43, 57, 180
Burgmüller, Johann Friedrich 151
Burnouf, Eugène 75
Busoni, Ferruccio 90–92, 93, 144
Byron, George Gordon, Lord 136

*The Cabinet of Dr. Caligari* (dir. Robert Wiene) 160
Cacavas, John 51
Caccini, Giulio 17, 131
Cagliostro, Count Alesandro 27, 28, 33, 143
*Cagliostro in Wien* (Johann Strauss) 33
Callow, Simon 188
Cameron, John 51
Cammell, Donald 184
Caplet, André 124, 157
Caporaso, André 20
Capra, Frank 56
Carerras, Sir James 153
Carson, John 141
Cary, Tristram 36
Castel, Père Louis-Bertrand 99
Cavendish, Richard 48, 131, 190
Chafey, Don 16
Chailley, Jacques 32
Chamberlain, Houston Stewart 79
*Chanson de Bilitis* (Pierre Louÿs/Debussy) 128
Charlot, André 122, 124
*Checkmate* (Sir Arthur Bliss) 158
*Chemical Wedding* (dir. Julian Doyle) 34–35, 188
Chopin, Frédéric 154
*La Chûte de la Maison Usher* (Debussy) 128–129
Cicéri, Pierre Luc-Charles 139, 150
Clarke, Arthur C. 25
Clayton, Jack 148, 149
*Cléopâtre* (Diaghilev ballet) 153
Clever, Edith 87
*A Clockwork Orange* (Anthony Burgess) 42, 43
*A Clockwork Orange* (dir. Stanley Kubrick) 42, 43
*Close Encounters of the Third Kind* (dir. Steven Spielberg) 5–6, 9, 16
Clurman, Harold 159
Cocteau Jean 127
Collins, Joan 185
*A Communication to My Friends* (Wagner) 84
Conan Doyle, Sir Arthur 175
*Concerning the Spiritual in Art* (Kandinsky) 96–97
*Conte fantastique* (André Caplet) 157
Cooper, Robert L. D. 27, 28
Copland, Aaron 159
*Coppélia* (Delibes) 152, 156
*Copying Beethoven* (dir. Agnieszka Holland) 42
Corman, Roger 107, 156
"Correspondance" (Baudelaire) 100–101

**Index** 209

*The Count of Monte Cristo* (Dumas) 138
*Countess Dracula* (dir. Peter Sasdy) 59
Courage, Alexander 8, 9
Court, Hazel 51, 67
Covach, John 90
Craft, Robert 174
*The Creation* (Haydn) 24, 39, 114
*The Creatures of Prometheus* (Beethoven) 39
Crowley, Aleister 20, 34, 117, 131–132, 176, 179, 180, 181–183, 185, 187, 188
Crowley, Suzan 20
Cushing, Peter 10, 52, 177
Cuthbertson, Iain 34
*Czárdás macabre* (Liszt) 59

"Dagobah" (Cyril Scott) 122
Daltry, Roger 55
*Damien: Omen II* (dir. Don Taylor) 65, 67, 188
*La Damoiselle élue* (Debussy) 128
D'Angelo, James 24, 26
Daniel, Jennifer 57
D'Annunzio, Gabrielle 128
Danot, Serge 164
*Danse macabre* (Saint-Saëns) 59
Dante 132
"Dark Flames" (Scriabin) 108
"Dark Hell" (Tchaikovsky) 55
*The Da Vinci Code* (Dan Brown) 127
Dawkins, Richard 190
Day, Robert 152
*Dead of Night* (dir. Alberto Cavalcanti, Charles Crichton, Basil Dearden) 148
*Death in Venice* (dir. Luchino Visconti) 42
"Death in Venice" (Mann) 42
*The Death of Alexander Scriabin* (dir. Ken Russell) 117
Debono, Leo 114
Debussy, Claude 7, 21, 122, 123, 124, 126, 127–129, 130
"Debussy and the Occultists" (Léon Guichard) 129
*Debussy et le Mystère* (Vladimir Jankélévitch) 129
*Debussy — His Life and Mind* (Edward Lockspeiser) 129
*Defence of Poetry* (Shelley) 115
Degas, Edgar 139
Dehlavi, Jamil 19, 20, 21
Dehn, Paul 149
Delibes, Léo 152, 156
Delville, Jean 116
Derbyshire, Delia 65
Deschamps, Emile 171
*The Devil Rides Out* (dir. Terence Fisher) 44, 46, 47, 49, 50, 56, 61, 131, 154, 163, 178, 184, 187
Diaghilev, Sergei 152, 153, 154, 158
Dickens, Charles 150
Dickinson, Bruce 188
Dickinson, Thorold 144, 148

*Dido and Aeneas* (Purcell) 68, 132
*Dies Irae* 52, 53, 54, 55, 61, 62, 65, 178
"Dies Irae Psychedelico" (Ennio Morricone) 56
Dieterle, William 174
Dietrich, Marlene 121
Disney, Walt 6, 56, 106, 157, 158, 174, 175
*The Divine Comedy* (Dante) 132
*Doctor Faustus* (Mann) 7, 39, 42, 68–69
*Doctor Faustus* (Marlowe) 188
*Doctor Who* 20, 36
*Doktor Faustus* (Busoni) 144–145
*Don Giovanni* (Mozart) 35, 53, 134, 137
*Donald Duck in Mathmagic Land* (dir. Hamilton Luske 1959) 6
*La donna serpente* (Carlo Gozzi) 170
The Doors 180
*The Doors of Perception* (Aldous Huxley) 107, 180
Doyle, Julian 35, 188
*Dracula* (Bram Stoker) 59, 140–141, 142, 159
*Dracula* (dir. Tod Browning) 151, 155
*Dracula A.D. 1972* (dir. Alan Gibson) 65, 177, 183, 185, 189
*Dracula Has Risen from the Grave* (dir. Freddie Francis) 56, 107
Dryden, John 24
*Duinese Elegien* (Rilke) 96
Dukas, Paul 106
Dumas, Alexandre 7, 33, 138
Du Maurier, George 58
Dunning, George 107, *181*
Dvořák, Antonín 163, 164
*Dynamic Triptych* (John Foulds) 125

*Earthly Powers* (Anthony Burgess) 180
*Ecce Homo* (Nietzsche) 182–183
Eckermann, Johann Peter 44
*Egypt* (Cyril Scott) 122
Einstein, Albert 90, 92, 191
Ekerot, Bengt 158
*An Electric Storm* (White Noise) 65
Eles, Sandor 59
Elgar, Sir Edward 124
"The Ensouled Violin" (Helena Petrovna Blavatsky) 65–66
"Entrueckung" (Stefan George) 90, 92
*Es ist genug* (J. S. Bach) 57
*Escalation* (dir. Robert Faenza) 56
Eschenbach, Wolfram von 83–84
Esterházy, Prince Nicolaus 28
"Eureka" (Poe) 179, 190–191
*Euridice* (Caccini/Rinuccini) 131
*Euridice* (Peri/Rinuccini) 131
Euripides 7
*Evelyn Innes* (George Moore) 58
*Evenings in the Orchestra* (Berlioz) 135–136
*Evolution* (Mondrian) 112
Ewing, Barbara 58

# Index

*The Exorcist* (dir. William Friedkin) 44, 46, 49, 56, 61, 69, 70
*Eye of the Devil* (dir. J. Lee Thompson) 61, 67

Faenza, Robert 56
*The Fairy Mythology* (Thomas Keightley) 161–162, 164–166
Faithfull, Marianne 183
Falkner, John Meade 62, 65
"The Fall of the House of Usher" (Poe) 128
*Fantasia* (dir. Norman Ferguson, et al.) 56, 106, 158
*Farbenlehre* (Goethe) 99
Faulks, Philippa 27, 28
*Faust* (Goethe) 3, 132
*Faust* (Gounod) 80
*Eine Faust Symphonie* (Liszt) 45, 59
*The Fearless Vampire Killers* (dir. Roman Polanski) 155–156, **156**
*Die Feen* (Wagner) 170
Fellini, Frederico 159
Ferrié, General Gustave-Auguste 100, 106
Ffrangcon-Davies, Gwen 163, 173
Ficino, Marsilio 16–17
*Fidelio* (Beethoven) 38
*The Fiery Angel* (Prokofiev) 145–146, 147, 148
Finzi, Gerald 124
*The Firebird* (Stravinsky) 45, 154
Firth, Peter 20
Fisher, Terence 10, 11, 44, 155, 159
*Five Pieces for Orchestra* (Schoenberg) 94
Fletcher, Ella Adelia 102–103
*Les Fleurs du mal* (Baudelaire) 100
*Der fliegende Höllander* (Wagner) 140, 142
Fludd, Robert 21–22, **23**, 51, 71, 72, 98, 127
Fokine, Mikhail 153, 154
Forman, Milos 11
Foulds, John 92, 124–126
Francis, Freddie 56, 58, 149
Franck, César 128
Frankel, Cyril 163
*Frankenstein* (Mary Shelley) 115, 136
*Frankenstein Created Woman* (dir. Terence Fisher) 10
Frazer, Sir James 61
Frederick the Great 41
*Der Freischütz* (Carl Maria von Weber) 45, 52–53, 135–136, 137
Freud, Sigmund 82, 129, 147, 152, 179, 180
Friedkin, William 44, 69
*From Hell* (Alan Moore) 32, 35
*From Hell* (dir. Albert and Allen Hughes) 32, 35
*From the City to the Stars* (David Bedford) 25
*Funeral Cantata for Joseph II* (Beethoven) 39
*Funeral Music for Queen Mary* (Purcell) 68

Galileo, Vincenzo 17
Galway, James 21
Gance, Abel 41
*Gandharva-Music* (John Foulds) 124
Gandhi 179
Gaona, Brian S. 39–41
*The Garden of Allah* (dir. Richard Boleslawski) 121
*The Garden of Allah* (Robert Smythe Hichen) 119–120
Gardiner, H. Balfour 173
*Gargantua and Pantragruel* (Rabelais) 181
Garner, Alan 165
*Gaspard de la Nuit* (Ravel) 66, 168
Gautier, Théophile 151, 153
Gawboy, Anna 105
Gébelin, Antoine Court de 28
Gebler, Tobias von 28
Geeson, Judy 104
George, Stefan 90
*Geschichte der neuren schönen Literatur in Deutschland* (Heine) 151
Gettings, Fred 118
Gibson, Alan 65, 177
Gilling, John 57, 131
*Giselle* (Adolphe Adam) 150–151, 154
Glass, Paul 69
*Die glückliche Hand* (Schoenberg) 88
Godwin, Joscelyn 99–100
Godwin, William 2
Goethe, Johann Wolfgang von 3, 36, 38, 44, 45, 46, 80, 88, 89, 99, 132
*The Golden Compass* (dir. Chris Weitz) 49
Goldsmith, Jerry 1, 36, 44, 51, 61, 62, 65, 67, 69
*The Gorgon* (dir. Terence Fisher) 155
*Götterdämmerung* (Wagner) 45–46, 102, 162, 164
Gounod, Charles 80
Gozzi, Carlo 170
Grainger, Percy 173
*Un Grand Amour de Beethoven* (dir. Abel Gance) 41
Graves, Robert 13
Gray, Allan 126
Gray, Charles 178
*Great Expectations* (Dickens) 150
Greenfield, Howard 174
Gregorovius, Ferdinand 57
Grieg, Edvard 161
Griffiths, D. W. 153
*Grogh* (Aaron Copland) 159–160
Guichard, Léon 129
Gull, Sir William 33
Gunning, Christopher 147
Gustavus III of Sweden 133
Gutman, Robert 77, 140

Haig, Justin Moorwood 123
Hall, Charles D. 153, 155
*Hamlet* (Ambroise Thomas) 134
Hammer-Purgstall, Joseph von 37
*Hammerhead* (dir. David Miller) 104–105
Handel, George Frideric 132–133

# Index    211

*Hands of the Ripper* (dir. Peter Sasdy) 146–147
Hannibal Lechter films 66
*Hänsel und Gretel* (Humperdinck) 143
Hanslick, Eduard 6
Hardy, Robin 190
Harker, Joseph 142
*Die Harmonie der Welt* (Hindemith) 18, 24
Harris, Steve 188
Harrison, George 126, 180
Hart, Charles 137
*The Haunted Ballroom* (Geoffrey Toye) 157
*The Haunting* (dir. Robert Wise) 149
Haworth, Jann 179
Haydn, Franz Josef 24, 28, 36, 37, 54, 56, 67, 114
Head, Raymond 118
*Heaven and Hell* (Swedenborg) 101
Heindel, Max 79–83, 84
Heine, Heinrich 7, 151, 162
*Hellas: A Suite of Ancient Greece* (John Foulds) 124
Helpman, Robert 158, 159
Hempel, Anouska 186
Herder, Johann Gottfried von 36, 37
Herheim, Stefan 87
Herrmann, Bernard 121
Herzog, Werner 140
Hesse, Hermann 96
Hichens, Robert Smythe 119–120
Hindemith, Paul 18, 24, 26
*His Dark Materials* (Philip Pullman) 49, 167, 175
Hitchcock, Alfred 33
Hitler, Adolf 158, 170, 179, 187
Hoffmann, E. T. A. 53, 55, 92, 103, 104, 151, 152, 161, 163, 167
Hofmann, Josef 7
Holbrooke, Joseph 124, 156, 157
Holland, Agnieszka 42
Holst, Gustav 17, 117–122, 124, 125
Holst, Imogen 119, 121
Holt, Seth 36, 42
*The Holy Blood and the Holy Grail* (Baigent/Leigh/Lincoln) 127
Holz, Karl 38
Honegger, Arthur 7, 66
Hopkins, Anthony 66
Horner, James 74–75
Hornung, Eric 28
Hughes, Margret Watts 100, 106
Hugo, Victor 127
Humperdinck, Engelbert 143
*Hunky Dory* (David Bowie) 187
Hunt, Marsha 177
Hunter, Meredith 185–186
Hurt, John 13
Huxley, Aldous 107, 179, 180
Huysmans, J. K. 50, 103, 128

Iamblichus 5

Ibsen, Henrik 161
*Immortal Beloved* (dir. Bernard Rose) 41
*The Immortal Hour* (Rutland Boughton/Fiona MacLeod) ) 163–164, 173
*Impressioni braziliane* (Respighi) 55
*In a Persian Market* (Albert Kètelbey) 122
*Indiana Jones* films 30
*The Innocents* (dir. Jack Clayton) 148–149
*Inspector Morse* (TV Series) 33–34
*Invitation to the Waltz* (Car Maria von Weber) 135
Iron Maiden 187, 188
Irving, Sir Henry 58–59, 142
Irwin, Robert 176, 190
*Isis Unveiled* (Helena Petrovna Blavatsky) 78
*The Isle of the Dead* (Rachmaninov) 55
*It's a Wonderful Life* (dir. Frank Capra) 56

Jackson, Michael 160
Jacobsen, Jens Peter 10
Jagger, Chris 185
Jagger, Mick 185
*Die Jakobsleiter* (Schoenberg) 88, 90
James, Henry 147
James, Jamie 17, 21, 87, 88, 90, 92
James Bond films 104, 106
James VI 27
Jankélévitch, Vladimir 129
Janowski, Horst 169
Jaspers, Karl 46
*Jaws* (dir. Steven Spielberg) 66
Jefferson Airplane 176
Jenny, Hans 25
Jesus Christ 79, 83, 115, 127, 179, 180, 182, 185
Jones, Chuck 106
Jones, Rev. Edward 165
Jones, Jim 180
*Joseph Balsamo* (dir. André Hunebelle) 33
Joseph of Arimathea 83
*Judaism in Music* 77
Jung, Carl Gustav 84, 85, 93, 179–180
Jurgens, Curt **60**

Kalipha, Stefan 20
Kandinsky, Wassily 95–97
Kant, Immanuel 71
Karajan, Herbert von 50
*Karma* (Cyril Scott) 122, 123
Karsavina, Tamara 154
*Katschei the Immortal* (Rimsky-Korsakov) 45
Katzin, Lee H. 101
Kayser, Hans 24, 26
Keightley, Thomas 161–162, 164, 165, 166
Keller, Jack 174
*Keltic Suite* (John Foulds) 124
Kennealy-Morrison, Patricia 180
Kennedy, John F. 185
Kepler, Johannes 22, 24
Kerr, Deborah 148
*Khamma* (Debussy) 127

# Index

Khan, Hazrat Inyat 12
Kinderman, William 40
Kinsky, Klaus 140
Kircher, Athanasius 21, 98, 106
Kirchner, Ernst Ludwig 96
Kirk, Robert 165, 166
*The Kiss of the Vampire* (dir. Don Sharp) 44, 55, 57, 67, 155, 156, 178
Kleist, Heinrich von 48–49
Klinger, Max 39
Klopstock, Gottlieb Friedrich 36
*Know Thyself* (Wagner) 77
Koechlin, Charles 127
Komeda, Christopher 178
Koonen, Alisa 112
Körner, Christian Gottfried 40
Korngold, Erich Wolfgang 174
*Kreisleriana* (E. T. A. Hoffmann) 103
Krick, Karen 87
Kubrick, Stanley 25, 42, 43, 46, 54, 107, 113, 119
Kutter, Michael 87

*Là-bas* (J. K. Huysmans) 50
Landau, Martin 101
Landis, John 160
*The Law of the Rhythmic Breath* (Ella Adelia Fletcher) 102
Lawson, Sarah 131
Leadbeater, C. W. 95
Led Zeppelin 183
*Led Zeppelin III* (Led Zeppelin) 183
Lee, Christopher 46, 48, 131, 134, 140, 153, 189, 190
Lee, David 67
Leigh, Richard 127
*Lélio* (Berlioz) 171
Lenau, Nikolaus 59
Lennon, John 179, 180–181, 182, 183
Leo, Alan 117–119
Leroux, Gaston 55
Lévi, Éliphas 127
Levi, Erik 47
Levin, Ira 178
Lewis, C. S. 12
Lewis, Matthew 155
Lichnowsky, Karl 36
Lichtenthal, Peter 62
Liebenfels, Lanz von 78
*The Life of Sethos* (Jean Terrasson) 27–28, 30–32
Ligeti, György 1, 54, 69, 107
Lincoln, Henry 127
*The Lion, the Witch and the Wardrobe* (C.S. Lewis) 12
List, Guido von 78
Liszt, Franz 1, 45, 55, 57, 58, 59, 60, 61, 92, 139, 154, 162, 164
*Lisztomania* (dir. Ken Russell) 55
Lockspeiser, Edward 129
Logan, Crawford 115

*Lohengrin* (Wagner) 45, 81, 84–85, 86, 87, 142, 170
Lom, Herbert 157
Lombroso. Professor Cesare 103
"Die Loreley" (Liszt/Heine) 162
*The Lost Stradivarius* (J. Meade Falkner) 62–64
Louÿs, Pierre 128
Lovecraft, H. P. 19, 61, 64
Lucan 132
Lucas, George 8
*Lucifer Rising* (dir. Kenneth Anger) 183–185, **184**
Lucretius 2
"Lucy in the Sky with Diamonds" (The Beatles) 54, 107
Ludwig II of Bavaria 157
Lugosi, Bela 151
*Luonnotar* (Sibelius) 122
Luske, Hamilton 6
*Lust for a Vampire* (dir. Jimmy Sangster) 56
Lutoslawski, Witold 61
Lutyens, Sir Edwin 117

*Macbeth* (Shakespeare) 133, 137
*Macbeth* (Verdi) 133
*Macchiette Medioevali* (Busoni) 91
MacDonald, Malcolm 124
MacGowran, Jack 155
Machen, Arthur 64, 117, 173
Mackenzie, Michael 186
MacLeod, Fiona 125, 163
Maeterlinck, Maurice 172–173
*The Magic Flute* (Mozart) 27–35, **29**, 52, 151
*The Magic Roundabout* (TV Series, dir. Serge Danot) 164
*The Magician's Nephew* (C. S. Lewis) 12
Magnus, Albertus 2
The Mamas and the Papas 178
*Man and Superman* (George Bernard Shaw) 190
Mann, Thomas 7, 16, 39, 46, 68–69, 141
Manson, Charles 61, 178, 183
Manson, Marilyn 187
Marais, Jean 33
Marlowe, Christopher 188
Marschner, Heinrich 137, 140, 170
*Le Martyre de Saint-Sébastien* (Debussy/D'Annunzio) 128
Marx, Karl 137
*Masonic Funeral Music* (Mozart) 35
"Masonic Murders" (*Inspector Morse* episode, dir. Danny Boyle) 33–35
*The Masque of the Red Death* (Cyril Scott) 124
*The Masque of the Red Death* (Holbrooke) 156–157
*The Masque of the Red Death* (dir. Roger Corman) 51–52, 67, 156
Massine, Léonide 158
Master, Quentin 185

# Index      213

Mathers, Samuel Liddell MacGregor 183
*A Matter of Life and Death* (dir. Michael Powell and Emeric Pressburger) 126
Matthisson, Friedrich von 38
McCartney, Paul 180–181
McDiarmid, Ian 34
McFarland, Gary 61
McKnight Kauffer, Edward 158
*The Medium* (Menotti) 146–147
Megadeath 188
*Die Meistersinger von Nürnberg* (Wagner) 151
*Memoirs of Hector Berlioz* 135
Mendelssohn, Felix 6, 162, 169
Menotti, Gian-Carlo 146–147
*The Mephisto Waltz* (dir. Paul Wendkos) 1, 44, 60–62, **60**, 69
*Mephisto Waltz No. 1* (Liszt) 59, 60, 61, 164
Mephisto Waltzes (Liszt) 59
*The Merchant of Venice* (Shakespeare) 19
Messiaen, Olivier 129–130
Metallica 188
Meyerbeer, Giacomo 52, 137–140, 150
*A Midsummer Night's Dream* (Mendelssohn) 170
*A Midsummer Night's Dream* (Shakespeare) 167, 169, 174
*A Midsummer Night's Dream* (dir. William Dieterle and Max Reinhardt) 174
*The Midwich Cuckoos* (Wyndham) 187
Miller, David 104
Milton, John 2, 23, 49, 115
Mitchell, Julian 33
Mondrian, Piet 1, 111–112
*The Monk* (Lewis) 155
*The Monster Club* (dir. Roy Ward Baker) 160
Monteverdi, Claudio 21, 131
Montgomery, Elizabeth 175
"Moon Landing" (Auden) 190
*Moonchild* (Crowley) 132, 176
*Moonfleet* (J. Meade Falkner) 61
Moore, Alan 32
Moore, George 58
Moreau, Gustave 116
Morienus, Romanus 84, 87
Morricone, Ennio 56
Morrison, Jim 180
Morrison, Simon 146
Morse, Barry 101
Moses 82, 92
*Moses und Aron* (Schoenberg) 89
Motte Fouqué, Friedrich de la 163, 167
Mourney, Gabriel 128
Mozart, Wolfgang Amadeus 11, 20, 27, 28, 30, 32–36, 43, 52, 53, 57, 62, 67, 134, 137, 143, 151, 167
Mozer, Alexander 105, 112
*The Mummy* (dir. Karl Freund) 151
Munch, Edvard 15
*Murder by Decree* (dir. Bob Clark) 32
Murnau, F. W. 140, 159, 159

*Music — Its Secret Influence Throughout the Ages* (Cyril Scott) 123, 125
"Music of Erich Zann" (Lovecraft) 19–20, 21, 64, 66
*Music Today* (John Foulds) 125
*Musical Offering* (J. S. Bach) 40
Mussolini, Benito 158
Mussorgsky, Modest 56, 106, 158
*Musurgia Universalis* (Kircher) 98
Myaskovsky, Nikolai 55
*Mysteries of the Great Operas* (Heindel) 80–83
*Mysterium* (Scriabin) 50, 104, 109, 110, 113, 114, 125

Nascimbene, Mario 16
Neame, Christopher 177
Neefe, Christian Gottlob 36
"*Nelson*" *Mass* (Haydn) 67
Newton, Sir Isaac 1, 90, 99, 112, 127
Nicholas, Paul 55
*Niels Lynne* (Jacobsen) 10
Nietzsche, Friedrich 76, 78, 110, 182–183, 185, 187
*Night on the Bare Mountain* (Mussorgsky) 56, 106, 158
*Nightmare Tales* (Blavatsky) 65
Nijinsky, Romola 152, 159
Nijinsky, Vaslav 153, 154, 159
Nimoy, Leonard 74
*Nirwana* (von Bülow) 72
Nixon, David 159
*Les Noces de Sathan* (Jules Bois) 128
*Nocturne symphonique* (Busoni) 91, 92, 144
Noll, Richard 179
Norman, Phill 61
*Nosferatu* (dir. F. W. Murnau) 159
*Nosferatu* (dir. Werner Herzog) 140
Nostradamus 3
Nouritt, Adolphe 139
Novalis 96
*The Nutcracker* (Tchaikovsky) 151–152, 164, 172

*Oberon* (Weber) 168–169
"Ode for St. Cecilia's Day" (Dryden) 24
Oehlenschläger, Adam 91
Offenbach, Jacques 158
Oldfield, Mike 44, 56
*The Omen* (dir. Richard Donner) 44, 49, 51, 61, 67
"On Betelgeuse" (Woolf/Holst) 122
"On the Suffering in the World" (Schopenhauer) 72
*One Million Years B.C.* (dir. Don Chafey) 16
O'Neill, Norman 173
*Optics* (Newton) 99
*Optique des couleurs* (Castel) 99
Order of the Golden Dawn 117, 128, 179, 183, 187
Order of the Rose + Croix 81, 126–127
*Orfeo* (Monteverdi) 131

# Index

**214**

Orledge, Robert 127, 128–129
Osborne, Ozzie 187
*Outline of a New Aesthetic of Music* (Busoni) 92
*Ouverture zum Märchen von der Schönen Melusine* (Mendelssohn) 162–163
*Overture: A Midsummer Night's Dream* (Mendelssohn) 169

Paganini, Niccolò 58, 61–62, 64, 66
Page, Jimmy 183
*Le Panthée* (Pèledan) 127
Paracelsus 2, 93
*Paradise Lost* (Milton) 23, 115
*Parsifal* (Wagner) 15, 45, 50, 75–78, **76**, 79, 80, 82, 83, 85–87, 89, 140–143, 151, 154, 170
Pärt, Arvo 159
Pasternak, Alexander 115
Pavlova, Anna 154
Pearce, Jacqueline 57
Peck, Gregory 67
*Peer Gynt* (Ibsen/Grieg) 161
Péledan, Joséphin 81, 126, 127, 128, 129
Penderecki, Krzysztof 1, 11, 46, 61, 69
*La Peri* (Burgmüller) 151
Peri, Jacopo 131
*Peter Pan* (dir. Clyde Geronimi and Wilfrid Jackson) 174
Petipa, Marius 150
*Petroushka* (Stravinsky) 158, 160
Pfeffel, G. C. 38
*Phaedo* (Plato) 9
Phillips, John 178
Phillips, Michelle 178
*The Philosophy of Modernism* (Cyril Scott) 98, 102
*Photographing Fairies* (dir. Nick Willing) 166, 175
*Piano Concerto* (Busoni) 91
*Piano Concerto in C major, K503* (Mozart) 143
*Piano Sonata No. 2 in F sharp minor, op. 13* (Myaskovsky) 55
*Piano Sonata No. 9 "Black Mass"* (Scriabin) 48, 65, 108, 117
*Piano Sonata No. 26 in E-flat major, op. 81a — "Les Adieux"* (Beethoven) 169
*The Picture of Dorian Gray* (Wilde) 179
Pink Floyd 176
Piper, Myfanwy 148
*The Pit and the Pendulum* (dir. Roger Corman) 107
Pitt, Ingrid 59
*The Plague of the Zombies* (dir. John Gilling) 131, 141
Planché, James Robinson 169
*The Planets* (Holst) 17, 117–119
Plato 8, 9, 11, 16, 17, 18, 21, 40, 88, 92, 98, 114
Pliny 2
Podgayetsky, Nikolay 48, 108
Poe, Edgar Allan 124, 128, 159, 179, 190–191

*The Poem of Ecstasy* (Scriabin) 109–111
"The Poet and the Composer" (E. T. A. Hoffmann) 167
Polanski, Roman 155–156, **156**, 178
Polidori, Dr. John 136
*Polymorphia* (Penderecki) 69
*La Porte héroïque du ciel* (Jules Bois) 128
Porter, Eric 147
Powell, Michael 158
*Prélude de la porte héroïque du ciel* (Satie) 128
*Première Pensée Rose + Croix* (Satie) 126
Prendergast, Roy 106
Pressburger, Emeric 158
Price, Alan 176
Price, Vincent 156, 157, 160
Procul Harum 176
Prokofiev, Sergei 145–146, 147
*Prometheus* (Delville) 116
*Prometheus — The Poem of Fire* (Scriabin) 99, 105, 106, 108, 110, 112, 113, 114, 116, 117, 190
*Prometheus Unbound* (Shelley) 49, 114
*Psychomania* (dir. Don Sharp) 51
Pullman, Philip 49, 167, 175
Purcell, Henry 68, 132, 166–167
Purse, Jill 12–13, 125
Pushkin, Alexander 143
Pythagoras 5, 6, 8, 9, 10, 11, 16, 18, 21, 24, 25, 26, 71, 74, 87, 90, 92, 98, 99, 123

*Quartet for the End of Time* (Messiaen) 130
*The Queen of Spades* (Tchaikovsky/Pushkin) 143–144
*The Queen of Spades* (dir. Thorold Dickinson) 144, 148
Quilter, Roger 173
Quittard, Henry 128

Rabelais, François 181–182
Rachmaninov 51, 159
Radcliffe, Ann 155
*Rainbow Trout* (Cyril Scott) 122–123
*Ramayana* 120
Rameau, Jean-Philippe 98
Rasputin 185
*Rasputin the Mad Monk* (dir. Don Sharp) 48
Ravel, Maurice 66–67, 129, 168
"The Raven" (Poe) 179
Rawlings, Margaret 147
*"Razumovsky" String Quartet, op. 49, no. 1* (Beethoven) 36
*Rebecca* (dir. Alfred Hitchcock) 44
*Recollections of Ancient Greek Music* (John Foulds) 124
*The Red Shoes* (dir. Michael Powell and Emeric Pressburger) 158
Reed, Oliver 117
Rees, Angharad 147
Reid, Beryl 146–147
Reinhardt, Max 174

# Index

*A Relation of Apparitions of Spirits in the County of Monmouth and the Principality of Wales* (Rev. Edward Jones) 165
*Religion and Art* (Wagner) 77, 87
Remick, Lee 67
*The Reptile* (dir. John Gilling) 57, 126
*The Republic* (Plato) 8, 9, 16, 40
*Requiem Mass* (Mozart) 67, **68**
Respighi, Ottorino 55
*The Revenge of Frankenstein* (dir. Terence Fisher) 159
*Rhapsody on a Theme of Paganini* (Rachmaninov) 55
*Das Rheingold* (Wagner) 101, 140, 164
*Richard Wagner in Paris* (Baudelaire) 101
*Rienzi* (Wagner) 140
*Rig-Veda* 121
*Rigoletto* (Verdi) 134
Rilke, Rainer Maria 96
Rimbaud, Arthur 112
Rimington, A. Wallace 105
Rimsky-Korsakov, Nicolay 45, 98, 152
*Rinaldo* (Handel) 132–133
*Der Ring des Nibelungen* (Wagner) 16, 52, 59, 78, 81, 152, 162, 163
Rinuccini, Ottavio 131
*The Rite of Spring* (Stravinsky) 67, 122, 157
Ritter, Karl 73
*Robert le diable* (Meyerbeer) 52–53, 138–139, **138**, 140, 150
Robinson, Bernard 150
Robinson, Harry 52, 55, 59, 156
Rogers, Anton 186
Rohmer, Sax 64, 65
The Rolling Stones 176, 185
*The Romance of the Forest* (Radcliffe) 155
*Romeo and Juliet* (Shakespeare) 170
*Romeo and Juliet Symphony* (Berlioz) 170–171
Rooney, Mickey 174
Rose, Bernard 41
Rose, Paul Lawrence 78
*Rosemary's Baby* (dir. Roman Polanski) 178
*Rosicrucian Cosmo-Conception* (Heindel) 79–80
Rossi, Bastiano de' 17
Rubinstein, Ida 153
*Rusalka* (Dvořák) 163, 164
Russak, Marie 122
Russell, Ken 55, 117, 159
Rutherford, Michael 16

Sabaneev, Leonid 105
*St. Matthew Passion* (J. S. Bach) 190
*Saint of the Mountain* (Cyril Scott) 145
Saint-Saëns, Camille 59
Salzedo, Leonard 159
Sangster, Jimmy 56
Sasdy, Peter 134, 146
*Satan Wants Me* (Robert Irwin) 176–178, 190
*Satanic Poem* (Scriabin) 108

*The Satanic Rites of Dracula* (dir. Alan Gibson) 51, 189
*Le Satanisme et la Magie* (Jules Bois) 128
*Satan's Treasures* (Delville) 116
Satie, Erik 124, 126, 127, 128, 129
*Savitri* (Holst) 121
"Scarbo" (Ravel) 66–67
Schaffer, Peter 11
Schaw, William 27
*Schéhérazade* (Rimsky-Korsakov) 152–153, 154
Schikaneder, Emmanuel 28, 31
Schiller, Friedrich 35, 36, 38, 40
Schindler, Anton 37
Schloezer, Tatyana 110
Schnittke, Alfred 159
Schoenberg, Arnold 10, 46, 68, 69, 70, 87–90, 92, 93–95, 125
Schopenhauer, Arthur 37, 44, 71–74, 86, 87
Schreck, Max 160
Schubart, Christian 132, 136
Schubert, Franz 158
Schumann, Robert 47, 103, 151
Schwabe, Carlos 81
Scorsese, Martin 11
Scott, Cyril 46–47, 98–99, 102, 122–124, 125, 144–145, 173
Scott, Marion M. 40, 41
Scott, Ridley 16
Scott, Sir Walter 136
Scriabin, Alexander 1, 47–48, 49, 50–51, 56, 59, 61, 65, 97, 98, 99, 103–104, 105, 106, 107, 108–117, 119, 122, 125, 190
Scribe, Eugène 133
Searle, Humphrey 149
*Sebastian* (dir. David Greene) 54
"The Second Coming" (Yeats) 148
*Second String Quartet, op. 10* (Schoenberg) 90
*The Secret Commonwealth of Elves, Fauns and Fairies* (Robert Kirk) 165–166
*The Secret Doctrine* (Blavatsky) 78, 111, 112, 113, 125
Semanski, Thomas 159
*Seraphita* (Balzac) 88–89, 90, 101
*Sgt. Pepper's Lonely Hearts Club Band* (The Beatles) 126, 179, 180
*The Seventh Seal* (dir. Ingmar Bergman) 158
Shakespeare, William 18–19, 133, 137, 140, 166, 167, 169, 170, 171–172
Sharngadeva 130
Sharp, Don 44, 48, 51, 155
Sharp, William 163; *see also* MacLeod, Fiona
Shaw, George Bernard 117, 190
*She* (dir. Robert Day) 152
Shearer, Moira 158
Shelley, Mary 2, 115, 136
Shelley, Percy Bysshe 1, 2, 3, 49, 114, 115
Sherpling, Nikolai 48
Shimada Toshiyuki 105
*The Shining* (dir. Stanley Kubrick) 46, 56, 69
Shostakovitch, Dmitri 55

# 216       Index

*The Shout* (dir. Jerzy Skolimowski) 13, *14*
Shrapnel, John 188
*Shrine* (Cyril Scott) 145
Shyer, Charles 33
Sibelius 52, 122, 164, 172
*Siegfried* (Wagner) 82, 102, 143
Simpson, Dudley 186
*Sita* (Holst) 120
Sitwell, Osbert 117
Skolimowski, Jerzy 13, *14*, 15, 16
*Sleeping Beauty* (dir. Clyde Geronimi) 174, 175
*The Sleeping Beauty* (Tchaikovsky) 151
Smithson. Harriet 55
*The Snow Maiden* (Hans Christian Anderson) 174
Socrates 8, 9, 16, 40
*Sonatina secundo* (Busoni) 91
*The Sorcerer's Apprentice* (Dukas) 106, 158
"Sorrows and Grandeur of Richard Wagner" (Mann) 141
*The Soul's Probation* (Steiner) 88
*The Sound of Music* (dir. Robert Wise) 149
Souza, Edward de 57
*Space: 1999* 101
Spencer, Edmund 166
*Sphinx* (Cyril Scott) 122
Spielberg, Steven 5, 66
Spring-Rice, Sir Cecil 118
Standing, John 58
*Star Trek* 8
*Star Trek: The Wrath of Khan* (dir. Nicholas Meyer) 74–75
*Star Wars* (dir. George Lucas) 8, 119
Starr, Ringo 180
Stassen, Franz **76**
Status Quo 186
Steele, Sir Richard 133
Steiner, Max 121
Steiner, Rudolf 79, 80, 81, 88, 89, 95, 104, 105, 111, 115–116
Stephens, Toby 175
Stevens, Martin 148
Stewart, Fred Mustard 60, 61, 62
Stiff Kittens 188
Stockhausen, Karlheinz 179, 180
Stoker, Bram 59, 136, 140–141, 142, 159
Stokowski, Leopold 106
Stoneground 177
Strauss, Johann 25, 33, 156
Strauss, Richard 74, 75, 116
Stravinsky, Igor 45, 67, 122, 154, 157, 158, 160, 173–174
"Strawberry Fields" (The Beatles) 54
Strindberg, August 164
*String Quartet in C-sharp minor, op. 131* (Beethoven) 40–41
Strysik, John 19, 66
*The Stud* (dir. Quentin Master) 185
Sturm, Christian 37
*Suite No. 3* (Tchaikovsky) 55

"Supernatural Horror in Literature" (Lovecraft) 64
*Swan Lake* (Tchaikovsky) 151, 175
*Swanwhite* (Strindberg/Sibelius) 164
Swedenborg, Emanuel 88, 90, 95, 101
Syberberg, Hans-Jürgen 87
Sydow, Max von 158
Sykes, Peter 69
*Les Sylphides* (Delibes) 152, 154, 155
"Sympathy for the Devil" (The Rolling Stones) 185
*Symphonie fantastique* (Berlioz) 54–55, 135, 171
*Symphony No. 3 — "The Divine Poem"* (Scriabin) 111
*Symphony No. 3 in D minor, WAB 103* (Bruckner) 49
*Symphony No. 3 in E-Flat Major, Op. 55 — "Eroica"* (Beethoven) 39
*Symphony No. 6 in F major, Op. 68 — "Pastoral"* (Beethoven) 102
*Symphony No. 8 in B minor — "Unfinished"* (Schubert) 151
*Symphony No. 9 in D minor, Op. 125 — "Choral"* (Beethoven) 35, 38, 40, 43, 69
*Symphony 103 in E-Flat — "Drumroll"* (Haydn) 54

*Tales of Chinatown* (Sax Rohmer) 64
*The Tales of Hoffmann* (dir. Michael Powell and Emeric Pressburger) 158–159
*Tannhäuser* (Wagner) 80, 81, 82, 101, 102
*Tapiola* (Sibelius) 52
Tarasti, Eero 45, 46, 47, 49, 50, 54
Tartini, Giuseppe 65
*Taste the Blood of Dracula* (dir. Peter Sasdy) 134
Tate, Nahum 132
Tate, Sharon 61, 178
Tchaikovsky, Pyotr 55, 143, 151, 152, 164, 172, 174, 175
"Tchériapin" (Sax Rohmer) 64–65
Tchérina, Ludmilla 158, 159
*The Tell-Tale Heart* (John Foulds/Poe) 124
*The Tempest* (Shakespeare) 171–172
*The Tempest* (Sibelius/Shakespeare) 172
Terrasson, Jean 27–28, 30
Teyte, Maggie 127
*Thamar* (Balakirev) 153–154
*Thämos, King of Egypt* (Mozart) 28
Thaw, John 33
*Their Satanic Majesties Request* (The Rolling Stones) 185
*Theory of Harmony* (Schoenberg) 93
Theosophical Society 78, 109, *109*
*Things to Come* (dir. William Cameron Menzies) 158
Thoma, Hans 174
Thomas of Celano 53
Thomas, Ambroise 134

## Index

Thomas, Damien 52
*Thought-Forms* (Leadbeater and Besant) 95
*Three Mantras* (John Foulds) 125
*Thriller* (dir. John Landis) 160
Tiomkin, Dimitri 56
*Titanic* films 150
*To the Devil a Daughter* (dir. Peter Sykes) 69
*Toccata and Fugue in D minor* (J. S. Bach) 106
*Tod und Verklärung* (Richard Strauss) 74
*The Tomorrow People* (TV series) 186–187
*Torture Garden* (dir. Freddie Francis) 58
Toscanini, Arturo 34
*Totentanz* (Liszt) 55
*Towards the Flame* (Scriabin) 108
Towers, Harry Allan 157
Townsend, Justin 105
Toye, Geoffrey 157
*Treatise of Orchestration* (Berlioz) 53
*Très Riches Heures de Duc de Berry* 117
*Trilby* (George Du Maurier) 58
*Tristan und Isolde* (Wagner) 58, 71, 72–74, 75, 77, 102, 129, 163
*Troilus and Cressida* 18
*Trois Sonneries de la Rose + Croix* (Satie) 126
*Tubular Bells* (Mike Oldfield) 44, 56
*Turangalîla Symphony* (Messiaen) 129–130
*The Turn of the Screw* (Henry James/Britten) 147–149
*Twins of Evil* (dir. John Hough) 52
*2001— A Space Odyssey* (dir. Stanley Kubrick) 25, 54, 69, 107, 113, 119

Ulmer, Edgar G. 51
*Undine* (E. T. A. Hoffmann/Friedrich de la Motte Fouqué) 163, 167–168
Unterberger, Ignaz 29

Valois, Dame Ninette de 157, 158
*The Vampire Lovers* (dir. Roy Ward Baker) 139, 156
*Der Vampyre* (Marschner) 136–137, 138, 140
"The Vampyre" (Polidori) 136–137
Varèse, Edgar 92–93
*Venus and Mars* (Botticelli) 118
Verdi, Giuseppe 133–134
*Vexations* (Satie) 126
Victoria, Queen 33
Vigano, Salvatore 39
Visconti, Luchino 42
Vorhaus, David 85
"Les Voyelles" (Rimbaud) 112–113

Wagner, Albert 137
Wagner, Cosima 73, 84
Wagner, Richard 6, 15, 16, 37, 45, 50, 52, 58, 59, 70–87, **79**, 89, 101–102, 103, 104, 105, 129, 137, 139–143, 151, 152, 157, 162, 163, 164, 169–170

Wähner, Friedrich 40
Walbrook, Anton 144
*A Walk in the Black Forest* (Horst Janowski) 169
Walken, Christopher 33
*Die Walküre* (Wagner) 81
Wallace, Oliver 174
Walpole, Horace 175
*War Requiem* (Benjamin Britten) 125
Warfare 188
Warhole, Andy 107
Warrack, John 169
Warren, Barry 57
Waxman, Franz 44
*The Way of Initiation* (Steiner) 95
Weber, Carl Maria von 1, 45, 52, 53, 135–136, 137, 163, 168–169, 170
Weiner, Marc A. 78
Wells, H. G. 158
Wendkos, Paul 1, 44, *60*
Wesendonck, Mathilde 72, 83
Whale, James 154
Whatley, Kevin 34
Wheatley, Dennis 1, 69, 116, 123, 131, 154, 177
Whitaker, David 104
*The Wicker Man* (dir. Robin Hardy) 190
Wieland, Christoph Martin 168, 169
Wiene, Robert 160
Wilde, Constance 117, 179
Wilde, Oscar 117, 179
Wilhelm, Richard 177
Williams, John 5, 6, 8, 16, 66, 119
Willing, Nick 166, 175
Willman, Noel 57
Wilmer, Douglas 104
Wilson, Colin 177, 183
Wise, Robert 149
*The Witch Boy* (Leonard Salzedo) 159
*The Witches* (dir. Cyril Frankel) 163
Wood, Sir Henry 117
Woodcock, Maude 124
Woodward, Edward 190
Woolf, Humbert 121
*The World as Will and Representation* (Schopenhauer) 71, 73–74
*World Requiem* (John Foulds) 124–125
Wronski, Joseph-Marie 100, 106
Wyndham John 187
Wyngarde, Peter 148

Yeats, W. B. 117, 125, 148
*Yellow Submarine* (dir. George Dunning) 107, 181, *181*
York, Susannah 13

*Zodiac* (TV series) 186, 187
Zoroaster 28, 34